THE URBANE VIEW

THE URBANE VIEW

Life and Politics in Metropolitan America

SCOTT GREER

New York   OXFORD UNIVERSITY PRESS   1972

Copyright © 1972 Oxford University Press, Inc.
Library of Congress Catalogue Card Number: 71–182424
PRINTED IN THE UNITED STATES OF AMERICA

To the memory of my mother,

Mary Lee Scott Greer

Acknowledgments

The following essays first appeared in these publications; thanks are due the holders of copyright for permission to reprint.

"Urbanism Reconsidered: A Comparative Study of Local Areas in a Metropolis," *American Sociological Review* 21: 19–25, January 1956.

"Urbanism and Social Structure: A Los Angeles Study" (with Ella Kube), in *Community Structure and Analysis*, edited by Marvin Sussman (New York: Thomas Y. Crowell and Company, 1959).

"Dispersion and the Culture of Urban Man," in *Urban Survival and Traffic*, edited by T. E. H. Williams (London: E. and F. N. Spon Limited, 1962).

"Individual Participation in Mass Society," in *Approaches to the Study of Politics*, edited by Roland Young (Evanston: Northwestern University Press, 1958).

"The Social Structure and Political Process of Suburbia," *American Sociological Review* 25: 514–26, August 1960.

"The Social Structure and Political Process of Suburbia: An Empirical Test," *Rural Sociology* 27: 438–59, December 1962.

"The Mass Society and the Parapolitical Structure" (with Peter Orleans), *American Sociological Review* 27: 643–46, October 1962.

"Dilemmas of Action Research on the Metropolitan Problem," in *Community Political Systems*, edited by Morris Janowitz (Glencoe, Ill.: The Free Press, 1961).

"The Rational Model, the Sociological Model, and Metropolitan Reform," *Public Opinion Quarterly* 27: 242–49, Summer 1963.

"Where is the Metropolitan Problem?" in *Applied Sociology*, edited by Alvin W. Gouldner and S. M. Miller (New York: The Free Press, 1965).

"The Political Side of Urban Development and Redevelopment" (with David Minar), *The Annals* of the American Academy of Political and Social Science 352: 62–73, March 1964.

"Ideology and Utopia: The Intellectual Politics of Urban Redevelopment," paper presented at the meetings of the Midwest Sociological Society, April 1970.

"Urbanization and Social Character," *The Quality of Urban Life*, Vol. III of the *Urban Affairs Annual*, edited by Werner Blumberg, Jr. and Henry J. Schmandt (Los Angeles: Sage, 1969).

"Policy and the Urban Future," *Studies of the Future*, edited by Wendell Bell (New York: Russell Sage, 1971).

Contents

THE URBANE VIEW

Introduction

I have chosen to call this collection of articles "The Urbane View" for two interlinked reasons. First, it is an attempt to look at cities from the viewpoint of the native and not that of the country man of yesterday, parochial in cultural time and space. By and large, Americans view cities as from the outside—from the fictive vantage point of small-town or open-country neighborhood: in the process they measure the urban texture against social systems and ways of life which it can never approximate nor was ever meant to. Such a view is usually pejorative.

I also want to indicate that I approach urban life and its structure in a certain frame of mind. I try to approach the city with the manner appropriate to polite society, one of open-minded inquiry and conditional good will; in short, I view the city as, first of all, *existing*. I have tried to understand urban structures as concrete reality. In a period when the simple-minded label all of the problems of society in these United States "the problems of the cities," I would like to have the reader keep two items in mind. One is the enormous preponderance of the wealth, work, talent, culture

1

(high and low), and intellect of the United States to be found in our metropolitan areas. Because cities are such repositories of value their troubles are important. The second is Poe's reply to the critic who accused him of merely copying German Gothic romances: "The terror of which I write is not of Germany but of the soul." Most of the "problems of the cities" are the problems, conflicts, and harsh dilemmas of the American soul.

To understand our cities, then, one must know something about the culture and organization of the United States as a whole; contrariwise, the study of urban structures should further illuminate that whole. Through the study over time of two of our great metropolitan areas, and through empirical research and analysis of two movements to improve the cities, I have attempted to identify some of the basic aspects of this society, the richest, most powerful, and in many ways most complex in history.

First I want to present an overview of the collection. Beginning in this chapter with some remarks on the state of the art of city-watching, *circa* 1952, I shall proceed through a discussion of my own theoretical leanings and aspirations. There follows a first set of studies which deals with a new, and to many frightening, phenomenon—the metropolitan area that resembles a scattered and many-centered network of people in places—that is, Los Angeles. The next set of studies deals with an almost polar opposite, a much older city which grew up on the Mississippi, expanded with the railways and, at the time I studied it, was still poorly equipped for the automobile age—St. Louis, Missouri. These are followed by several articles dealing with the movement to create a single metropolitan government for the sprawling, subdivided metropolis of today and two focusing upon urban renewal. The last section deals with some futures.

THE STUDY OF THE CITY CIRCA 1952

I first began serious empirical study of urban structure in 1952; the postwar years were over, the Eisenhower years had begun. We were in another of those periods of massive city-building which have recurred in the history of the country; each year of the decade the metropolitan population increased by an average of three and a half million, and the new urban growth was chiefly made up of diffuse settlements on the peripheries of the older centers. The tract development, shopping center, and industrial park became the major components of new urban settlement within the dominant framework of the giant express-highway grid.

Our investigation, theories, and knowledge of urban society were not growing proportionately. As I pointed out in *The Emerging City,* social science suffered a failure of nerve in the face of the apparent urbanization of the entire society or (to put it less dramatically) a mood of indifference to cities as isolable units of study had seeped through the social science community.[1] Thus the art of city study in 1952 was somewhat archaic, non-empirical, and frequently ideological.

One old and continuing line of inquiry was that of the ecologists, sometimes known as the Chicago school. Derived from the ideas of McKenzie, Park, Burgess, and lesser figures, it concentrated upon the eco-system, the structure of activities in space.[2] Suppressing the notion of human consciousness as an important aspect of urban behavior, the ecologists continued their plotting of human structures on maps. Thus we knew that there were, usually, certain patterns of land use in American cities; they were either developed in concentric zones, from the dense commercial center outward to the suburban fringe; or they grew in sectors which, having similar characteristics, extended continuously from center to edge; or they were a mixture of these two patterns.

Ecologists proposed to explain the city's structure as a result of competition for space among different kinds of

1. Scott Greer, *The Emerging City: Myth and Reality* (New York: The Free Press of Glencoe, 1962).
2. Representative examples may be found in *Contributions to Urban Sociology,* edited by Ernest W. Burgess and Donald J. Bogue (Chicago: The University of Chicago Press, 1964).

users. Contrariwise, the pattern of uses in space was to be a clue to the nature of the social order which had created the shops and plants, residences and throughways of the city. It was an approach with which one could not quarrel, yet it seemed in its disciplinary asceticism to have eliminated most aspects of urban society which were worth studying. Furthermore, in the new and rapidly expanding cities of the West and Southwest, as well as on the outskirts of the older cities, what was occurring did not seem to fit any of the spatial patterns. This suggested that new forces were creating new imprints on the city—that perhaps a new kind of city was coming into being.

Another strand of thought which had eminent origins and a long (if empirically unused) tradition was the social psychologism of Simmel, later adapted to American conditions by Louis Wirth.[3] In this view, the process of urbanization changed every aspect of human life and most aspects of human consciousness. The primary community of the peasant gave way to the marketplace in labor, goods, and space; kinship became attenuated; the neighborhood declined and all but disappeared; the church waned as an influence on life. The individual became highly conscious of himself and his differences from others, became blasé, manipulative, and lived in a world where his real self was very private indeed and separated entirely from his public self. The operator, the middleman, the "wheeler-dealer" became very critical in such a social order, for these types integrated the great formal organizations which controlled work and politics. At the same time, most urbanized personalities became in some degree operators, middlemen, and wheeler-dealers themselves. The urban consciousness was viewed, then, as inherently different in quality from the folk consciousness of earlier, agrarian man.

3. Georg Simmel, *The Sociology of Georg Simmel,* translated, edited, and with an introduction by Kurt H. Wolff (New York: The Free Press, 1964), especially Part Five, Ch. IV, "The Metropolis and Mental Life." For Wirth, see Louis Wirth, "Urbanism as a Way of Life," *American Journal of Sociology,* 44:1–24.

Closely akin to this approach was the rather vague culturalism of Tönnies.[4] Building upon his perception of the shift from a society held together by status to one based upon contract, Tönnies presents two ideal types: the *Gemeinschaft,* or primary community, and the *Gesellschaft* or formal, secondary community. His notions relate to those of Maine and are paralleled by Spengler's distinction between "culture," the mother of morals, art, and religion, and "civilization," the giant human society in which the original primitive drives are exhausted and community collapses. From status to contract, from sacred to secular, from custom to law, the organizing principles of human society are transformed and the question is raised: Can such a society survive?

Most of these concerns are united in the work of Durkheim, though without a specific focus upon the city.[5] In the transformation of the folk society (called mechanical), whose solidarity is based upon similarity of beliefs and norms, into the large-scale society (called organic), with solidarity based upon the division of labor, a great expansion of human energy and capacities is achieved. However, the cost is a very great danger: that, as men grow everywhere more interdependent, their ability to integrate their behavior in necessary and meaningful patterns will not keep pace. Put differently, as men lose commonality of beliefs and values the danger of anarchy increases; as the danger of anarchy grows so does the likelihood of tyranny developing as a counter-force. Between anarchy and tyranny liberal democracy maintains a precarious balance.

These various interpretations of urbanization as process and the city as product rested upon rather scant data. Ecologists mapped types of use and types of population in space. They occasionally carried out careful ethnographies of particular types of neighborhoods, but they relied mostly upon

4. Ferdinand Tönnies, *Community and Society,* translated by Charles P. Loomis (East Lansing: Michigan State University Press, 1957).
5. Emile Durkheim, *The Division of Labor in Society,* translated by George Simpson (New York: The Free Press of Glencoe, 1949). See especially the author's "Preface to the Second Edition."

inferences from mass data interpreted in terms of their own everyday experience. Simmel was a shrewd observer of the urban scene and his analyses are frequently fascinating, whether accurate or not. Tönnies relied upon history, particularly German history, and the tradition of "folk psychology" which rested in part on observation, in part on a kind of mysticism. Durkheim pioneered in the use of mass data for the study of solidarity. Very much a part of his time and its history, he always remembered the range of preliterate societies and insisted upon the continuity of social evolution, as well as the emergent properties of organic society.

Interesting as these various formulations were, none of them was particularly well established. The best documented approach, that of the ecologists, was also the narrowest, with the least to say about the great changes that urbanization was continuing to produce in American life in 1952.

Some Concerns of My Own

It is very difficult to recall accurately one's state of mind after eighteen years. Yet I am quite certain of one overall concern, and certain specific applications of it. Looking around at the huge, bland and, from most perspectives, formless urban texture of Southern California, I was aware of a great order implicit. It was not a kind of order that could easily be translated into the ideas discussed above, nor did these ideas seem all clear and in order among themselves. Conceptually they were fruitful, for they generated intellectual problems, but what did they mean empirically? Did they have any explanatory or predictive power?

I was convinced that the analysis of social organization was the way such problems should be translated into empirical research. That is, between the masses described conveniently by census data and the individual psyche postulated by social psychology there seemed to me a missing connection; that connection was the social aggregates in which men perforce did most of the work of their world. Thus the implicit order in the urban texture should be derivable from the larger order of the society, specifically: the giant organizations of work and government; the national market in land, labor, capital, and product; the smaller orders of kinship, friendship, the local community, and neighborhood. All had to be taken into account.

Another consideration in approaching the city was *change,* ubiquitous and rapid. The order of the city must be seen within a context of *organizational transformation.* One could see this process at work in the expansion of economic enterprise, the development of new products and processes, the broadening of markets over space, and the recurrent tendency towards giantism in the resulting enterprises. One could see parallel trends in the labor union movement, the Protestant denominations and, equally striking, in the structures of government at every level.

The trend of change seemed unidirectional then, towards larger and more powerful organizations, interrelated in many and inescapable ways. In summary, the very scale of the society was increasing, and I conceived of this increase as measurable by the diameters of the networks of interdependence. Clearly this is akin to Durkheim's notion—societal evolution was bringing great masses into closer relationships, in some degree ordered but without any guarantee of a persisting order. The creation and maintenance of such integration was a task forced upon human actors; the problem increased, *pari passu,* with the scale of the society.

These human actors obviously differed greatly in their social characteristics. Indeed, the increasing scale of the society was a causal factor in further differentiating them, for the process included the recruitment of labor from far and wide, the development of an enormous variety of skills, and wide variation in the scope of action allowed any given actor. In general, it seemed reasonable to postulate a "natural history" of the entry, socialization, and success of any given population in the large-scale society. Beginning at the bottom in skills and therefore rewards, coming from less urban societies and handicapped in manipulating the city scene, coming with strange language and looks from other cultures, the beginners would be found living a small-scale life within a cell of that giant matrix, the large-scale society. They would continue to live much of their lives as in their homelands.

As they were socialized to the city, they would move upwards in the job hierarchy; as jobs demanding greater skill became accessible, so would greater rewards. As they became more accustomed to the city, their ability to survive and flourish in the new scene, to exploit the new freedoms, would increase their choice. And as they ceased to seem distinctly "different" in their ethnic origins, they would suffer less discrimination and at the same time present fewer grounds upon which to base such discrimination. In a word, social mobility upwards together with acculturation to the urban world would increase social choice.

Thus the varieties of urban social types could be seen as lying on a continuum, from the transplanted ethnic peasant to the native urbanite—literate, prosperous, cosmopolitan. As the nation became increasingly a network of urban city-states, one giant metropolis should provide, in the mass and variety of its neighborhoods, almost the entire range of social types. Thus the great diversity of the society could be analyzed in terms of an order, and the order was one generated by the very forces of change, for differentiation implies integration. Much of that integration is based upon the concentration and segregation of unlike subpopulations who, in cooperation, keep the city operating.

The city could be viewed, then, as a distribution of neighborhoods in attribute space. Forgetting physical space, each neighborhood could be ranked in terms of urbanization (acculturation to urban life styles), segregation (ethnicity as reflected in extraordinary concentration of populations by origin), and social rank, or position in the hierarchy of skills and rewards that obtained in the society at the time. One could then ask what variations and what commonalities obtained across the array of neighborhoods. One could also ask: What was the social order specific to a given kind of neighborhood according to its place in attribute space?

The metropolis as a whole could be differentiated, through the use of census data, along the dimensions of attribute space. Then sample neighborhoods (census tracts) could be used to represent the types. Each tract could be studied through the then relatively new technique of the sample survey; a few hundred people could accurately stand for the thousands of people living in neighborhoods of a given type. Each person interviewed would be an informant concerning the type of life he lived, his personal variation in participation, and his integration in the larger organizations controlling work, religion, government, and play. His "participation profile" could be compared to those of others and the dominant types of neighborhoods could be compared among themselves. Organization of the larger whole would be to some unknown but, it was hoped, large degree, identified through the lives of these sample neighborhoods and sample residents.

There were certain biases implicit in this approach. One does not apologize, for any perspective generates in some degree "tunnel vision"; however, one does take note. In part they were probably reflections of the *Zeitgeist,* for it was an ebullient era when growth was proceeding at a prodigious rate accompanied by unprecedented prosperity. After the Great Depression and World War II, Americans were enjoying a long economic summer; nowhere was it more balmy than in Southern California. While I describe the place as it was in a later section I should like to underline now certain conditions: (1) the city had a relatively small and recently arrived black population which had improved its conditions considerably by migration there, the Mexican population was quiescent, and the Jewish one prosperous; (2) the overall income level was very high, as was the skill level; (3) unemployment was low; (4) housing quality was very high—though there was some shortage of low-cost housing, the construction industry was building tract houses at a rapid rate; (5) the country was at peace.

Thus it was easy to assume unilinear trends. Each decade, the population was increasing its income, education, and average skill level of occupation. As it acculturated to the city, it became more urbane; reproduction was controlled, women became part of the larger world through work outside the household, and children became results of choice. This increased the possibility for women to have careers, increased household income, and maximized the opportunities for all members of the household to enjoy the markets in leisure and the exotic landscapes of California. Further, as the ethnic populations moved upward in social rank, they moved outward in culture to be eventually assimilated into one golden type, the urbane American. Middle classification, in short, was under weigh with a full head of steam.

Today the unilinear trends are wavering; unemployment and inflation coexist with increased racism, black and white, while an unpopular war drags on. For some the basic structure of the society is in question; liberal democracy and market capitalism, our translation of the liberal humanitarian ideology, are both on the defensive. Many liberals and some capitalists are suffering a failure of nerve, while others are trying to exploit the *Zeitgeist* for their own ends.

Yet I think it is only a wavering in the long-run trends, producing a certain trembling of the national soul not infrequent in our history. The enormity of the task we have undertaken, to make one democratic and harmonious society of that fantastic array of people from all over earth, may quite easily induce vertigo. The wealth and power of organizations are in themselves dangerous; we have achieved a great height from which to fall. Yet despite the malaise which all of us feel from time to time, the lingering fear that mass democracy may not work after all, the processes described in these essays continue.

We continue to grow wealthier, and much of that wealth is devoted to educating the seven million students in colleges and universities. The black population is improving its relative position in the labor market and in the income distribution. We have become conscious of our impact on our non-human environment and are, slowly, beginning to act in that awareness. We are somewhat closer to a state of mind which would allow long-range planning in respect to our resources, our cities, and our people.

But the American system of government remains rigid and awkward. First we build a government designed to limit action by checks and balances; then we find it actually produces stalemate and inaction; then we improvise some means for circumventing the structures so that finally, however inefficiently or illegally, something can be done. Until this system can be changed, the rapid increase in scale of the private sector will continue to call most of the tunes for all.

If the system is to be changed, we shall have to develop a political culture and an art of statecraft appropriate to the scale and rate of growth of the society. Our political culture must become less static, less legalistic, and less given to ancestor worship; we must remember that the risk involved in keeping older governmental structures intact may be as great as that of innovating. Further, we must see beneath the legalistic surface to the norms of equality in participation which undergird the democratic doctrine, while recognizing that the truth is not always a matter of personal preference. Expertise far beyond the competence (or interest) of most citizens will be necessary for a governmental process adequate to the problems generated by change in other areas of the society.

Perhaps a new social character will be necessary for such

a political culture to emerge and dominate; perhaps such a social character is in process of becoming. The rapid acculturation of all social types to a new one, appropriate to an urban world, may go a long way towards solving the problem of government. For it is unlikely that, in a mass democracy, governmental intervention can go far beyond the median citizen's desire; only insofar as that desire is informed by understanding of the possibilities and limits of complex problems can a new art of statecraft be invented.

Such an art would assume commonalities of ultimate values which allowed direct communication between the temporary occupants of office and the citizenry. Reform would be based on an exploration of the true nature of the problem, rather than on slogans from the past. Governors would cease to talk down to the governed; the governed would cease to distrust the governors' words and aims. The expert could be used, not abused, in the process of reaching decisions which are never simply a matter of technical determination, but whose outcomes are almost always limited by such determination. In short, the experimental society would be possible within a democratic framework.

1

LOS ANGELES, CITY OF THE FUTURE

1

Mapping the Urban Order: Los Angeles

It would be difficult to find a more unlikely unit for organizational analysis than the contemporary American city, and Los Angeles in 1952 represented the extreme of the trends that make it so. Large but loose, decentralized, with no political unit below the municipality as a whole, city government was conducted by newspapers and television, administrators and demagogues. Non-partisan in nature, with councilmen elected at large, it was difficult to know whom the city council represented. There was the usual scatteration of suburbs, some completely encapsulated by the City of Los Angeles but exercising municipal autonomy. County supervisors were elected by districts—of some 500,000 each. While there were around two hundred "named places," Angelenos frequently had to rely upon the intersection of main thoroughfares to indicate their neighborhood.

The very rapid growth of the city had other effects. In 1950, one-fourth of the households had lived in their residence for a year or less. Their neighborhoods were apt to be built almost instantly, in large units of the same house type,

15

and very recently. At the same time, the giant grid of freeways, already well developed and extending apace, made possible movement from one edge to the other in an hour or so of driving.

What was needed in approaching Los Angeles as a subject for organizational analysis was a new kind of theory. Organizational theory in general is dependent for its success upon the tightness and clarity of the organized unit; here the metropolis was loose in structure, and what structure existed was unclear. In short, Los Angeles demanded a tighter theory for looser phenomena than organizational analysts usually study. To say it was unorganized was patently absurd: millions moved with considerable precision across the sandy littoral, operating giant enterprises and maintaining pleasant neighborhoods—constituting, indeed, the third largest metropolitan area in the United States.

The general focus of the Los Angeles studies was the way of life among the excluded middle of urban studies, the non-ethnic middle class. Neither rich nor poor, they made up the overwhelming bulk of the population, yet their ways were only sketchily understood. We sampled neighborhoods a little above median social rank, with tiny fractions who were non-white or foreign-born; we varied them by an index which seemed to identify variations in life-style—from the child-centered neighborhoods to those whose inhabitants were chiefly adults involved in the urban order through work and the market. We expected the latter kind of population to approximate Wirth's "urbanism as a way of life," if anyone did. The former should approximate small-town or rural America.

Thus we took a participation profile of our subjects. We interviewed in each of four areas, ranging from the most urbane to the most familistic among the non-ethnic middle class. We hypothesized that the more urban the population (and its neighborhood), the more isolated would our respondents be, and thus the more anonymous. They would be, so we thought, isolated from kinsmen and neighbors. Their friends would be work associates and they would spend a great deal of their time and energy in the world of mass entertainment—movies, theater, lectures, automobile shows—or else at the beach or in the mountains. They would be involved with formal voluntary associations, but not with church; they would live not in a neighborhood, but in the metropolis as a whole. With relatively few of the old supports of the individual—church, kin, community—they would have a higher likelihood of becoming *anomic*. That is, they would live in a subjective world with few norms, few limits, and would feel a corresponding sense of vertigo, aloneness, indifference, and mistrust of the objective social world.

Alas, on inspection things proved to be otherwise. The urbanites were, it is true, less involved with their neighbors; however they were as kinfolk-oriented as anyone, and as prone to have close personal friends in substantial numbers. They were not involved in mass entertainment to any striking degree, and five or six nights a week they were stay-at-homes. Their friends were not often work associates. They did not participate in voluntary organizations in great frequency or with great intensity; indeed, the majority were quite indifferent to such activity. A large minority were regular churchgoers.

With such findings it is no surprise that the urbanites were no more apt to be anomic than were the inhabitants of suburbia. In neither kind of neighborhood was there much evidence of anomie. Surprises continued: the less urban the neighborhood the *more* involvement in the local community through formal voluntary organizations, as well as the neighboring we had postulated.

Thus the extremes of life-style did not seem so strikingly different. Urbane or familistic, these middle-class people lived a life centered in home and work, friends and kin. The major difference, though unexpected, was quite logical: the more familistic the neighborhood the richer the individual's participation in formal voluntary organizations or, put differently, the denser the texture of associations.

2

Urbanism Reconsidered: A Comparative Study of Local Areas in a Metropolis*

The investigation of the internal differentiation of urban population has been concerned chiefly with economic rank and ethnic diversity, and with the differences which accompany variations in these factors. Such studies throw little light upon the broad, non-ethnic, cultural differences generated in the metropolitan environment, i.e., upon "urbanism as a way of life." While there has been much concern, theoretically, with the effects of the metropolitan ambit upon all social relationships, most of the empirical basis of urban theory has been the study of small "natural areas" or the study of gross regularities in census data, arranged spatially for analysis.

Perhaps the best evidence bearing upon this larger question of "urbanism" has been the study of urban neighborhoods. The work of Donald Foley, for example, indicates that

* Revised version of paper read at the annual meeting of the American Sociological Society, September, 1954. The study was carried out by the Laboratory in Urban Culture, a research facility of Occidental College, with the support of the John Randolph Haynes and Dora Haynes Foundation. I wish to express gratitude to Ella Kube, Research Associate, for assistance in the computation and analysis upon which the report is based.

19

in a sample of Rochester residents (1) the neighborhood pattern still exists to some degree, but, (2) many individuals do not neighbor and do not consider their local area to be a social community.[1] Such studies approach the propositions that urban society is functionally rather than spatially organized and that urbanites are mobile, anonymous, and lacking in identification with their local area.

To gauge the generality of Foley's conclusions, however, one needs to know where the neighborhoods he studied fit in an array of neighborhoods. Because wide variation exists, the relation between the area studied and others is crucial for the hypothesis tested; most of Rochester may be much more neighborhood oriented, or much less so, than the area studied.

The Shevky-Bell typology of urban sub-areas is useful in this connection, for it allows any census tract to be located simultaneously in three different arrays by means of three indices constructed from census data.[2] It is hypothesized that these represent three dimensions within urban social space, each statistically undimensional and independent of the others. The dimensions are social rank, segregation, and urbanization.[3] The last largely measures differences in family structure, and, it is assumed, indicates corollary differences in behavior. Thus, when social rank and segregation are controlled, differences in the index of urbanization for specific tract populations should indicate consistent variations in social behavior. One purpose of the present research was to

1. Donald L. Foley, "Neighbors or Urbanites? The Study of a Rochester District," *The University of Rochester's Studies of Metropolitan Rochester,* Rochester, New York, 1952.
2. Eshref Shevky and Wendell Bell, *Social Area Analysis,* Stanford, California: Stanford University Press, 1955. See also, Eshref Shevky and Marilyn Williams, *The Social Areas of Los Angeles,* Berkeley and Los Angeles: The University of California Press, 1948.
3. For a description of the statistical analysis and testing of the typology, see Wendell Bell, "Economic, Family, and Ethnic Status," *American Sociological Review,* 20 (February, 1955), pp. 45–52.

determine the nature of such corollary differences, and particularly differences in social participation.

This report is based upon a pilot study of differences in social participation between sample populations in two Los Angeles areas (census tracts 35 and 63).[4] The two tract populations are nearly identical with respect to two of the indices (social rank and segregation) and differ on the third, urbanization. For simplicity in presentation the tract with the higher urbanization index score (tract 63) will hereafter be called the high-urban tract, the other (tract 35) the low-urban tract.

The two sample tracts compare as follows. *History:* the low-urban tract is in an area that thirty years ago was separately incorporated for a brief time; the high-urban tract has always been a part of Los Angeles proper. *Location:* the low-urban tract is approximately fifteen minutes from the city center by auto; the high-urban tract is about half as far. (The low-urban tract is adjacent to the competing centers of Glendale and Pasadena.) *Social rank:* both tracts fall within the large middle range, being slightly above the median for the County. The social rank index for the low-urban tract is 68, for the high-urban tract, 66, as of the 1950 census of population, based upon the standard scores developed by Shevky with 1940 census data. *Ethnicity:* in neither tract does the foreign-born and non-white population amount to more than 5 per cent. *Urbanization:* the two tracts represent the extremes of the middle range of the urbanization index, within which a majority of the Los Angeles County census tracts lie. The low-urban tract had an urbanization index of 41, the high-urban tract, 57. There are much more highly urban tracts at middle rank, and much lower ones, in the County.

4. The extension of the study to include two additional sample tracts will be reported later; results are generally consistent with the findings reported here. Rank and segregation are the same in the added tract samples, but the new tracts extend to the extremes of the urbanization index within middle economic rank. See Chapter 3.

The sample is weighted against the instrument, so that if striking and consistent variations appear in this middle range, they probably indicate more extreme variations at the poles.

THE FIELD PROCEDURE AND THE SAMPLE

The field study included scheduled interviews on the participation of adult members of households in formal organizations, neighboring, cultural events, visiting, domestic activities, the mass media, the kin group, and other social structures.

Visiting was measured by questions concerning friends or relatives who were visited regularly at least once a month. The respondent was asked to give the address of the residence visited, both as a control over the accuracy of the information, and as a clue to social space position in the Shevky-Bell typology. Neighboring was measured by Wallin's "Neighborliness Scale," which was developed for a similar population in Palo Alto, California.[5] The scale assumes that neighborliness is unidimensional and can be measured by a small battery of questions referring to the degree of interaction with neighbors. The reproducibility for the present sample has not yet been determined. Cultural events were recorded and categorized in the manner devised by Queen, in his studies of social participation in St. Louis.[6] Individuals were asked about their attendance in the past month at movies, classes and study groups, athletic contests, lectures and speeches, museums and exhibits, musical events, and stage shows. They were also asked the location of the event and who accompanied them. Special schedules of questions were developed for the purpose of describing participation in formal organizations of various sorts, definitions of the local area, domestic participation, neighborhood play of children,

5. Paul Wallin, "A Guttman Scale for Measuring Women's Neighborliness," *American Journal of Sociology*, 49 (November, 1953), pp. 243–246.
6. Stuart A. Queen, "Social Participation in Relation to Social Disorganization," *American Sociological Review*, 14 (April, 1949), pp. 251–256.

and other aspects of participation which will not be reported here.

An area random sample was interviewed in each tract, with 161 respondents in the low-urban tract, 150 in the high-urban tract. These households represented approximately 7 per cent of the populations of the two census tracts chosen. The housewife was the respondent, and the response rate was over 85 per cent, being higher in the low-urban area. Interviewers were advanced and graduate students at Occidental College, and the average interview time was approximately one hour.

The two samples of households compare as follows:

Income: 20 per cent of the households in each area had less than $3,000 annually; 37 per cent in the low-urban area and 31 per cent in the high-urban area had annual incomes between $3,000 and $5,000; 35 per cent in the low-urban area and 38 per cent in the high-urban area had over $5,000 annually. Those who did not know or declined to state were 8 per cent in the low-urban area, 11 per cent in the high-urban area. The chief difference was a preponderance of middle income households in the low-urban area, with somewhat more heterogeneity in the high-urban area. *Occupation:* using the blue collar-white collar break, the samples were identical. In both areas, 72 per cent of the employed respondents were white-collar. Seventy-two per cent of the husbands in each area were in clerical jobs or higher.

Education: if education is divided into three classes, elementary or less, some high school or completed high school, and some college or more, the low-urban sample is slightly more homogeneous. Both respondents and husbands are 60 per cent high-school educated, with approximately 15 per cent below and 25 per cent above this class. In the high-urban sample the middle category accounted for only 50 per cent, with approximately 25 per cent below and 25 per cent above this class.

Such differences are not great but seem to indicate a consistent tendency towards somewhat more heterogeneity in the high-urban sample. It includes a slightly higher proportion of low-income, low-education persons, and also a slightly higher proportion of high-income, high-education persons. The high-urban sample is also more heterogeneous with respect to ethnicity. Although the percentage of non-white and foreign-born is similar in the two samples (9 for the low-urban sample, 11 for the high-urban) differences in religious affiliation indicate more ethnic diversity in the high-urban sample.

The low-urban area sample is much more homogeneous and Protestant in affiliation and preference. The high-urban sample, however, includes sizeable representations of the minority American religious beliefs: Jews and Roman Catholics are, together, only 20 per cent of the low-urban sample; they are 37 per cent of the high-urban sample. This heterogeneous and non-Protestant population in the high-urban sample is probably, to a large degree, made up of second and later generation ethnic individuals. Since the census tracts with high indexes of segregation in middle economic ranks are usually found in the more highly urbanized areas of the Shevky-Bell grid, it is likely that "later generation ethnics" (not identified in census data) are also concentrated in the more highly urbanized tracts of the middle social rank.

Such a correlation between second and later generation ethnic populations and urbanization, however, does not allow the reduction of the urbanization dimension to the ethnic component. In truth, many of these individuals are in process of leaving their ethnic status behind. Instead, it may be said that one of the attributes indicated by the urbanization index is apt to be the presence of second and later generation ethnics in the midst of acculturation. Such heterogeneity between faiths and within faiths is one of the conditions that give highly urbanized populations their particular characteristics.

EMPIRICAL FINDINGS

Table 1 gives differences in participation between two areas with respect to the localization of community. The low-

TABLE 1. LOCAL COMMUNITY PARTICIPATION IN TWO URBAN AREAS

TYPE OF SOCIAL PARTICIPATION	LOW URBAN*	HIGH URBAN*
Per cent of respondents with high neighboring scores		
(Scale types 2 through 5)	67†	56†
N of respondents	(162)	(150)
Per cent of respondents with friends in the local area	50	29
N of respondents	(162)	(150)
Per cent of all respondents' friends who live in local area	41	25
N of all friends	(441)	(316)
Per cent of respondents attending cultural events in local		
area, of those attending any cultural events	45	18
N attending any events	(101)	(92)
Per cent of respondents' formal organizations which meet in:		
Local area	62	26
Other areas	35	71
No response	3	3
N of organizations	(126)	(67)
Per cent of respondents' formal organizations with the majority of members residing in:		
Local area	57	33
Other area	18	18
Scattered over the city	23	45
No response	2	4
N of organizations	(126)	(67)
Per cent of husbands' formal organizations (as reported by respondent) which meet in:		
Local area	21‡	5‡
Other areas	73	86
No response	6	9
N of husbands' organizations	(104)	(57)
Per cent of husbands' formal organizations (as reported by respondent) with the majority of members residing in:		
Local area	25	10
Other area	23	12
Scattered over the city	45	77
No response	7	1
N of husbands' organizations	(104)	(57)

* P (χ^2) < .01, with exceptions noted below.
† P (χ^2) slightly above .05 level: $\chi^2 = 3.77$.
‡ P (χ^2) between .01 and .02 levels.

urban sample differed sharply and consistently in the direction of more participation in the local community. Their neighboring score was higher, they were more apt to have friends in the local area, and these constituted a larger proportion of all close friends, i.e., those visited at least once a month. They were more apt to go to cultural events such as movies, athletic contests, stage shows, and study groups, in the local area, and they were more apt to use local commercial facilities of certain types.

The low-urban sample had a higher rate of membership and participation in formal organizations other than church, and, more important, a larger proportion of their organizations were local in nature. A large majority of the respondents' organizations held meetings in the local area, and although the husbands' organizations usually met outside the area, still a much larger proportion met locally than did in the high-urban sample. Furthermore, the members of formal organizations to which the low-urban sample belonged were more apt to live in the immediate local community. In the high-urban sample other members were most apt to be scattered over the metropolis as a whole.

Further indication of the differential importance the local based organization had for these two samples is the greater familiarity of the low-urban sample with local community leaders. (See Table 2.)

TABLE 2. RESPONDENTS' ABILITY TO NAME LEADERS
OF THE LOCAL AREA AND OF LOS ANGELES

	LOW URBAN	HIGH URBAN
Per cent of respondents who could name at least one local leader	32*	21*
N of respondents	(162)	(150)
Per cent of respondents who could name at least one Los Angeles leader	38†	37†
N of respondents	(162)	(150)

* P (χ^2) between .02 and .05 levels.
† Difference not significant.

While the samples were equally able (and unable) to name Los Angeles leaders, there was a significantly higher proportion who could name local leaders in the low-urban area sample. This probably indicates a uniform engagement of the middle-rank populations in the affairs of the metropolis as a whole, but definite variations in their interest and involvement with respect to local affairs.

It is sometimes stated, almost as an axiom, that the urban milieu results in the extreme attrition of kin relations. The present study indicates this to be questionable. The most important single kind of social relationship for both samples is kinship visiting. A large majority of both samples visit their kin at least once a month, and *half of each sample visit their kin at least once a week.* These data, reported in Table 3, are

TABLE 3. KIN VISITING IN TWO URBAN AREAS

PER CENT VISITING KIN	LOW URBAN*	HIGH URBAN*
Once a week or more often	49	55
At least once a month, but less than once a week	24	21
A few times a year, but less than once a month	11	8
Never	5	9
No kin in Los Angeles	11	7
N of respondents	(162)	(150)

* No significant difference between low and high urban area samples.

consistent with the findings of Bell in his comparable study of social areas in the San Francisco Bay Region.[7]

Both samples indicated complacency with their neighborhood and said they were satisfied with it as a home, but in giving their reasons for liking it, they tended to differ. The low-urban sample described their area as a "little community," like a "small town," where "people are friendly and neighborly." The high-urban sample, on the other hand, most frequently mentioned the "convenience to downtown

7. Wendell Bell (with the assistance of Maryanne Force and Marion Boat), "People of the City," (processed) Stanford University Survey Research Facility, Stanford, California, 1954.

and everything," and spoke often of the "nice people" who "leave you alone and mind their own business." The high-urban sample seemed less committed to remaining in their present area—a higher proportion stating that there were other neighborhoods in the city in which they would rather live.

A tendency toward differential association with populations at a similar level of urbanization is indicated in the visiting patterns of the two samples outside their local areas. The residences of close friends and the meeting places of social circles are almost mutually exclusive for the two samples. Furthermore, when the census tracts in which are located the homes of the friends they visit are categorized by urbanization scores, clear differences appear. The low-urban sample is more apt to have friends in other low-urban areas, while the high-urban sample is apt to visit in other high-urban areas. (See Table 4.) When it is recalled that these two

TABLE 4. RESIDENCE OF FRIENDS VISITED, OUTSIDE OF THE LOCAL AREA, BY URBANIZATION INDEX SCORE*

	LOW URBAN†	HIGH URBAN†
Per cent of friends living in tracts with urbanization index score of		
1–20	13	12
21–40	35	25
41–60	41	33
61–80	8	19
81–100	3	11
N of friends visited	(180)	(162)

* Friends' addresses which could not be coded (80 in the Low Urban area, 65 in the High Urban) are excluded.
† $P (\chi^2) < .001$.

samples are almost identical with respect to social rank and segregation, the importance of the urbanization dimension is underlined. These visiting patterns refer to well structured friendship relations of probable importance. Such differential association may result from proximity, as well as selective visiting by levels of urbanization. The relative importance of proximity will be measured through the use of the intervening opportunities model. However, even if such differential association is to a large degree a function of spatial proximity, its significance in certain respects would remain. For, if populations at given levels of urbanization interact more intensely within those levels than with other populations, such interactions should result in fairly stable networks of informal communication and influence. The content of such communication should vary with urbanization.

SUMMARY AND INTERPRETATION

In order to investigate empirically the complex of notions surrounding the nature of urban social behavior, the Shevky-Bell typology, applied to sub-areas in Los Angeles County, was used to select two neighborhoods which differed clearly on the index of urbanization. Social rank was not used as the chief factor accounting for differential social participation, as was the case in the studies of Komarovsky, Goldhamer, and others.[8] Instead, rank was controlled, and the urbanization dimension was tested for broad differences in social participation.

It should be noted that this study investigates the effects of urbanization at a *particular* level of rank and segregation; at other levels, the effects of urbanization remain problematical. It is hoped that future studies will clarify, for example, the effects of differential urbanization at higher and lower social ranks, as well as in segregated populations. The Shevky-Bell typology, based upon a three dimensional attribute-space model of urban society, calls attention not only to three

8. Mirra Komarovsky, "The Voluntary Associations of Urban Dwellers," *American Sociological Review,* 11 (December, 1946), pp. 868–896; Herbert Goldhamer, "Voluntary Associations in the United States," unpublished Ph.D. thesis, University of Chicago, 1942.

separate factors, but also to the possibility that the particular effects of one may be transformed as either or both of the others vary.

However, the urbanization dimension was the focus of the present study. It was not identified with the older notion of urbanism which implies that all city populations are changing in the direction of atomistic, mass society.[9] Instead, it was assumed that there is a continuum of alternative life-styles at the same economic level and that these are concentrated in different urban sub-areas. In this framework, the low-urban areas are just as characteristic of modern urban society as are the high-urban areas. Both types continue to be alternatives in the urban complex. In this view, the Shevky-Bell index of urbanization is a putative means of identifying such variations in "ways of life." Instead of concentrating on urbanism as *a* way of life, the present study was focused upon the variations possible.

Two social aggregates, inhabiting tracts with similar economic rank and ethnicity but varying with respect to the urbanization index, were sampled. The sample populations were then studied by means of reported social participation.

The findings are consistent with the hypothesis that, where rank and ethnicity are equal, differences in the urbanization index will indicate differences in social behavior. Had the index identified populations not significantly different, doubt would have been cast upon its utility at the level of individual social behavior, for the urbanization dimension of modern society, as conceived by Shevky in his theoretical structure, implies such differences in social behavior.[10] However, the present study indicates that the index, constructed primarily with items related to family structure, does identify differences in social participation which are associated with variations in family structure but not derived solely from them.

9. See Louis Wirth, "Urbanism as a Way of Life," *The American Journal of Sociology*, 44 (July, 1938), pp. 1–24.
10. Shevky and Bell, *op. cit.*, especially Chapter II.

The general validity of the hypothesis must rest upon further studies in Los Angeles and other urban complexes. Although this study and that of Bell indicate the urbanization dimension does affect social participation to an impressive degree, the regularity with which these differences form a continuum at this intersection of social rank and segregation, and the nature of the hypothesized continuum, remain to be spelled out. Still, in the interpretation of the findings here reported, the following implications come to mind:

1. The local area in the contemporary American metropolis may be viewed as attracting population, not only by the economic rank and ethnic composition of the population already in the area, but also by the degree of urbanization characteristic of the area—the way of life common to the older inhabitants.

2. Such areas may attract populations on at least two different functional bases: (1) the demographic and the cultural characteristics of the older settlers, who give the area its "tone," may attract people, as seems true in the low-urban sample, or, (2) the area as a socially neutral, but convenient, base of operations for various segmental interests, may attract people as in the high-urban sample. Such different principles of attraction would tend to produce greater homogeneity of background and interest in low-urban areas, and from this similarity a higher degree of community-type behavior and of conformity would be expected.

3. A continuum is hypothesized for non-segregated, middle-rank areas. At one pole lie the local areas which select a predominantly "old American" population with similar jobs, aspirations, incomes, who wish to raise children, neighbor, participate in local community groups, and, in brief, carry on a life in many ways similar to that of the small towns described by Warner and his associates.[11] At the other pole lie those areas of the city which are more heterogeneous, with fewer children and little interest in the local

11. See, for example, W. Lloyd Warner and associates, *Democracy in Jonesville*, New York: Harper and Brothers, 1949.

area as a social arena. Such areas may approach, in many ways, the ideal type of urban environment hypothesized by Wirth.[12]

4. In this perspective, the local area is important as a framework for interaction, as a "social fact," just where it is least representative of the total urban society. The small community, as studied by Warner and others, is a very poor example of the urban complex, since it will include the fewest elements of urban society as a whole. At the same time, the high-urban tract as a sample of urban society is only slightly less biased, for in it the local area as a social fact disappears altogether. Thus it is not possible to use either the model of a small, spatially enclosed community or the stereotype of the continually more atomistic mass society in describing social participation in the contemporary metropolis.

There are, however, certain common structural threads running through the fabric of modern society. As Paul Hatt noted, the indices developed by Warner and others to measure social status may be generalized to the total society, since the various methods correlate highly with one universal attribute—occupation.[13] The present approach is, then, to ask: How does this attribute become defined and organized, how does it influence participation, in different sub-areas of the metropolis?

A tentative answer is that the individual's social position is defined differently and his social participation is patterned differently as the focus shifts from the low-urban populations to the high-urban populations. One may envisage the low-urban areas as somewhere between the small town and the conventional picture of metropolitan living. Where the local area is a social fact, where common interests and associations obtain, generalizations derived from small community studies

12. Wirth, *op. cit.*
13. Paul K. Hatt, "Stratification in the Mass Society," *American Sociological Review*, 15 (April, 1950), pp. 216–222.

may have validity. For here the individual's status will result, in part, from participation in a known and used local organizational structure and from family ties that are publicly understood.

When, however, high-urban populations are considered, social participation is organized around position in other organizational contexts, as for example, the corporation, politics, the labor union, or perhaps, as Riesman has suggested, categories derived from the popular culture of the mass media.[14] Here also are many individuals whose life, aside from work, is ordered by participation in small informal groups, and informal groups only, floating within the vast culture world of the market and the mass media. In such populations the locally defined community is largely irrelevant to status and participation. Associations are spread geographically, but ordered and concentrated in terms of selected interests. Family, in this context, is still important. It is slightly more important in the high-urban sample described. But it is probably much more private in its reference. In fact, kin relations may be seen as growing in importance just because of the diminished reliance placed upon neighborhood and local community.

What has been sketched above is a tentative model which will allow the use of contributions from earlier research, (studies of small cities, natural areas, the apartment house family, the suburban fringe) within a framework which integrates and orders them in relation to one another. Such a frame of reference also relates, eventually, to the increasing importance of large-scale organizations in a society which allows many alternative life patterns for individuals at the same functional and economic level.

14. David Riesman, in collaboration with Reuel Denny and Nathan Glazer, *The Lonely Crowd, A Study of the Changing American Character*, New Haven: Yale University Press, 1950, especially Chs. X, XI, XII.

3

Urbanism
and Social Structure

(with ELLA KUBE)

The historical growth of sociology has correlated closely with urban growth, and many of the theoretical and practical problems with which sociologists are concerned result from the forces which create great cities. In fields as diverse as demography, social psychology, and industrial sociology, the concepts of the "urban industrial society" and "urbanism as a way of life" are basic to much reasoning and research.

But while interest in urbanism is widespread, there is no general agreement on how it may be studied most profitably. It sometimes is treated as a dependent variable, a result of those vast transformations in the socio-economic system which Wilson and Wilson have termed "increase in scale." [1] It may also be treated as a set of conditions which alter the very nature of man's psychic existence and his self-image—as Simmel and Tönnies have done. Or, following Wirth, certain features of large cities may be taken as given—size, density, and

1. *The Analysis of Social Change,* G. and M. Wilson (London: Cambridge University Press, 1944).

heterogeneity—and one may attempt to deduce from them the conditions of social interaction among urban dwellers.[2] It is apparent that the method of study is not dictated by the subject matter (whose nature is largely unknown) but by the particular interests of the investigator.

In this study the writers have been particularly concerned with urbanism as a process which greatly increases variations in social behavior. However, the authors have been less concerned with extreme cases (such as "the gold coast and the slum") than with those variations in way of life which characterize the great middle range of the population. Forgetting, for the moment, the dramatic extremes of urban living, we wish to consider the important differences among the non-ethnic population of middle income, occupation, and education.

Such differences are difficult to isolate from the mass data made available by the Bureau of the Census unless one has a clearly defined criterion for selection. One such criterion is that developed by Shevky and Bell (see chapter 1); their work has produced a method of classifying urban subpopulations on three scales, those of social rank (or economic level), segregation (or ethnicity), and urbanization (or familism).[3]

The urbanization index grew out of various observations of the effects of urbanism upon social structure. As societies become more urban in nature, there is an increase in the individual's dependence upon large formal structures such as the corporation, the state, and other bureaucracies. As this occurs, the family ceases to be a major structure for carrying on productive activity, and its members find employment outside the home. At the same time the absolute values of "familism" decline; the procreation of children is no longer con-

2. Louis Wirth, "Urbanism as a Way of Life," *The American Journal of Sociology*, vol. 44 (July, 1938), pp. 1–24.
3. Eshref Shevky and Wendell Bell, *Social Area Analysis* (Stanford: Stanford University Press, 1955).

sidered necessary for every family, but now becomes a matter of personal choice. And, as family values decline and women become employees, the type of dwelling changes; the apartment may better serve the needs of the highly urban family than the detached, single-family dwelling.

Thus the urbanization index is based upon the proportion of women working outside the home, the proportion of the population living in single family dwelling units, and the fertility ratio. The urbanization score, *as an index,* points toward broader areas of differentiation. Thus, it indicates relative commitment to family and also to neighborhood, local area, and kinship ties. Or, conversely, it points toward the greater involvement of highly urban populations in the larger metropolitan world and lesser dependence upon the neighborhood and other vestiges of primary community.

Historically there has been a strong association between urban growth and decreasing fertility; however, it is doubtful if such an association will continue indefinitely in highly urban societies. Like most projections from past correlations, it is vulnerable to any change in the structure which produced those regularities. And the structure of modern American society is changing basically, producing a world which has never existed before—one in which a surplus of time, energy, and economic value is available to the population as a whole and not to just a small leisure class. It is the authors' belief that this increase in surplus allows an increasing freedom to choose—to vary one's way of life—and that the urbanization index measures an increasingly important dimension of urban society.

Empirically, the index may be thought of as identifying a continuum of life styles in which the relative importance of home, family, and children is one key factor. (The importance of this factor has led Bell to prefer the term "family status" for the index.) At one extreme we may speak of the "urbanism" of the densely inhabited apartment district and, at the other, of the "familism" of the suburbs. The aim of the present study has been to explore the meaning of differences on the urbanization index for social participation.

THE SETTING OF THE STUDY AND
THE STUDY DESIGN

Los Angeles is one of the most telling examples of change in total society and in the nature of cities. A product of twentieth-century technology, it arose in a most unlikely place, violating the rules which have generally governed the location of great cities. On a semi-arid coastal plain, without natural resources other than petroleum and without a harbor, it grew from a city of 200,000 in 1900 to become the nation's third metropolis, an urban complex of some 5,000,000 people, by 1956.

Wealthy, expanding, riding the crest of technological change, it capitalized on such developments as the invention of the movies, television, and radio, the increasing importance of petroleum, the growth of the electronics and aircraft industries, and the demand for consumer goods. At the same time the metropolis experienced a corollary increase in the white-collar occupations. Increase in the professional, semiprofessional, and clerical workers necessary to order large-scale enterprise, as well as the sales and service workers for the market, made the work force especially representative of a large-scale and still expanding society. Here, if anywhere, is a modern American city, a place to study the growth of American society and its culture. The meaning of urbanism should become apparent here in the variations of life-styles its residents choose.

With these research objectives in mind, it was necessary to select a number of neighborhoods with varying social characteristics, as measured by the Shevky-Bell indexes. Four were chosen, all within the legal "city" of Los Angeles, all named places, and all at least thirty years old as settled areas. They were chosen so as to have approximately the same socio-economic level, in order that the effects of variation on "urbanization index" scores might be clear. At the same time, they were tracts without large ethnic populations. Approximately a third of the Los Angeles area population is within ten percentile points above or below these sample census tracts in occupational and educational level. This is the great middle range of urban society—neither poor nor rich, a modal population with a modest prosperity. The most highly urban tract is one in central Hollywood, a neighborhood of apartment houses inhabited, not by "stars," but by ordinary working people. The tract more urban than average is called Silver Lake, the tract slightly below average, Eagle Rock, while the tract lowest in urbanism is in Temple City, a suburban settlement in the San Gabriel valley.

In each of the sample tracts an area random sample of dwelling units was selected, and the wife of the head of the house, the female head, or (where there was no family) a randomly chosen female, was interviewed. The total number of interviews was 150 in each tract except Eagle Rock; there it was 162. Eighty-four per cent of the eligible respondents were interviewed, and these interviews are the basis for the data to be reported.

The four areas had similar social rank scores: there was a variation of only 6 points in social rank among the four areas.[4] They differed sharply, however, on the urbanization index; scores ranged from 26 in Temple City to 36 in Eagle Rock, 55 in Silver Lake, and a high of 80 in Hollywood. None had a concentration of ethnic population above average for the Los Angeles area. They represent the range from the most "familistic" to the most "urban" nonethnic population at middle social rank.

The socio-economic level of the four tracts is about the same, as measured by the Shevky-Bell index. The four samples are also similar, as indicated by the descriptive statistics in table 1. The variation in houschold income vould indicate

4. "Social Area Scores for Los Angeles," Laboratory in Urban Culture, Occidental College (1954).

TABLE 1. SELECTED CHARACTERISTICS OF FOUR URBAN SAMPLES

	HOLLY-WOOD	SILVER LAKE	EAGLE ROCK	TEMPLE CITY
A. Socio-Economic Characteristics				
Occupation: percentage employed residents and husbands in white collar jobs	61.0	56.0	57.5	66.0
Education: percentage residents with some high school	77.6	80.7	86.4	81.3
Household income: percentage under $3,000	25.8	20.7	19.8	21.3
B. Social-Demographic Characteristics				
House type: percentage single family	38.4	51.3	82.7	96.0
Women working: percentage residents employed	51.0	42.0	39.8	26.7
Marital status: percentage single, widowed, or divorced	36.0	25.3	24.7	14.7
Family roles: percentage mother and wife	24.7	38.6	43.8	48.0
Family isolation: percentage single and living without kin	24.0	15.3	12.3	6.7
C. Background Characteristics				
Mobility: percentage living in Los Angeles for 2 years or less	13.2	7.3	8.7	3.3
Regional origin: percentage whose place of longest residence is the Far-Western states	21.8	32.0	42.2	40.0
Original nationality: percentage whose family was originally from North Europe	68.9	74.7	90.2	90.7

less wealth in Hollywood, but the average size of household is also smaller there, so that per capita income is similar for the four samples. Temple City and Hollywood, the two extreme tracts on the urbanization index, are slightly higher in social rank than are the middle tracts; the general similarity in socio-economic level is, however, great.

As similar as these samples are in their socio-economic characteristics, they vary widely in the social attributes usually associated with "urbanism as a way of life." In house type, percentage of women working, marital status, and family roles, they differ widely. They differ also, though not so sharply, in mobility—the length of time they have lived in the city—and in their regional origin. Heterogeneity is indicated by the percentage of variation of families whose original nationality was North European. (This is not a direct measure of ethnicity, as this origin may have been many generations in the past.) By these attributes, urbanism increases consistently from Temple City to Eagle Rock to Silver Lake and is most clear-cut in the Hollywood sample. Thus the Shevky-Bell index does isolate populations which vary according to the general notions of increasing urbanism. Once differing population types are isolated, other aspects of social behavior must be investigated—aspects which cannot be derived from mass data.

One approach to social behavior is through the study of interaction, or social participation. The writers chose this approach because, whatever its psychological meaning, participation is a fact of importance in itself, because reported participation may be quantified in a relatively unambiguous manner, and because, no matter how interpreted, participation is factual and unlike attitudes it cannot easily be explained away. The major part of the scheduled interview was devoted to an inventory of the individual's social life; we were interested in where he interacted, with whom, and how often. We measured neighboring, domestic participation, kinship relations, friendship visiting patterns, church participation, and formal organizational participation. We gathered, in fact, a short case history of social involvement. These data were supplemented by items on the respondent's definition of his neighborhood, social class and political behavior, and certain attitude scales.

THE RESEARCH FINDINGS: URBANISM
AND SOCIAL PARTICIPATION

The results will be presented in three contexts: (1) the general frequency of participation in different social relationships among the respondents in each of the four areas, (2) the relative importance of the local area as a social fact in each of the samples, and (3) variations among the four area samples on attributes other than participation.

Frequency of Participation

There was considerable variation among the four areas with respect to participation in both formal and informal social relationships. We shall first consider informal relationships—those existing outside the formal organizational structures. In domestic participation, neighboring, and kinship relations, there were consistent differences between the familistic and the highly urban neighborhoods (See table 2).

TABLE 2. The Social Participation of Four Urban Samples

	HOLLY-WOOD	SILVER LAKE	EAGLE ROCK	TEMPLE CITY
A. Informal Participation				
Domestic: percentage spending three or more evenings a week at home with others	67.0	72.0	77.0	83.0
Neighboring: percentage with moderate to high neighborliness scores	37.4	40.0	50.0	62.0
Kinship: percentage visiting relatives once a month or more	64.6	73.3	72.3	83.3
Work associates: percentage visiting once a month or more	28.0	37.3	28.9	32.0
Other friends: percentage visiting once a month or more	74.7	70.6	76.6	82.0
B. Formal Participation				
Church: percentage attending once a month or more	35.9	34.6	40.4	50.6
Clubs and organizations: percentage who belong and attend	40.0	40.0	51.0	60.0

Eighty-three per cent of the Temple City sample spent three or more evenings a week at home with family members, but only two-thirds of the Hollywood sample did so. Neighboring varied even more; as measured by Wallin's "Neighborliness Scale" only 37 per cent in Hollywood had moderate or high

scores, against 62 per cent in Temple City. Kinship participation varied from 64 per cent in Hollywood who visit kin
once a month or more to 83 per cent in Temple City. The
variation in amount of kin visiting results from the fact that
residents of the less urban neighborhoods are more apt to
have relations in the metropolitan area. This does not, however, reduce the importance of this variation. The family
in-laws and relatives outside the home are less important in
the highly urban neighborhoods, while neighboring declines
sharply.

There are less striking differences in visits with work associates and other friends. One feature of interest, not reported in table 2, is the variation in the proportion of respondents who visit with work associates once a week or
more. This increases with urbanization, from 7 per cent in
Temple City to 16 per cent in Hollywood. This is partly
due to the large number of employed respondents in Hollywood, but when only employed respondents are considered,
those who visit with work associates this frequently are 25
per cent of the Hollywood sample and 10 per cent of those
in Temple City. One-fourth of the employed Hollywood
respondents visit with work associates very frequently.

The amount of visiting with friends who are neither neighbors, relatives, nor work associates is high in all areas; from
70 to 82 per cent visit with such friends at least once a month.
Thus in each area a very large majority has close relationships
with relatives and with friends, while neighboring, kinship,
and domestic participation decrease with urbanism. It is important to note, however, that the percentage of persons
totally isolated from informal relationships was almost non-
existent.

Turning now to participation in formal organizations, we
find the same tendencies toward increasing participation in
the less highly urban neighborhoods. Church participation
increases from 36 per cent to just over one half, and participation in other formal organizations increases from 40 per cent

in Hollywood to 60 per cent in Temple City. Thus a slight majority in Temple City participates in formal organizations, as against a substantial minority in Hollywood.

Many of these respondents only belong to one organization in which they actively participate. It is important, then, to consider the "joiners" who participate in two or more organizations other than church. This class increases from 13 per cent in the Hollywood sample to 35 per cent in Temple City, with Silver Lake and Eagle Rock falling between.

Some data are available on the formal participation of the respondents' husbands. In general, the difference between areas is consistent with the findings for the respondents; however, the husbands belong less frequently to churches and participate less in churches, while they are more apt to belong to other formal organizations in all areas excepting Temple City. In this area husbands and wives have similar participation rates in clubs and other organizations.

THE LOCAL AREA AS A "SOCIAL FACT"

An important notion in the study of urban society is that the local area is becoming less important. Briefly stated, the hypothesis is that as functions become organized as segments in large formal structures, the local area in the metropolis ceases to be the basis for meaningful interaction among its residents and becomes instead a mere spatial location. Residential areas become dormitory districts and not in any sense communities. Yet many observers have noted the existence within large urban complexes of highly individual "named places." These may be survivals of earlier conditions, or they may have a contemporary reason for existence. In order to test the present importance of the four named places studied here the authors have relied upon several measures: the location of important groups in the local area, informal interaction in the area, access to communications and information concerning the area, and the residents' definitions of the area.

The Location of Groups in the Area. There is a consistent

tendency for the proportion of respondents participating in local groups to decline as urbanism increases. This is accompanied by a decreasing participation in groups whose members are chiefly local residents. At the same time, the proportion attending local churches declines while the proportion of respondents attending churches where they see neither friends, relatives, nor neighbors increases. One-fourth of the Hollywood church-goers attend churches where they have no other social relationship with any of those present.

The importance of local organizations in some urban areas is clear when it is noted that the 150 Temple City respondents belong to and participate in 111 organizations besides church which meet in Temple City. In contrast, the Hollywood respondents belong to 53 local organizations (still a surprisingly large number, until it is remembered that Hollywood is many times as large as any of the other "named places"; this inflates the importance of the immediate locale for these respondents' answers).

Informal Interaction in the Area. The clear and consistent decrease in neighboring as the neighborhood becomes more urban has already been noted. About one-third of the Hollywood respondents are "neighbors" in a meaningful sense, as against some two-thirds of those in Temple City. Close friendship, however, does not follow this pattern. There is very little difference between Hollywood and Temple City in the proportion having friends in the area. (A check of the friends' addresses indicates that the size of the Hollywood area does not determine this.) Thus close friendship does not follow the pattern of neighboring; it is freer of spatial limitations and allows greater choice.

ACCESS TO COMMUNICATION CHANNELS IN THE AREA

One important communications channel is formal organizations, and we have indicated that participation in local organizations varies consistently with type of neighborhood. Another important channel is neighboring. However, a third

TABLE 3. MEASURES OF COMMUNITY IN FOUR URBAN AREA SAMPLES

	HOLLY-WOOD	SILVER LAKE	EAGLE ROCK	TEMPLE CITY
A. Social Relationships				
Local groups: percentage who belong to any meeting locally	18.0	19.0	36.0	46.0
Local groups: percentage who belong to any with all local members	16.0	10.0	32.0	42.0
Local churches: percentage who attend	21.0	17.0	29.0	39.0
Local friends: percentage who visit once a month or more with at least one local friend	46.0	29.0	51.0	46.0
B. Information about the area				
Community press: percentage of readers	60.0	66.7	78.9	78.0
Local leaders: percentage naming one or more	14.0	21.3	31.7	26.7
C. Definition of the area				
Preference: percentage preferring other areas for residence	54.0	51.0	37.0	25.0
Felt permanence: percentage expecting to live there "more than ten years" or "all my life"	48.7	62.7	70.8	70.0
Satisfaction: percentage who like living in the area	85.0	87.0	84.0	97.0

channel of considerable importance is the local community press; Janowitz has made clear the power it has in creating social bonds in local areas.[5] In Hollywood 60 per cent read the community paper, two-thirds of the Silver Lake sample did so, whereas just under 80 per cent were readers in Eagle Rock and Temple City.

One measure of effective communications is the ability to name "local leaders." This varied considerably; fourteen per cent in Hollywood could name at least one leader, as against 32 per cent in Eagle Rock and 27 per cent in Temple

5. Morris Janowitz, *The Community Press in an Urban Setting* (Glencoe, Ill.: The Free Press, 1952).

City. (When controlled for length of residence, the percentage naming leaders was about the same for the two latter areas.) Few women in any area could name local leaders, but the percentage who could was twice as high in Temple City as in Hollywood. The ability to name two or more leaders declines consistently, from 17 per cent in Temple City to less than 5 per cent in Hollywood. In contrast there was no significant difference in ability to name leaders of the metropolitan area as a whole. Roughly 40 per cent in each area could name such men.

THE RESPONDENT'S DEFINITION OF THE LOCAL AREA

Here the respondent made evaluative judgments of the area. When asked if "there is any neighborhood in which you would rather live than here," 54 per cent of the Hollywood sample said "Yes," as against one-fourth of the Temple City respondents. (See table 3.) Preference for other areas is related to length of residence, for the area tends to keep as long-time residents those who like it; still, when length of residence in the area is controlled, the residents of highly urban neighborhoods consistently prefer other areas more frequently than do those of the familistic neighborhoods.

When the respondents were asked how long they expected to live in the area, those who expected to stay less than one year increased from 9 per cent in Temple City to 23 per cent in Hollywood. Those who expected to stay more than ten years or all their lives decreased from 70 per cent in the suburban areas to 48 per cent in Hollywood.

While these samples show great variation in their degree of "felt permanence" in the local area, there is little difference in the percentage saying that, in general, they like living where they are. Eighty-four per cent or more agreed in all areas.

In summary, these sharp variations in localism indicate that the disappearance of the "local community" and neighborhood in the city is far from complete. It is most nearly true in the highly urban area, but in those neighborhoods characterized by familism there is considerable vitality in local associations. This is evident in neighboring, local organization and church participation, readership of the local community press, and ability to name local leaders. It is accompanied by an attitude of commitment to the area as "home"—a place from which one does not want or expect to move. In participation and in felt permanence, the highly urban areas had a much weaker hold on their residents.

URBANISM AND ANOMIE

It is often assumed of urban man that he is "anomic," that as he loses his primary group ties in the neighborhood, the extended family, the local community, and other structures characteristic of rural society, he ceases to be identified with the social whole and is, at the same time, less controlled by the norms of his society. Such theorists as Durkheim, Ortega, and Sorokin have emphasized the isolation and malaise of modern urban life; they have been echoed in general sociological thinking, particularly in the field of social disorganization.

If it has been demonstrated that the four neighborhoods studied do include representative urban social types, of which the Hollywood sample is the most characteristically "urban," then a test of these hypotheses is possible. The authors have used Srole's anomie scale to make such a test. The scale includes five questions measuring such things as confidence in the future and in one's fellow man.[6] We have grouped the respondents into three types on the basis of total scores; these are the "anomics," the "semi-anomics," and the "non-anomics." The distribution of each type in the four areas is shown in table 4.

6. We are indebted to Leo Srole for an early opportunity to use the scale, (letter, Srole, 1953). See Srole, "Social Dysfunction, Personality, and Social Distance Attitudes," paper read before the American Sociological Society, Chicago (1951).

TABLE 4. ANOMIE IN FOUR URBAN SAMPLES

	HOLLY-WOOD	SILVER LAKE	EAGLE ROCK	TEMPLE CITY
A. Distribution of Anomie Scores				
Percentage anomic	12.5	12.0	8.6	8.7
Percentage semi-anomic	30.5	22.0	31.7	23.0
Percentage nonanomic	57.0	66.0	59.0	67.0
B. Socio-Economic Status and Anomie				
Low occupation: percentage non-anomic in blue-collar households	50.0	61.0	53.0	59.0
Low education: percentage non-anomic with less than H.S. education	27.0	45.0	32.0	36.0
Low income: percentage nonan-omic with income under $3,000	41.0	39.0	37.0	50.0

Though the differences in the percentage of "anomics" are not significant, there are important variations in the percentage of the "nonanomics." However, there is no consistent trend apparent; while Temple City has the highest percentage of nonanomic respondents and Hollywood the lowest, Eagle Rock is nearly as low as Hollywood and Silver Lake almost as high as Temple City. The percentage of "anomics" is very low in each area.

Certain alternative hypotheses were tested, for it is possible that there is sufficient variation in the samples on other grounds to explain differences in anomie scores. The distributions of anomie scores were examined, with nationality background, occupational status, educational level and income being held constant. There was no significant difference between respondents with North European and non-North European background. When respondents were divided into those who are employed and those not employed, there was no difference in anomic responses in any area excepting in Hollywood; in that area, where half the women are employed, those who are working are significantly less likely to be anomic. This would suggest that the neighborhood is much better adapted to the needs of the employed woman than to the housewife; the latter does not participate in the larger world of occupations, and she cannot participate in the smaller world of the neighborhood.

When the sample was divided by the occupational class of the head of the household (using the respondent's own occupation when she had no husband) consistent differences occurred between the "white-collar" and the "blue-collar" households. For each urban area the percentage giving non-anomic responses is higher in the white-collar group. There is also a consistent association between education and anomie scores. In each area, anomie decreases as educational level goes up. And for the combined sample, one-fifth of those with grammar school education are anomic; ten per cent of those with some high school are anomic; only 4 per cent of those with some college are anomic. The percentage *nonanomic* increases from 35 per cent to 63 per cent to 79 per cent for the same educational classes. The trend indicated for occupational and educational level is equally clear with respect to household income level. When the sample is divided into income groups of under $3,000, $3,000 to $4,999, and $5,000 or over per annum, the percentage giving nonanomic responses increases by striking and statistically significant degrees at each higher level.

In summary anomic or nonanomic attitudes do not seem to vary consistently with the character of the urban neighborhood as measured by the Shevky-Bell index of urbanization. Nor do they vary with nationality background. However, they do vary consistently and significantly with each of the conventional measures of socio-economic status, for the sample combined and for each area separately. The anomic respondents are those with low occupational and educational levels and low family incomes; this indicates that for this kind of a population anomie is chiefly the result of social class and perhaps economic frustration.

While anomie does have meaning in relation to these measures of socio-economic status, it must be noted that the proportion of extremely anomic respondents is quite low in each area and for the entire sample is only slightly above 10 percent. The highest proportion is in Hollywood (one-eighth), and the lowest, in Eagle Rock, is one-twelfth of the total.

SUMMARY AND INTERPRETATION

At many levels of social participation there are striking differences in the ways of life found in the familistic suburban areas and the highly urban apartment house district. As urbanism increases, neighboring declines, as does domestic social participation. There is a similar decrease in church participation, membership, and attendance at the meetings of formal organizations and in multiple membership in formal organizations.

Yet certain types of interaction, while decreasing as the area becomes more typically urban, have a considerable stability at the middle social rank. These include the extreme importance of kinship and friendship in all areas. And, as participation in voluntary formal organizations is lowest in the highly urban area, such organizations are also much less important as frameworks within which friendship develops. Almost half of the friends in the Hollywood sample were met outside of organizations, work, the neighborhood, churches, or clubs. Forty-seven per cent of all friends were met in this way, compared to 32 per cent in Silver Lake, 25 per cent in Eagle Rock, and only 21 per cent in Temple City. It is in small, intimate circles, through relatives, other friends, or childhood friends, that the highly urban sample meets half of its friends.

Much of urban sociology theory has postulated an increasing importance for formal, voluntary organizations with increasing urbanism, and a decrease in intimate, primary relationships. Our data indicate the exact opposite occurs within the metropolitan area; as the neighborhood grows more characteristically urban, friendship and kinship become a larger proportion of *all* social interaction. This is, perhaps, largely by default; organizations and churches have a shrinking active membership as populations become more typically urban. At any rate, the association of individuals is more predominantly informal and moves more often through personal channels. The formal structure of society affects such populations chiefly through work, the market, and commercialized play. Yet they are isolated, not from other people, but from groups larger and more formal than "social circles."

It is our present hypothesis that the more "urban" an area the less important are formal voluntary organizations and the more important are informal, face-to-face primary relations. Such primary relations are less often created through residential contacts or formal organizations and are more apt to be the result of choice. Such relationships may be more truly "primary" in nature than are those which result from the ascribed ties of kinship, neighborliness, or peer group membership.

There is slight variation in anomic respondents among the four urban areas, and it is not consistently related to urbanism. In general, the anomie scores were remarkably similar and low in all areas. (Only among respondents with low education, occupation and income levels was anomie high.) It is possible that primary relations compensate for whatever loss of "community" occurs in the highly urban neighborhoods. If Srole's scale is a valid measure, the inhabitants of Central Hollywood are not unusually disorganized or demoralized personally; nor are they socially disorganized. They are merely organized in different ways.

Another focus in this study was upon the local areas as communities. In general, the findings indicate that the more familistic areas tend to recreate a meaningful local community in the midst of the great urban complex. Such a community is a product of various factors. Individuals are originally attracted to an area by a wide range of considerations, yet an area selected tends to result in a relatively homogeneous population. The residents may share common interests and commitments (home ownership, with all that it entails, children and all they entail) and just from living closely together people may form associations which bind them together socially. These associations limit and control the individual, and to the outsider searching for a home they seem to affect the character of the neighborhood.

The highly urban apartment house area attracts other types of people—on other grounds. Such individuals lack common interests and commitments and, particularly, any commitment to the local area as "home." Though all of the population in Hollywood did not fit this pattern, a sufficiently large proportion who do so may prevent the "good neighbors" from interacting. This may be illustrated by an interesting finding on "neighborliness."

Less neighboring would be expected for employed respondents than for those who were housewives and mothers and, in general, the employed respondents had low neighboring scores (a majority in all areas, from 55 per cent in Temple City to 71 per cent in Silver Lake). Perhaps more important, however, is the variation in the neighborliness of those who did not work. The percentage with low scores increased spectacularly, from 32 per cent in Temple City to 41 per cent in Eagle Rock, 52 per cent in Silver Lake and 63 per cent in Hollywood. In Hollywood the employed respondents neighbored as much as those who stayed at home.

Our interpretation is as follows: as employed women become a larger proportion of the total female population the opportunities for neighboring decline. Since they typically neighbor less than those not employed, the woman who wishes to neighbor in a highly urban area simply has no opportunities to do so. Thus the particular distribution and location of given population types in an area also set limits on the kinds of interaction possible in the area.[7]

In conclusion we may ask why, in view of the data reported, so many writers have emphasized the isolation and anomie of the urban individual, his reliance upon secondary relationships, and his loss of community. Why has the urbanite been pictured as a lost individual, a particle in a social "dust heap"?

One answer might be based on time lag; much of the theory of urban society derives from work done around the turn of the century by Tönnies, Durkheim, and Simmel. Perhaps things were different then, and the urban individual was an isolate. Sociology, like the French generals, typically fights the last war and describes a world that existed thirty or forty years ago.

However, we doubt that such conditions ever prevailed for the great bulk of urban dwellers. We suggest that the traditional picture of urban life, glamorous and dramatic as it has been, has been based upon small and highly biased samples. Those who studied "urbanism" in the past looked, usually, for the striking example, "the gold coast and the slum," the "ghetto" and the "hobohemia." Such areas and their populations constitute a very small portion of the people in a great urban center; Zorbaugh's study area was considerably less than one-twentieth of the Chicago area at the time and very unrepresentative of the rest. Furthermore, such studies have generally confused "urbanism as a way of life" with "poverty as a way of life," "wealth as a way of life," or "ethnic identity" as a way of life.

When one separates these dimensions, as Shevky and Bell have done, into socio-economic rank, ethnicity, *and* other variations in a way of life, it becomes apparent that our no-

---

7. Similar limits result for the play of children; over twice as many of the women with children in Hollywood as in Temple City say their children do not play with any children in the neighborhood. The opportunities (ie., presence of other children) do not exist.

tions of urbanism have rested upon an unanalyzed abstraction. In general, we suspect that the "anomie" of the urban dweller is the complaint of the poor and ethnic urban dweller; individualism, a luxury of the wealthy and of students not in the labor force. The mosaic of worlds which "touch but do not interpenetrate" is probably a much more complex fabric than has been thought. The evidence from this study of four middle rank, nonethnic areas in Los Angeles indicates that "style of life" varies widely even at the same social, economic, and family levels. Furthermore, the populations we have studied, while duller, are more recognizably human than the denizens of the urban world as they appeared to earlier scholars.[8]

8. The study was carried out through the Laboratory in Urban Culture, a research facility of Occidental College, with the support of the John Randolph Haynes and Dora Haynes Foundation. A fuller report of the findings is presented in *Urban Worlds: A Comparative Study of Four Los Angeles Areas,* Occidental College (1955).

4

Dispersion and the Culture of Urban Man

The metropolitan Los Angeles area is the third greatest urban concentration in America, a city more than five times as large as the most generous estimates of Imperial Rome. Yet, in the eyes of many, it is no city at all. Sprawling over some 2500 square miles between the mountains and the sea, its 6,000,000 or so inhabitants live scattered and far apart. The average density is far below that of such cities as Chicago or New York; nowhere does it approach the older model of an American city. Thus the derogatory remarks about it; it is called "a dozen suburbs in search of a city," and "the biggest suburb in the history of the human race." Nor are such comments always good-humoured; there is a curiously moral bitterness in the stranger's response to the city. Mr. Marples* seemed obsessed with it; whatever the other valuable information he carried back to Britain, a chief item was his image of Los Angeles. This may have affected Britain's transportation policy—since he spoke

* Minister of Transport in the U.K. at the time.

strongly of his determination that Britons never, never shall be like Los Angelenos.

Responses of this sort are to be expected in the face of any massive social change. Los Angeles symbolises such changes in an area close to home—changes in the communities where we live. The changing space-time ratio, greatly reducing the time and energy cost of short-time movement and communication, has radically changed the building lay-out of the city. For space has no fixed meaning; its meaning to human organisation is provided by its role as a channel for, and a barrier to, integration of human activities. With our contemporary revolutions in transport and communication, the whole meaning of space for human behaviour has radically shifted.

The age of the railroad provided the preconditions for the creation of cities—large, densely settled concentrations of population existing in an exchange relationship with their hinterland, other cities, and the world. The railroad did not, however, much affect movement within the city. The city of the age of steam was one in which movement was by foot and carriage. However, the electric railway, the buses, and finally the wide distribution of private automobiles, successively changed the meaning of space within the city and always in the direction of a greater control over space in the same period of time.* Each improvement in the flexibility and speed of intra-city movement meant an extension of the distance over which human activities could be just as closely co-ordinated as before. This, in turn, meant that vast areas of geographical space became accessible for shops, factories, residential districts, and the other structural needs of urban populations. The result has been the increasing spread of structures on the outskirts and the increasing amount of land per structure.

The horizontal nature of Los Angeles is, then, a result of

* For an extensive discussion of the social consequences of technological changes in transport, see Fred Cottrell, *Energy and Society*, New York: McGraw-Hill Book Company, 1955, especially Chapter 5.

the automobile revolution. The need for intensive inter-action in a very small area declines as other areas become easily accessible; the down-town district of Los Angeles is, in fact, less impressive than that in cities one-fifth its size, where such cities were built in the earlier technological ages. Nor is Los Angeles unique in this respect; all of the very new American cities—those built largely during the age of the automobile—are similar: all reflect the new locational freedom consequent to the changing space-time ratio.

However, there are many large American cities which are divided between a central area of extreme density and out-lying areas of extreme dispersion. This is particularly true of the cities east of the Mississippi; settled earlier in tech-nological time, growing to large size in the age of steam, they have heavy commitments to the structures built in that period. On their growing edges, however, one finds the typ-ical western pattern—a loose texture of tract development, suburban shopping centre, fields and industrial parks, all knit together by the super highways. The investment in older structures is such that one cannot take advantage of the newer opportunities provided by truck transport, a decen-tralising labour force, and the electric power grids. Such in-vestments, however, lose value rapidly; the loft-buildings and multiple-storey factories in the centre of New York, Chicago and St. Louis, cannot compete with the horizontal plants in the suburbs. There are frequently high vacancy rates in the centre of the city.

As a consequence of this dichotomisation there are, visu-ally, two cities in each of the older metropolitan areas. There is the residential mecca of suburbia, symbolised by the miles of billboards along the Los Angeles freeways, extolling the competitive virtues of this year's model house. At the same time, there is the enormous older central city, a congerie of aged neighbourhoods where the houses are compact, close together, and dark, with little space for yards and little in-sulation from the neighbours. These areas have been called "grey areas" for they have value, yet they are a drug on the market for middle-class, white, residential housing.

On the other hand, they are a boon for the segregated populations (Negroes, Puerto Ricans, Mexicans) who cannot move freely to the suburbs. (As a colleague remarks, perhaps the term "grey area" simply refers to the mixture resulting when black people move into formerly all-white neighbourhoods.) Though the older neighbourhoods of the central city are abandoned by the white-collar workers and the non-ethnics, they have a great relative value to the ex-slum dwellers, the manual labourers and the coloured populations. Thus the two cities of the metropolis become increasingly distinguishable: the central city is working-class and ethnic, while the suburbs are higher in occupational level and white. This schism is complemented by a governmental split—for the central city is a unified government, while outside its borders dozens or hundreds of small municipalities govern the suburbanites. One result of this is that the central cities are typically one-party states, controlled by the Democratic party as representative of the manual workers and the ethnics; the suburbs tend to be Republican in their voting.*

In the meantime, many major tasks which stem from the total metropolitan area, and can be handled only through area-wide devices, are left half-done, or undone. To consider only one, few American cities have any adequate transport programme, much less an existing transport grid which satisfies the citizens. Such a grid would require an area-wide polity—and this is almost impossible for general government because of the split between suburbs and central city. With each half of the population jealously guarding its sovereignty, plans for "metropolitan government" have been turned down in area after area. One reason for this is the competing

* See the author's analyses of the situation in metropolitan St. Louis, Missouri, in *Path of Progress for Metropolitan St. Louis,* University City, Missouri: 1957, The Metropolitan St. Louis Survey, Part One, "The People."

images of the city which exist today. Many still hold to an older ideal of the centralised city controlling all its neighbourhoods, its down-town the symbol and hub of the metropolitan community. For such persons, all roads should lead to the centre—and the retrieval of the use values in the centre is a basic objective. Others, however, including many of the younger, home-owning suburbanites, seem to see the city as a loose structure of separate and virtually autonomous incorporated neighbourhoods bound together by a circulatory system which makes all parts of the metropolis easily accessible to all. Such persons want, not a complex mechanism to enforce the use of mass transport into "town" and therefore the rejuvenation of the centre, but a vast super highway system which uses the centre as an interchange.*

It is, in fact, unlikely that the older image will prevail. Without a metropolitan area government the transport system will be handled in isolation—by separate district governments, or by subsidies from the national government. The system will be adapted to present demand, and that demand is pre-eminently determined by the suburban millions. Thus we can probably expect an accelerated dependence upon the automobile, a consequent deterioration of public transport, and an increasing dispersion of the population. Furthermore, as the circumferential highways develop around the outer edges, we find an increasing number of "super shopping centres" rising at the intersection of arterials and circumferentials. Such shopping centres symbolise and hurry on the decentralisation in all classes of retail trade; serving populations of a quarter million or more, they create a polynucleated structure for the metropolis. As a result, the commercial activity of the down-town stagnates or declines.

Americans, committed to the automobile, are also committed to a new type of urban community. It is one which spreads far and wide, with enormous concentrations of ac-

* These propositions are documented by the author in the forthcoming research report of the Metropolitan St. Louis Survey.

tivity in suburbs far from the centres—one in which hundreds of thousands of citizens live from year to year without entering the central business district. It is in many respects a radical development of human community. Ecologically, it is somewhat like a village society, yet it is the major form of community within the largest-scale human society ever developed. And, because of the technological revolutions in communication and transport, its villagers range far in their daily journeys, and have immediate access to the news of the world. Let us consider, in some detail, the emerging culture of these urban villagers.

LIFE IN THE SUBURBS

Just as the newer metropolitan communities are subject to derogatory comments by the patriots of an older kind of city, so are the suburban neighbourhoods objects of scorn. Both in the popular periodicals and in the scholarly and semi-scholarly literature, there has been a widespread criticism of suburban life. It is described as a world of "dormitory communities," where the organisation men with few roots or loyalties beyond their job retire to a bovine peace. Riesman speaks of the "suburban sadness," a result of isolation and the diminishing scale of social life: his "other directed" people seem to be, preponderantly, suburban in their residence. The government of suburban municipalities is described as "trivial" and "amateurish." In short, many see the suburbs as negating the great advantages for human development that would seem implicit in a metropolitan society. Their criticisms stem from a basic disillusionment with the quality of life in the greatest cities of the wealthiest nations.

In recent years there has been a substantial amount of research into the nature of life in the American suburbs. Sociologists have investigated the suburbs of Los Angeles, New York, Chicago, St. Louis, Milwaukee, and other larger cities. The findings are quite similar, and allow us to make some general statements about the life of the suburban villagers. We shall discuss: their reasons for moving, the nature of their investments in the suburban neighbourhoods, their life-space, their community social life, their political life, and their cultural activities.

Studies of the reasons for movement from central city to suburb all result in the same interpretations. Urban Americans, increasingly committed to a life-style which we have called "familism," value highly a household which is an adequate scene for an intense family life and the raising of a number of children. Such a scene includes private space, indoors and out; a physically pleasant and safe location; neighbours with similar commitments who can be trusted to help maintain a safe social environment. All these are found in the residential developments on the outskirts of the city, just as they are scarce within the older and denser neighbourhoods of the central city. And, as the familistic populations of middle social rank move outward, these older neighbourhoods are down-graded on the housing market: they fill up with persons of lower social rank, and frequently, of different ethnic identity. Rightly or wrongly, the middle-rank white population interprets this as a threat to the kind of life which they wish to live. Thus their continued movement away from the older urban neighbourhoods.

Although it is true that the great majority of suburban residents do not earn their living in their immediate community, and many work within the central city, it is quite misleading to speak of the suburbs as only "dormitory communities." They are the seat of most men's treasure—the site for the home to which he is committed and the setting for the everyday life of his wife and children. Their work, education, play and social circles all centre on the suburban community. And the breadwinner himself, with diminishing work weeks in most occupations, spends more of his waking hours in the suburb than in the central city where he works. Furthermore, his limited income and high aspirations lead him to invest a remarkable amount of his free time in improving his home: from gardening to mosaic tile setting, Americans are supplementing their money wages with home crafts—oriented towards their suburban worlds.

Socially, suburbanites are intensely involved with friends in their neighbourhoods, and extensively involved with many people who are simply "neighbours." They live within a complex network of friendships, local voluntary organisations of the suburban communities, relatives (most of whom are also suburban) and neighbours. This network makes of the suburban community a social fact and not simply a geographical contiguity. Because of the homogeneous life-styles within the local community, each household has much in common with its neighbours. The local schools are of major importance, but there is also concern for the location and maintenance of public space in parks and playgrounds, shopping centres and local governmental organisations. In short, there is intense interdependence, based upon common locale and common interests: these maintain and are in turn sustained by the neighbouring, friendship, and organisational relationships of the suburban citizens.

Thus their political life has a specific and important content. Though most suburbs evince a high degree of consensus with respect to the proper nature the community should maintain, the methods of that maintenance require public consideration. Land use, the location of highways and schools and other facilities, the amount of the taxes and bonds necessary to support adequate governmental goods and services, the nature and cost of new developments—such are the issues of suburban politics. Ordinarily such politics do not operate through a party structure; though tending to Republican preference at the national level, most American suburbs are "non-partisan" in their local affairs. Typically the suburbs are governed by a "good government caucus," a selected sample of the home-owners in the community, who nominate one slate of officers: these run without opposition. With little differentiation of population, with consensus on the image of the neighbourhoods, and with few persons making a living from government, suburban municipalities show little inclination towards either dishonesty or violent schisms in respect to polity. They tend to be administered, rather than governed. As they are small in size, their citizens trust the local municipality governments and find them very accessible when they have complaints or suggestions to register. It is a government of friends and neighbours. The local suburban community press gives form to these affairs by reporting, in detail, the social and political life of the locality.

Still, the very smallness of the suburban communities militates against certain activities we think of as characteristic of an urban way of life. Cities of ten to fifteen thousand cannot support symphony orchestras or museums of art—not to speak of universities and research centres. They can hardly maintain adequate libraries. Instead, the public life of the suburbs is dominated by affairs at the local public schools—plays and musical performances by children and amateurs—and small reading and dramatic "circles." Indeed, the culture of the suburb is remarkably similar to that of the country towns in an earlier America. To be sure, the central city, with its fortresses of the arts, is available to the suburbanite; however, it is far away in time and space at the end of a working day. It is an expedition to attend a cultural event, rather than a normally expected activity. Thus the small scale of suburban cultural events—and what Riesman calls the "suburban sadness," the turning away from a larger world.

There is, however, little evidence that most suburbanites miss such experiences. Indeed, they are typically ebullient in their expressions of fondness for, and commitment to, the suburb of their choice. They like it there and they intend to stay there. Between 75 and 95 per cent of the residents in middle-rank suburbs will say that there is no place in the entire metropolitan area in which they would rather live. Few speak with regret of what they have left behind in the city. And indeed, we must remember that many of the present suburbanites saw little of the desirable and glamorous aspects of the city: they did not patronise the opera and the museum often when they lived in the central city. Then, as now, the mass media were their chief window on the world of art and thought: and they have, within their living room, the major medium of communication in the great world as they see it—the television set.

Thus the lifeways of suburban Americans, whose communities are the result of our new locational freedom in the cities, are similar in many respects to those of a small town. They are neither residents nor citizens of the greater polity. They take no responsibility for the central city or the metropolis as a whole; where local government is concerned they do not see far beyond their municipal boundaries. Though many of them are men of great power in the corporate and professional worlds, they do not commit themselves to the community where their work is located—the central city. Instead, they involve themselves in the affairs of the little suburban municipality with the pretty name. Meanwhile, the government of the central city rests upon the politics of the ethnic minorities, the working class, and the professionals of the Democratic party. It is a schizophrenic community.

What Has Been Lost?

We have lost, probably forever, the highly centralised city, the classical centre of civilisation. We have lost the concentrated focus of all the urban population's attention upon the activity at the centre. The cultural events and public monuments, as well as the glittering shops and hotels of downtown no longer mean, to the average prosperous citizen, the city. Instead he sees the centre as a declining and dingy commercial area, surrounded by slums, public housing, industry, and the mile upon mile of "grey area." As David Riesman recently noted, Americans once escaped from the stifling atmosphere of the small provincial towns to the greater life of the city; now they escape from the deteriorating, depressing and dangerous city to the safe and pleasant life of the suburbs.

More important, we have lost the ancient structure of the city as a *polis,* a republic of committed and patriotic citizens. The recent essay by Don Martindale, introducing a translation of Weber's essay on *The City,* emphasises the lack of congruence between the classical cities of Greece and Italy, the walled communes of Europe, on the one hand, and contemporary cities on the other. The city is, in this view, no longer the major arena where dynamic forces change and create the polity—nor is it the prime stage upon which *virtu* is displayed and glory is won. It is, instead, a convenience of location for the organisations and the population of a contemporary society.

And indeed, the classical city is anomalous in large-scale society. The revolutions in transport, communication, and energy transformation, which have created large-scale economic and political systems, make obsolete the encapsulated political community. The same changes which have dispersed the metropolitan neighbourhoods have increased the total urban population—through increasing the interdependence of city and total society. Both the increasing control of local affairs by giant extended organisations, which span the entire society, and the increasing dominance of the national government, detract from the particular importance and value of City Hall. At the same time, the increasing perfection of the mass media allows communication without the assemblage of the citizens at the centre. In short, the revolution in the space-time ratio has made obsolete the older urban community forms.*

IF WE PROJECT . . .

However, the increase in scale of the society creates as it destroys. It is precisely because our degrees of freedom have been multiplied that we no longer huddle at the centre where railroads, canals, and rivers cross. And, looking into the future, it is difficult to see a reversal. First, one can only expect a continued and increasing use of the new media of transport and communication, along with technological innovations which will speed and cheapen short-haul movement. Furthermore, the older structures at the centre will continue to decline in value unless their central location is the key to their use. They will be socially amortised and abandoned. At the same time we are increasingly committed to the newer structures of the dispersed city.

The city that emerges is, then, more of a regional structure than a highly concentrated complex of tall buildings. It will spread over areas larger than entire states, bound together by a transport and communications grid which will be as efficient in relation to geographical extension as that of fifteenth-century Florence. It will be polynucleated, with dozens of large decentralised markets for all the necessities of life. At the same time, there will be greater communication from city to city, and a greater involvement in the nationwide culture and the national polity.

This decentralisation is already in full swing. However, the conservatives of an older urban tradition continue to insist that the centre, and the centre alone, is the proper location for many agencies of the local community. As this prejudice gives way to the forces of the various markets (not only

---

* For an extensive discussion of increase in scale and its consequences for the total society, see *The Analysis of Social Change* by Godfrey and Monica Wilson, Cambridge: The University Press, 1954.

for retail goods, but for varied services) we can expect the spread of other activities among the regional sub-centres. Thus it is quite possible to develop a network of art museums throughout the metropolitan complex, with travelling shows. There is no reason why the metropolitan symphony orchestras should not "tour" their own suburban centres—particularly since the major market for the performing arts is among the white-collar workers who have left the central city. In short, if we get over our prejudice in favour of suffering, and recognise that many persons may like theatre, opera, concerts and the plastic arts, but still dislike the long drive to the centre and back in the evening, we may rediscover the audiences which can give vigorous support to such activities.

Meanwhile, the mass media are most certainly here to stay. Such developments as F.M. radio, high-fidelity recording, and paid television, promise to make the greatest performances available to the greatest number of citizens in the large-scale society. In losing the cultural concentration of the older city, we may well escape from a kind of parochialism which becomes discernible only when we can compare it with the new opportunities.

In conclusion: contemporary western societies are rapidly increasing in organisational scale. This is accompanied by a spreading urbanism, a culture general throughout the nation state—a way of life which cuts across the various communities, neighbourhoods, regions, provinces, of older societal patterns. Historically, these two processes have been empirically situated in cities—dense, heterogeneous agglomerations of people. Today, with our new media of transport and communications, cities as we have known them are no longer necessary—and very likely, no longer possible. Instead, we are developing region-spanning complexes of human activities, accessible from end to end for each citizen.

5

Individual Participation
in Mass Society

The participation of the individual in his community is of importance on two grounds. Theoretically, an understanding of such behavior aids in the clarification and extension of our picture of modern society as a system. And, from a normative point of view, the nature and degree of such participation sets the limits and indicates the possibilities of social control in a nonhierarchical society. The dissolution of traditional orders, reflected in our fluid class structure and the uncertain basis for legitimacy, presents a major problem for modern society. Further, if we assume that the solvents destroying these older forms of order emanate from the process of rational transformation and increase in scale in the society, we may be confident that the problems experienced in America and the West are potentially universal problems.

The general ideology identifying the problem and indicating its solution is for Westerners some variation of the democratic dogma. We assume that for the hierarchical order of the past we may substitute an order based on individual option, control through the consent of the governed.

In making such normative decisions, however, we are also making certain empirical assumptions about the nature of modern society. We assume the existence, at some level, of subcommunities, in which the individual has interest, influence, and concerning which he has some realistic information. Such subcommunities are the necessary condition for individual participation in the vast totality of society (though they are not sufficient conditions), and whoever says "democracy" is, in effect, positing such groups.

However, the western societies in which modern democratic political systems were first devised have changed radically since their democratic birth. America, approximately five per cent urban at the time of the Revolution, is today over sixty per cent urban and this predominantly urban, centralized society differs radically from the nation assumed by the framers of the democratic constitutions. While the rural population and the smaller cities still have their importance, the social structure of the large urban complex is crucial for the study of social participation and democratic process in contemporary society. It is upon individual participation in very large cities that this paper is focused.

Many current interpretations of the large city sharply contradict the empirical assumptions implied in the democratic dogma. The analyses of Louis Wirth [1] and Georg Simmel [2] emphasize these aspects of the city: (*a*) its heterogeneity (*b*) its impersonality (*c*) its anonymity and (*d*) the consequent social fragmentation of the individuals who make up the urban world. Such views are congruent with the long-run trends envisaged by Durkheim,[3] Tonnies,[4] Park,[6] and others —trends from a simple homogeneous society possessing an automatic *consensus universalis* and resulting solidarity, towards a complex, heterogeneous society, in which order results from functional interdependence of differentiated groups, and solidarity within groups leads to dynamic relations between them. In this view (there are important differences between these theorists, but in major respects they are similar) the primary-group structure of society is in a process of rapid dissolution. Kinship groups, neighborhood groups, the church, and the local community are losing their importance. Their strength in controlling individual behavior is shifted to formal, secondary groups, which organize work, religion and politics. Even play is controlled by the large commercial organization.

From such a position, the theorist who wishes to emphasize the viability of democratic structure and process must, like MacIver,[7] accept the formal organization as the effective subcommunity—one which is capable of performing the function of organizing individuals in meaningful wholes which may then participate in the control of the larger society. The "Associational Society" is seen as the alternative to the hierarchical society of the past, based upon primary communities and hereditary strata.

These formulations concerning urban social structure are largely the result of keen observation and analysis, rather than large scale empirical studies. Their influence is largely due to two facts: (*a*) they are based upon observations available at random in any large city, and (*b*) they fill, neatly, a gap in the theoretical system of sociology. However, in the past decade, and even more in the last few years, a substantial body of work has been accumulated dealing with the specific area of participation in the urban community. It is possible, on the basis of this work, to sketch a tentative description of the modes of participation which occur among urbanites—a snapshot of the organizational topography of the modern city. Such a description serves as a test of earlier assumptions and the basis for new interpretation.

THE DISENCHANTMENT OF THE CITY:
EMPIRICAL RESEARCH

The studies to be summarized are focused upon participation in formal organizations—Kommarovsky,[8]—the local area as community—Janowitz,[9]—the urban neighborhood—

Foley,[10]—and these together with other areas of participation —Axelrod,[11] Bell,[12,13] Greer.[14,15] The urban complexes included are: New York (Kommarovsky), Chicago (Janowitz), Los Angeles (Greer), San Francisco (Bell), Detroit (Axelrod) and Rochester (Foley). The net is thus spread wide, and the results are remarkably consistent—so much so that the discussion of findings will emphasize common trends, rather than variations. The following loci of participation will be discussed: kinship, the neighborhood, the local area, formal organizations, friends, work associates, and the mass media.

Some Empirical Fndings. A. Kinship. One of the most striking results of this research is the extreme importance of kin relations for the urban residents. The results, in Detroit, Los Angeles, and San Francisco, all indicate the same fact: kin relations, as measured by visiting patterns, are the most important social relations for all types of urban populations. Half of the urbanites visit their kin at least once a week, and large majorities visit them at least once a month. Even the extended family is important; one-third of the Los Angeles sample visited uncles, cousins, and the like at least monthly. The conjugal family is of basic importance; the urbanite, in any local area, is apt to spend most of his evenings in the bosom of his family; this is true even in Hollywood, and extremely so in the suburbs.

B. The neighborhood. There is much more differentiation here—the range is from a substantial number of people who are intense neighbors to a substantial number who hardly neighbor at all. The degree of neighboring varies by local area, and within the city there is a wide range, but the average urban resident has some informal neighboring relationships.

C. The local area. Much like their neighboring behavior, urban residents indicate wide variation in their degree of "local community" identification and participation. Janowitz found a majority of his Chicago samples to be identified with their local area as their "true home," and in Los Angeles this was true of some areas, but varied considerably between areas.

D. Formal organizations. Although a majority of urban residents belong to churches, a minority which varies around forty per cent attend as frequently as once a month. Aside from church participation, most urban individuals belong to one organization or none. Low socio-economic rank individuals, and middle-rank individuals, usually belong to one organization at most, and it is usually work-connected for men, child- and church-connected for women. Only in the upper socio-economic levels is the "joiner" to be found with any frequency. When attendance at organizations is studied, some twenty per cent of the memberships are usually "paper" memberships.

E. Friendship. Informal participation in friendship relations, with individual friends or friendship circles, is an extremely frequent occurrence. Friendship, outside any organizational context, is a near-universal in the city. The urbanite is seldom isolated from this type of primary group.

F. Work associates as friends. Here one of the important hypotheses of urban theory is in question. As the primary community and neighborhood decline, friendship was expected to be more closely related to work organization. However, studies by Axelrod, Bell, and Greer all indicate that work associates are a minor proportion of the individual's primary relations when he is away from the job. Only in the upper socio-economic levels (where friendship is frequently instrumental for economic ends) is there a change. Work relations are usually insulated from free primary-group participation of the urban-dweller.

G. Mass entertainment. Cultural participation in organized entertainment is relatively unimportant for urban adults. Most of the Los Angeles samples attended fewer than three events a month. One-third attended no event, one-third one or two, and a few attended as many as ten or more. Most attendance was at movies, but the real importance of the mass entertainment media was in the home—television and radio are extremely important, but it is in the context of family participation.

In summary, the urbanite's individual "path" through social structure crosses these six areas of possible involvement and participation. According to one theory of urban society, his involvement should be increasingly intense with respect to formal organizations, work associates as friends, and mass entertainment; it should be correspondingly weak with respect to kin, neighbors, the local community, and primary groups other than these. The studies cited indicate no such clear-cut development. Instead, the usual individual's involvement in formal organizations and work-based friendship is weak; the mass media are most important in a family context; participation with kin and friendship circles is powerful, and with neighbors and the local community's groups it varies immensely by area.

The picture that emerges is of a society in which the conjugal family is extremely powerful among all types of population. This small, primary group structure is the basic area of involvement; at the other pole is work, a massive absorber of time, but an activity which is rarely related to the family through "outside" friendship with on-the-job associates. Instead, the family-friendship group is relatively free-floating, within the world of large scale secondary associations. The family is usually identified, although weakly, with the local community; it "neighbors," but strictly "within bounds." By and large, the conjugal family group keeps itself to itself; outside is the world—formal organizations, work, and the communities.

Such a picture is remarkably similar to that which Oeser and Hammond[16] present, from their studies in Melbourne, Australia. Melbourne, like the American cities studied, is a mushrooming metropolitan complex in a highly urbanized society. Its people are largely "middle rank" economically, neither poor nor wealthy. Its social order centers around the single family dwelling unit, the conjugal family, selected kinfolk, the job, and the mass media—the latter largely consumed in the home. Neither in Melbourne nor in American cities do we find much participation, by most people, in formal organizations or the community. The family retires to its domain, to work in the garden, listen to radio or television, care for children, and read.

A Typology of Urban Populations. Such findings as these are important in two respects: first, in their sharp departures from what would be considered the conventional picture of metropolitan life, and, second, in their consistency. The agreement between the various American studies, and between these and the Australian study, leads us to suspect that such participation patterns are a result of powerful trends in modern Western society. In explaining the average, and variations from it, it is useful to base a description upon social trends.

The Shevky-Bell typology of urban subpopulations[17,18] is one such method of describing and accounting for the varieties of urban areas. Based upon Colin Clark's studies of economic history,[19] and on analysis of the long-term changes in the nature of production, the organization of work, and the composition of the total society, the typology posits three dimensions along which urban subpopulations vary. These are: social rank (economic and occupational status), segregation (the proportion of segregated ethnic populations in a community), and urbanization. The latter refers to variations in life-styles; it ranges from the family-centered, home-centered life at the low-urbanization pole to an opposite pole where one finds many single individuals and couples without children. Studies have indicated that the urbanization of an area is closely associated with the importance of the local area as a "social fact," as a community. And this, in turn, is associated with political participation.

The results of the Los Angeles study of four census-tract populations at middle social rank, without segregated populations, but varying from very highly-urban to very low-urban areas, were summarized as follows:

> In general, our findings indicate a growing importance of the local area as a social fact, as we go from the highly urbanized areas . . . to the low-urban areas. Neighboring, organizational location in the area, the residences of the members of organizations in the area, the location and composition of church congregations, all vary with urbanization and increase as urbanization decreases. Readership of the local community press also increases, as does the ability to name local leaders and intention to remain in the area indefinitely.
>
> Thus the studies of the small community, with its local organizational structure and stratification system, may apply in the low-urban areas; they are not likely to fit in the highly-urban area. We may think of the urbanization dimension as having, at the low pole, communities much like those studied by W. Lloyd Warner, August Hollingshead, and others. At the highly urbanized pole, we encounter the big city population of the stereotype, organized not in community terms, but in terms of the corporation, politics, the mass media, and the popular culture. But predominantly, the highly urban populations associate in small, informal groups, with friends and kinfolk.[15]

A comparison was made between the political attitudes and behavior of the very highly-urbanized population and the very low-urban population studied in Los Angeles. The latter were more involved in their local community (they could name more local leaders), had a more consistent voting record, were more certain of the social class position of their "community" (middle-class) and of their political preferences. This data is reinforced by that of Janowitz, who found that, among his Chicago sample:

Family cohesion and primary group contacts seemed more relevant for predisposing an individual toward acceptance of the community's controlling institutions and associations.[9]

Janowitz took community newspaper readership and identification with the local community as indexes of community participation.

Regardless of the respondents' political affiliations, relative confidence in the effectiveness and honesty of local politics—projective measures of personal political competence—tended to be associated with high community newspaper readership.[9]

We may summarize the findings in this manner: (a) urban subpopulations may be arranged in a meaningful typology, based upon their place in arrays derived from indexes of social rank, segregation, and urbanization. (b) As the type of area varies, participation patterns vary. As urbanization declines, there is an increase in neighboring and participation in the local community in all its forms. (c) This participation is associated with more political involvement and a higher degree of political competence.

The picture of participation in the metropolis must be qualified in these ways: the highly-urbanized populations are atypical—they are an extreme of a continuum. Their behavior deviates from the stereotype of the atomistic man in their great involvement in the family and their intensive participation in primary groups. However, the majority of the population in a great urban complex does not lie in the highly-urbanized segments; instead, it is of middle to low urbanization, and middle social rank. At the extremely low-urban pole, the local area becomes a definite community—it is a social fact, as well as a geographical fact.

The galaxy of local residential areas which make up a great city may be seen as differing in their level of living (social rank) and their style of living (urbanization). At each level of social rank there are vast differences between areas of high and low urbanization. In general, the highly urban areas lie within the central city, and the low-urban areas lie towards the suburbs. One may keep in mind the image of the urban apartment house districts, on the one hand, and the tract developments and suburbs on the other. As one moves towards the latter, community participation in the local area increases, and political behavior in general changes.

However, even as few urban subareas approach the anonymity and fragmentation of the stereotype, fewer still approach the kind of subcommunity envisaged in the democratic ideology. Although more respondents can name local leaders in the suburbs than in the highly-urbanized areas, less than forty per cent can do so anywhere. And the percentage who cannot even name one city-wide leader is considerable. With this qualification in mind, the differences between the polar extremes are sharp and suggestive. What is the meaning of this great variation in "normal life style"—what accounts for it, and what are its consequences?

COMMUNITY—AND MODERN URBAN SOCIETY

The word *community* is an ambiguous one, with many theoretical meanings and varying empirical referents. Two core meanings, however, stand out in the theoretical and empirical uses of the term. In one, community connotes certain modes of relationship, in which the individual shares values, is understood and identifies with the aggregate. In the other meaning community indicates a spatially-defined social unit having functional significance, reflecting the interdependence of individuals and groups. In the first sense, the modern metropolis is not a community; in the second, it must be by definition.

Rather than choose one meaning, it is preferable to indicate the empirical interrelation of the two aspects. For it is likely that, when we refer to community, we have in the back of our mind the picture of the *primary community*—preliterate society, feudal holding, or peasant village. Such communities fulfilled both definitions: they were extremely significant functionally, providing all or most of the conditions for individual and group life, and they had a high degree of consensus and communion. Such is manifestly not the case with the urban community today, and the reasons lie deep in the nature of modern society.

The chief difference between societies based upon primary communities and urban societies is one of scale—modern urban society is the result of a vast increase in scale. Wilson and Wilson[20] have studied this process in Central Africa, tracing its nature and its effects upon three small village cultures. They noted the autonomy of the societies at the early stage—each small group had its own means of subsistence and order, and each was independent of the other. The process of increase in scale was one of increasing commitments to widespread social groups and dwindling dependence upon immediate associates. The wealthy Central African farmer, for example, became free of local economic coercion by the village head man at the same time he became dependent upon the international ground-nuts market. Thus, if one conceives of social organization as a network of mutually-sustaining activities, based upon necessary functions, one may say that the radius of this network was short in the primary community of village society; with the increase of scale, there is a lengthening of these radii of functional interdependence.

Such extension of interdependence is not necessarily the result of rational undertaking, nor are the results all functional. However, once such interdependence exists, the human need for predictability (and the demand for predictability in ongoing organized groups) tends to result in a flow of communication and a mutual ordering of behavior. To paraphrase Freud, "Where interdependence is, there shall organization be."

The process may be traced in the development of modern industry (Florence[21]). The need for a predictable source of supplies results in "vertical integration"; the need for a predictable market results in monopoly, oligopoly, and cartels; the need for predictable work-flow results in bureaucracy, and indirectly in some form of labor organization. The organization of one function acts as a catalyst producing further organization; thus industrial cartels produce national labor unions, and unions in turn force the further integration of management groups.

Returning now to the concept of the primary community, we note that in such communities the radii of many functional interdependencies were short, coinciding with the same aggregate of persons. The result was, for the individual, a complete dependence upon this community leaving him few choices; for the community, it was autonomy from outside groups. There was a coincidence of many organizational networks, based upon functional interdependence for various social products in the same small aggregate. The result was an extreme density of interaction. When such density of interaction occurs, a secondary function results: the social process. This may be defined as communication as an end in itself; it is identical with many meanings of *communion*, and it is the basis for that aspect of association which we call the primary group.

Interdependence based upon the need for the various social products (protection, economic production and consumption, etc.) and upon the need for the social process, or communion, thus creates an extremely strong social group coterminous with the spatially-defined collective. Such a group satisfies both the meanings of community advanced earlier: it is both a mode of relationships and a spatially-defined social unit having functional significance. In such a society the village is, to a large degree, one primary group. (For a more extended presentation of this theory, see Greer.[5,22])

The process of increase in scale, however, results in both the lengthening of the radii of interdependence (spatially and socially) and the disjunction of the different radii, representing the organizations fulfilling different functions. Not only is the small local area no longer autonomous—the boundaries of the organizations upon which it is dependent no longer coincide. Work, government, education, religion—each is a congeries of organizations which include parts of the local area's population in their various spans, while this area is thrown with many others into various society-wide networks.

In this sense of the word, America has never been to any large degree a society based upon primary community for Western society was already large in scale and rapidly expanding when America became a colony; the very nature of colonialism insured dependence upon the imperial and international markets. There are, however, degrees and it is likely that, until the twentieth century, community existed in a widespread fashion in open-country neighborhoods, villages, and the country towns. Such community, less complete than in the peasant village to be sure, was infinitely stronger than that to be found in any part of the modern metropolis. Scattered data from the novels celebrating the "revolt from the village," the criticisms by intellectuals like Thorstein Veblen, and studies of contemporary backwoods settlements in the Hispañola country and the southern Appalachians indicate that spatial isolation produced a marked degree of community.

Such community disappears under urban conditions; it has no hold over the individual, for its functions are preempted by large specialized organizations in the interest of rational control, while the individual is highly mobile and is isolated in the local area only when he chooses to be. As the functional bases for intense interaction disappear, communion goes with them.

As this occurs, the small conjugal family becomes increasingly important for the individual and, indirectly, for the total society. The reason is partly one of default; as the primary community leaves the spatially defined group, the conjugal family remains and is today probably the strongest basis for communion available to most people in the large city. At the same time, in a society of increasing scale, the family is relatively free from community norms (where there is little interaction there can be neither surveillance nor sanctions), and great individuation of family patterns is possible. With the surplus of freedom, of leisure, and of money, the individual can choose between family and nonfamily living—and the family can choose between community-oriented and noncommunity local areas to live in.

Thus the variations in urbanization, and in local community participation, found in the various studies cited can be understood as part of the large-scale process which (a) destroys the primary community, (b) releases its individual components for duty in large, segmental organizations, and (c) releases much time, expenditure, and behavior from community-enforced norms. The large scale society is, in this sense, one of emerging freedoms.

IMPLICATIONS FOR POLITICAL CONTROL

The results of this brief excursus may now be compared with the empirical assumptions underlying democratic political structures. Much of that ideal pattern relies upon the belief in stable subcommunities, viable wholes through which the individual may clarify in social discourse and affect through social action the objects of his grievances and desires. Such a group requires sufficient communication and involvement to result in the ordering of individual behavior. It must then be important to a large part of its constituency. Our ideal example from the past is the New England township, and its image still has an overweening importance in our thinking. It is something of an archetype.

The local area today, however, particularly in the metropolis, no longer represents such a community. Instead of a primary community it is necessarily what Janowitz calls a "community of limited liability." The individual's investment is always small, and if he "loses" he can cut his losses by getting out—the community cannot hold him. Even among the most community-oriented, "small town" areas, those at the low-urbanization pole within the city, there is great variation in the importance of the area to the individual. The local merchants have more of a stake than the home-owning residents with children, and these are more invested than the couple without children who rent an apartment. However, even the most deeply involved can withdraw from the local community, and satisfy all needs elsewhere—and the withdrawal need not be physical.

The reasons may be restated: by community in the double sense we mean a spatially defined aggregate which is a powerful social group. Such groups exist only where there is functional interdependence (as the local community in the suburbs is most functional for the merchants, least so for the childless couple who rent). Only where such functional interdependence occurs is participation strong: constraint is, in this sense, the key to community.

If this is true, then it follows that primary communities are not possible in modern society save in a very few areas—in such survivals as the backwoods communities noted earlier, and in such institutional aggregates as the prison, the monastery, and the army. However, aside from such atypical collectives, there are other groups in which the individual must interact continuously and for a large share of his waking life. One such is the work organization.

The functional interdependence, the flow of communication, and the consequent ordering of behavior at the place of work bulk large in the individual's life. Some theorists, of whom Mayo[23] is the best known, imply that a primary community of work is therefore possible. Certainly economic production, a share in the surplus, and status in the general society are basic functional supports of such primary communities as the peasant village. However in a most cursory inspection of modern industry, several factors appear which make such a strong work community very unlikely. These include freedom of labor, the conflicting functions of the work organization, and their results in the labor union on one hand and the hierarchical organization of industry on the other.

Free labor, which is functional for the total economic system, allows the individual to leave a given work group and join another. His needs may be served as well or better—and likewise the functional demands of industry; however, his relations with others in the group are conditioned by this freedom. Even work is a commitment of limited liability.

Equally important is the hierarchical organization of work in our society. The "scalar principle" is undoubtedly necessary in large organized groups; still the net effect is that the most important social group outside the family is ordered in a way which contradicts the assumptions of democratic process. Further, the common interest of workers and management is so channeled, through the unstable division of the product into profits and wages, as to create a well-structured division of interest as well. This schism between the leaders of work and their followers drastically reduces the common ground of values, and the unions have arisen in response.

Finally, the division of labor at present is so great as to weaken the common conscience of the different levels of workmen. Durkheim postulated a solidarity, a group *élan,* based upon teamwork; however, to the routine worker his job is frequently merely the payment of a pound of flesh (Oeser and Hammond).[24] A large proportion of most work organizations is made up of routine workers, and their lack of control over their work, their competition with management for economic rewards, their organized voice, the union, and their ability to leave the job, all represent limiting conditions. It is difficult to see how strong communities could arise within such market-oriented organizations.

Thus the major institutional order of work is unable to supply the basis for primary community; the local area is functionally weak; the kinship system is most important at the level of the small conjugal family. The remaining possible structure for individual participation is the formal voluntary organization. A brief review of the findings cited earlier, however, indicates that such organizations are relatively unimportant "at the grass roots." They are arenas for intensive participation to only a small minority of their members, and many individuals have no formal organizational membership at all.

One possible exception is the labor union. Here is an organization whose functional importance is great indeed for its members. Unlike industry, it is an organization based upon the assumptions of the democratic ideology: participation in decision-making is quite easy. Finally, it is an organizational type which is extremely widespread—it is probably the most important single kind of formal organization outside the churches. What of union participation?

Many studies indicate that the average attendance of members at a local union's routine meetings is extremely low—from less than one per cent to perhaps 20 per cent.[25,27] Most of those who attend are the same group, over and over, and these, together with the paid professional staff, have undue influence upon the organization. For the average member, on the other hand, the union is almost an aspect of government. He pays his dues, and, as in the national elections, frequently does not vote. His leaders, with the best will in the world, far overreach their responsibility—for there is nobody else to take responsibility. Most often the leaders "run the locals" (with some restraint from the small cadres of actives) and the members act as a "plebiscitary body" in Herberg's phrase.[26] Far from constituting a "real community" for the workers, the union is simply another service organization. It can mobilize the members to strike, but not to participate in the organization's routine functioning where the basic grounds for strikes are considered and argued out.

In summary, it is apparent that in a society with a democratic political structure and ideology democratic processes are relatively rare. Shared decision-making, control through consent, is most common in the conjugal family and friendship groups, but it is hardly transmitted through them to larger entities. The other areas where individual participation is possible, local community and formal organization, engage only a minority in more than token participation, and the organizations of work—most important of all in many respects—are structurally unfit for democratic processes. The following picture of participation in urban society results.

There is a plethora of formal organizations, labor unions, business and professional groups, churches and church-related groups, parent-teacher's associations, and the like. They exert pressure and they influence the political party—another formal organization. However, the leadership in such organizations is largely professionalized and bureaucratized, and such leaders become, in effect, oligarchs. At the same time the members participate in an erratic manner, and frequently "stay away in droves" from the meetings. The organization is a holding company for the members' interests; they exercise an occasional veto right in the plebiscites.

The local area is either not a community in any sense, as in the highly urban areas of the city, or it is a community "of limited liability"; communication and participation are apt to be segmental here as in any formal organization that is ex traterritorial. And many are utterly uninvolved, even in the strongest "communities."

Formal government is highly bureaucratized and, aside from votes in national elections and (very occasionally) in local elections, the individual participates very little. Most party "clubs" are made up of professionals, semiprofessionals, and a handful of "actives."

The organization of work is nondemocratic in its nature, and the individual's participation is largely a matter of conforming to directions and decisions made far above him in the hierarchy. This is of great importance, for with the rise of professional leadership in all formal organizations—from labor unions to churches, Boy Scouts, and even recreation in general—the most intense participation in all groups is apt to be that of the official, for whom the organization is his *job* in a job hierarchy.

Thus interpreting the participation of the average individual in democratic society is a somewhat bizarre experience: by and large he does not participate. Since this is true, it is difficult to make a case for the widespread importance of the democratic processes for most people, except in the home and friendship circle. The democracy we inhabit is, instead, largely a democracy of substantive freedoms, or what Fromm[28] calls "freedom from." Produced by the struggles between various professionally directed interest groups, largely quite undemocratic in their control processes, freedom of choice for the individual is something of a by-product. It exists, perhaps, through the balance of "countervailing forces."

This freedom is, however, a considerable area of the average person's "life space." It is manifest in the urbanite's ability to choose his marital and family status, his local area and degree of community participation—his life style. He may privatize his nonworking world, and turn inward to his single family dwelling unit and his conjugal family (which he does); he may refuse to participate in many activities and yield only a token participation in others (and he does).

Though his commitments to the job and the family are constant and have a priority in time and energy, he exercises freedom of choice—in the market, the large sphere which

Riesman[29] calls consumership. He also has a freedom in the symbol spheres which has never been widespread before in any society—the variety of media and of messages is overwhelming. (There are approximately 1,000 hours of television available each week to the Los Angeleno.) His relative wealth, literacy, and privacy allow an exploration of meaning never possible before. In his homelife he experiments with leisure—the hobby industries, the do-it-yourself industries, the flood of specialized publications and programs bears testimony to the increasing use the urbanite makes of this choice. He is part of the *nouveau riche* of leisure.

His rise is a measure of the leveling of the hierarchical orders; their remnants remain in the relatively higher rates of participation and leadership for the "upper ranks" in most of the formal organizations. Most people, however, are the equivalents and descendants of the illiterates of a hundred years ago. They have neither the vested interest nor the tradition of responsible participation—and they have a great freedom from forced participation in work. They exercise it in fashioning the typical life-patterns adumbrated, in avoiding organizations, politely giving lip-service to the neighbors and local leaders, avoiding work associates off the job, orienting themselves towards evening, week ends, and vacations, which they spend *en famille* looking at television, gossiping and eating with friends and kin, and cultivating the garden.

The bureaucratic leadership and the plebiscitary membership, the community of limited liability, and the privatized citizen are not images many of us hold of a proper democratic society. Perhaps it cannot last—perhaps power is accumulating too rapidly and in too few centers. On the other hand, the picture is less frightening than that of the atomistic man adrift in mass society, *anomic* and destructive. Furthermore, the picture of participation in the primary community is a rather strenuous one. Perhaps a revision downwards, toward effective "limited community" participation, and effective "plebiscites" might result in an adequate check upon the formal leadership groups—enough to represent a modest achievement of democratic participation and control through consent.

REFERENCES

I. Images of the City

1. Louis Wirth, "Urbanism as a Way of Life," *The American Journal of Sociology*, XLIV (July, 1938), 1–24.
2. Kurt Wolff, trans. and ed., *The Sociology of Georg Simmel* (Glencoe, 1950).
3. George Simpson, trans., *Emile Durkheim on the Division of Labor in Society* (New York, 1933).
4. C. P. Loomis, trans. and ed., *Fundamental Concepts of Sociology* (Ferdinand Tönnies, *Gemeinschaft und Gesellschaft*) (New York, 1940).
5. Robert Redfield, *The Folk Culture of Yucatan* (Chicago, 1941).
6. Robert E. Park, *Human Communities* (Glencoe, 1952).
7. Robert M. MacIver and Charles H. Page, *Society: An Introductory Analysis* (New York, 1949).

II. Empirical Studies

8. Mirra Kommarovsky, "The Voluntary Associations of Urban Dwellers," *American Sociological Review*, XI (Dec., 1946), 868–896.
9. Morris Janowitz, *The Community Press in an Urban Setting* (Glencoe, 1952).
10. Donald E. Foley, "Neighbors or Urbanites? The Study of a Rochester District," *The University of Rochester's Studies of Metropolitan Rochester* (Rochester, 1952).
11. Morris Axelrod, "Urban Structure and Social Participation," *American Sociological Review*, XXI (Feb., 1956), 13–18.
12. Wendell Bell, "Urban Neighborhood Types and Participation in Formal Organizations," *American Sociological Review*, XXI (Feb., 1956), 25–34.
13. Wendell Bell (with the assistance of Maryanne Force and Marion Boat), "People of the City," (processed) Stanford University Research Facility, Stanford, California (1954).
14. Scott Greer, "Urbanism Reconsidered: A Comparative Study

of Local Areas in a Metropolis," *American Sociological Review*, XXI (Feb., 1956), 19–25.

15. Scott Greer and Ella Kube, "Urban Worlds: A Comparative Study of Four Los Angeles Areas," (processed) Laboratory in Urban Culture, Occidental College (1955).
16. O. A. Oeser and S. B. Hammond, eds., *Social Structure and Personality in a City* (New York, 1954).

III. *A Typology of Urban Populations*

17. Eshref Shevky and Marilyn Williams, *The Social Areas of Los Angeles* (Berkeley and Los Angeles, 1948).
18. Eshref Shevky and Wendell Bell, *Social Area Analysis* (Stanford, 1955).
19. Colin Clark, *The Conditions of Economic Progress* (London, 1940).
20. Godfrey Wilson and Monica Wilson, *The Analysis of Social Change* (London, 1945).

IV. *Community—and the City*

21. P. Sargant Florence, *The Logic of British and American Industry* (London, 1953).
22. Scott Greer, *Social Organization* (New York, 1955).
23. Elton Mayo, *Human Problems of an Industrial Civilization* (New York, 1933).
24. Oeser and Hammond, op. cit., Part V, "The Workers: Social Hierarchies."
25. Scott Greer, "The Participation of Ethnic Minorities in the Labor Unions of Los Angeles County" (unpublished Ph.D. dissertation), Department of Anthropology and Sociology, University of California at Los Angeles (1952).
26. Will Herberg, "Bureaucracy and Democracy in Trade Unions," *Antioch Review*, III (Sept., 1943), 405–417.
27. Seymour Martin Lipset, "The Political Process in Trade-Unions: A Theoretical Statement," in *Freedom and Control in Modern Society* (New York, 1954).
28. Erich Fromm, *Escape from Freedom* (New York, 1941).
29. David Riesman (in collaboration with Reuel Denny and Nathan Glazer), *The Lonely Crowd, a Study of the Changing American Character* (New Haven, 1950).

II

ST. LOUIS,
A CITY WITH A PAST

6

Putting the Political In:
An Introduction

In comparing St. Louis with Los Angeles the difference in age was most dramatic. Not only was St. Louis older, but it was a city built upon nineteenth-century technology. Its location at the confluence of the Missouri and Mississippi rivers was its original reason for being, and it grew to be the third largest city in the country with the coming of the railroads. Thus it was not laid out with the automobile in mind, and in 1956 had only three miles of express highway, built before World War II. Its narrow streets and massive slums contrasted sharply with the open texture of Los Angeles, the city on wheels.

Yet in their newer areas, at the growing edge of suburbia, the cities were not really very different. As some have called Los Angeles one great suburb, so one may call the suburban developments around the country extensions of L.A. The same shopping centers, industrial parks, and housing developments, tied together by the same system of super-highways, containing the same kind of familistic population, occur from Buffalo to San Diego. All that really differs is climate and terrain, and, perhaps, civic culture. Many people in St.

Louis mourned for the days when it was the third largest metropolitan area, wealthy and contemporary, with a rich and impressive center near the river. This was one of the strands in the tangled ideological skein called the movement to solve "the metropolitan problem."

The Metropolitan St. Louis Survey was organized to describe and analyze the government, economy, and social structure of St. Louis, Missouri, for the purposes of evaluation and reform. As chief sociologist of that enterprise, I carried out a series of studies from 1956 through 1959, concerned with the participation of citizens in local government.

As I have noted, St. Louis in 1956 was, in many respects, the polar opposite of Los Angeles. It was an old city, by American standards, and it looked it. It was not only ill used; it was abused. While the incumbent mayor had, in his previous post as director of the smoke abatement agency, cleaned up the air fouled with soft coal smoke, the souvenirs of its presence for the last hundred years were everywhere. The downtown of the city was sooty and unprosperous; the great riverfront with its historic associations extraordinarily unkempt and undeveloped. The City of St. Louis, about half the metropolitan area, was a half circle with the river for its straight side; it corroborated the concentric zone hypothesis in the sense that blight, overwhelming in the pre-Civil War housing near the center, slowly declined as one approached the city limits. Halfway out from the center lay a district, near St. Louis University, known as "midtown." It was an abortive second nucleus whose growth had been halted by the Depression. With theaters, shops, and some tall buildings it was, by 1956, already blighted.

The area of new growth lay beyond the city, in suburban St. Louis County. The county seat, Clayton, lay due west of the boundary line, in the midst of prosperous to opulent neighborhoods. It contained the most lucrative shopping center in the metropolitan area, and it was thus the commercial and political center for the amorphous galaxy of suburbs known as "the County." Here the Metropolitan St. Louis Survey set up shop. In 1956 the air was not filled with concern over the central city, its slums and its poverty and its blacks, as the major problem of America, and it is symptomatic that we located so far from the center. Our suburban location doubtless contributed various biases, including a certain aloofness—reinforced by the fact that several major figures in the Survey organization were from elsewhere. Our assignment was to study the city in a systematic way.

Coming to St. Louis directly from the studies of Los Angeles neighborhoods, it seemed sensible to continue the line of investigation I had begun in the newest of our great metropolises. The relationships between the type of population in a local area and its associational structure seemed highly relevant to the St. Louis research problem. One of the major aims was to assess the reasons for, and consequences of, a metropolis divided into one very large municipality, the City of St. Louis, and ninety-seven small suburbs, the County. It was believed that the small suburbs in their number and fractiousness prevented true government for the metropolitan area as a whole. On the other hand some argued that the small scale of politics in the little municipalities brought government close to the people, making for greater accessibility and more accountability of officials. A key element in such a state of affairs would be, then, citizen participation informally and formally in the associational structure of the local community.

Indeed, a key focus of the sociological studies in St. Louis was suburbia, as ideal type and discernible fact. In those days the air was full of disparaging comments on the vast areas of horizontal housing surrounding the central city. The "split-level mousetrap" and the "crack in the picture window" were polemics against the horrors of massified suburban living. It was generally thought by civic ideologues that the suburbs were symptom and cause of a general anemia in American social and cultural life. Nowhere had I seen suburbs and central city so sharply differentiated as in St. Louis; and the Los Angeles studies had provided a method for identifying what difference, if any, suburban residence made in social life.

But, as Walter Martin had pointed out, suburbs could be defined in several ways. They were political entities separate from the center; they were populations of a certain type— white, middle-class, and fertile; they were neighborhoods in which people lived a certain kind of social life, which emphasized neighboring, child care, and informality. One way to approach the definition of suburbia was to measure the census tracts of central city and suburbia by social rank, ethnicity, and life-style.

When we did so, we found a considerable overlap between central city and suburban county. Middle-rank, non-ethnic, familistic populations made up the middle majority of each. At the extremes, however, they differed; the city had more than its share of ethnics (and nearly all of the blacks), the poor, and the urbane in life-style. Still, in the suburbs there were many census tracts inhabited by working-class people and some of them were quite poor; there were a few blacks and one all-black suburb; there were scattered white ethnics, and one substantial middle-class suburb predominantly Jewish; there were also neighborhoods of the urbane middle class, near the city and around the nucleus of the County, Clayton. (There were, of course, the great majority of all the rich.) Social space did not translate very accurately into geographical or political space.

This variety of populations in the sub-areas of the County was related to variety in their associational structure. The more familistic the area the more neighboring and community participation, whether in central city or suburb; since the suburbs had a larger proportion of familistic population, they also had a denser associational network at the local level. The same was true for social class. When these two variables were controlled, ethnicity was of little importance.

More important for our purposes in St. Louis, however, was the question of political participation. Did the smaller suburban municipality bring government closer to the people? How transitive was the organizational network of friendship, kinship, voluntary organization, and neighborhood to the political process?

In general, it seemed that the familistic neighborhoods, with their dense networks of neighboring and voluntary organizations, did produce more involvement and informed political action. However, the size of the municipality made a difference: the kind of people who were local political actors in the suburbs were much less likely to be so in the City of St. Louis. So, organizational type of neighborhood and political unit had independent effects. In general, the type of sub-area (urbanism-familism) predicted the proportion of local actors, but their *political* activity was affected by the organization of the polity.

Given the same kind of population in center city, incorporated suburb, and unincorporated County, there were still important differences. Thus you could argue that the small municipality was most conducive to political competence and activity among those most concerned; the city would activate more people, regardless of their political competence; the unincorporated areas would provide no opportunity to those who would and could participate responsibly in a municipality.

But in all kinds of census tracts, with all kinds of population, one still found the local "isolates." These people were educated or not, ethnic or not, but they were uninvolved in any local organization and they were political neutrals. They had opted out. Even in the most familistic and high-rank areas of suburbia, one-fifth to one-fourth were in this category. They were, in Janowitz's phrase, participating in "communities of limited liability."

7

The Social Structure
and Political Process
of Suburbia I*

Three aspects of suburban society are emphasized in the recent literature: the demographic characteristics of the population, the associational structure, and the political structure. Suburban population tends to be more middle-class, ethnic, and family-centered than that of the central city; in the suburb the neighborhood and perhaps the local community are more important *loci* of association than in the city; and suburbia characteristically has smaller governmental units than the cities, and has more of them.

General theory is hazy, unarticulated, and incomplete with respect to the manner in which these three aspects of suburban society are related. Those committed to each approach neglect the others, or assume a non-existent integration. Duncan and Reiss, who emphasize differences in population composition, accept political boundaries as meaningful for

* An expanded and revised version of a paper read at the annual meeting of the American Sociological Association, September, 1959. I wish to thank, for their critical reading and creative suggestions, Aaron Cicourel and Harold Guetzkow of Northwestern University, and Wendell Bell of The University of California, Los Angeles.

their analyses.[1] Those who are more concerned with ecological processes derive demographic differences from ecological position and the economic dependence of suburbs upon the central city, paying little attention to the political structures which contain and define their data.[2] On the other hand, Robert Wood's recent treatment of suburban political structure emphasizes the political form of the municipality in the suburbs as a determinant for both recruitment to suburbia and the staying power of the suburban governmental enclaves.[3] Wood does not, however, explore the interrelations between political structure and the variables emphasized by the demographers and ecologists; again, a "loose fit" is assumed. Finally, recent work by Bell postulates a "quest for community" which implies that associational structure is a major selective factor in migration to suburbia and a stabilizing factor in the suburban trend, but one which cannot be subsumed under the "housing market" or the "political climate" of suburbia.[4]

In this paper an effort is made to integrate and order these three aspects of suburbia and to develop a systematic theory of the relationships among population type, associational patterns, communication system, and political structure congruent with the present state of research findings and capable of further test and evaluation. The paper emphasizes the organizational level of analysis, and concentrates upon the explanation of the immediate organizational structure—that is, the spatially defined group as it exists in the suburbs.

1. Otis Dudley Duncan and Albert J. Reiss, Jr., *Social Characteristics of Rural and Urban Communities: 1950*, New York: Wiley, 1956.
2. E.g., Walter T. Martin, "The Structuring of Social Relationships Engendered by Suburban Residence," *American Sociological Review*, 21 (August, 1956), pp. 446–453.
3. Robert C. Wood, *Suburbia, Its People and Their Politics*, Boston: Houghton Mifflin, 1959. See especially Chapter 4, "The Nature of Suburbia."
4. Wendell Bell, "Social Choice, Life Styles, and Suburban Residence," in W. A. Dobriner, editor, *The Suburban Community*, New York: Putnam's 1958, pp. 225–247.

This strategy differs from several current and traditional approaches. It does not move directly from the most general levels of societal structure to the observables (ordinarily the person-to-person relationship) or *vice versa*, as is common in the work of Durkheim, Parsons, Riesman, Weber, and other analysts of large-scale society.[5] Nor does this approach assume away the nature of interaction, as in much work by contemporary ecologists.[6] Both general theory and ecology are "macroscopic" approaches which emphasize the congruity and interdependence of social trends at a high level of abstraction. If, however, one takes seriously the intermediate-level constructs implied by these approaches—social class, bureaucracy, and occupational strata—one finds striking anomalies when studying the local community. Thus suburbanites, disproportionately made up of white-collar bureaucrats (the "organization men" and the "other directed"), are precisely the people who cling most fiercely to the autonomy of the small municipalities when merger with the central city is in question. Their involvement in large-scale organizational systems does not determine their behavior in the com-

5. Emile Durkheim, *Suicide*, translated by John A. Spaulding and George Simpson, edited with an Introduction by George Simpson, Glencoe, Ill.: Free Press, 1951; Talcott Parsons, *The Social System*, Glencoe, Ill.: Free Press, 1952; David Riesman, Reuel Denney, and Nathan Glazer, *The Lonely Crowd*, New Haven: Yale University Press, 1950; Max Weber, *The Theory of Social and Economic Organization*, translated by A. M. Henderson and Talcott Parsons, edited with an Introduction by Talcott Parsons, New York: Oxford University Press, 1947. To bring matters up to date, see the work of the Detroit Area Study, which moves immediately from individual characteristics to such societal dimensions as the stratification system: *A Social Profile of Detroit, 1956, A Report of the Detroit Area Study of the University of Michigan,* Ann Arbor: Detroit Area Study, Department of Sociology and the Survey Research Center of the Institute for Social Research, 1957.

6. Amos H. Hawley, *Human Ecology: A Theory of Community Structure,* New York: Ronald, 1950; Otis Dudley Duncan and Beverly Duncan, "Residential Distribution and Occupational Stratification," *American Journal of Sociology,* 60 (March, 1955), pp. 493–503; Leo F. Schnore, "The Growth of Metropolitan Suburbs," *American Sociological Review,* 22 (April, 1957), pp. 165–173.

munity. In view of the viability or staying power of the suburban communities, one must ask: To what extent is this
behavior appropriate to occupational scenes transferred, if
at all, to the residential area? To raise this question is to require that the relevant area of social action, the residential
community itself, be approached with a conceptual scheme
appropriate to its own characteristics as a field for social
action.

Thus, the strategy adopted here is to move from the macro-
level, using census data for an aggregate description, but
spelling out the steps by which one reaches the micro-level of
household organization. This procedure provides a method
of analyzing the social structure of the suburb—neighborhood, local residential community, and municipality. Such
an approach then leads back to the macro-level. Indexes
based upon census data, however, now become measures of
conditions under which spatially defined social groups become probable.[7]

POPULATION TYPE AND LIFE STYLE

The transformation of a predominantly agricultural and
rural nation into an increasingly metropolitan nation may be
summarized as an increase in societal scale. Many sequences
of change are fundamental causes of this process and many
secondary changes ensue.[8] For present purposes, changes in
the kind of *differentia* which cut across the societal unit are
emphasized. Occupation, for example, is a rather unimportant differentiator within small-scale society, and ethnic variations are usually absent. In modern cities, however, nothing

7. In the exposition of the theory that follows, the author has assumed the
   dogmatic but simplifying device of expressing many discrete hypotheses as
   valid propositions. These hypotheses, couched in testable form, conclude
   this paper.
8. See, e.g., Fred Cottrell, *Energy and Society*, New York: McGraw-Hill, 1955;
   Godfrey and Monica Wilson, *The Analysis of Social Change*, Cambridge:
   At the University Press, 1954; Eshref Shevky and Wendell Bell, *Social
   Area Analysis*, Stanford: Stanford University Press, 1955.

is more impressive than the differences in culture, life chances, deference, and power associated with variations in occupation and ethnic identity.

A third dimension emphasized here is urbanism, or life style. By urbanism we refer to the life-ways of sub-segments which have become differentiated on a continuum ranging from a familistic to an extremely urban mode of life.[9] Such a continuum first emerged from the analysis of census tract populations, and the indexes developed to measure it apply to such aggregates.[10] Toward the urban end of the continuum are neighborhoods of apartment houses with single persons, childless couples, and one-child families predominating; toward the other end are single-family dwelling units inhabited by families with several children, in which the woman, not a member of the labor force, plays the role of wife and mother. This definition of urbanism, emphasizing household organization and its consequences, excludes much that is usually encompassed in the term, but this limited meaning appears to be especially relevant to the present analysis of spatially defined groups in the metropolis.

The familistic type of neighborhood approximates, of course, the typical image of suburbia. Although surburbs have no monopoly of such populations, they tend to be more consistently inhabited by familistic households than any other

9. The term *urbanism* is used to refer to a concept Shevky has denoted as "urbanization" and Bell as "family status" or "familism." In general, urbanism implies that the higher the index reading, the nearer the approach to an ideal typical "urbanism as a way of life." Both the earlier terms are awkward, have disturbing connotations in the literature, and are sometimes downright misleading.

10. The index of urbanism is discussed in Shevky and Bell, *op. cit.*, pp. 17 and 55–56. For evidence of the independence and importance of this dimension, see the factor analysis studies: Wendell Bell, *A Comparative Study of the Methodology of Urban Analysis*, unpublished Ph.D. thesis, University of California, Los Angeles, 1952; Maurice D. Van Arsdol, Jr., Santo F. Camilleri, and Calvin Schmid, "The Generality of Urban Social Area Indexes," *American Sociological Review*, 23 (June, 1958), pp. 277–284. For a test of the index, using sample survey data, see Scott Greer and Ella Kube, "Urbanism and Social Structure," in Marvin Sussman, editor, *Community Structure and Analysis*, New York: Crowell, 1959, pp. 93–112.

part of the urban agglomeration. One important reason for such concentration lies in the demand and supply of sites for family living. Studies of suburban residents indicate the high evaluation they place on the physical and social facilities for child-rearing and home-making, including the prerequisite for this life, private space, indoors and out. The site demanded is one which allows for the play of children in safe and "pleasant" places, space for growing flowers, vegetables, and grass, for keeping pets, for patio exercise, and the like.[11] With the existing patterns of land allocation in urban regions, however, a large area per person is available at moderate price only on the outskirts of the built-up districts. To be sure, the relationship between demand and supply is far from perfect; as Schnore implies, many persons might settle for equivalent lodgings in the middle of the city.[12] But the point is moot—until new, single-family dwellings, rather than high-rise public housing developments, replace the tenements and row-houses near the centers, we will not know how many "suburbanites" are fleeing the city and how many are forced to move outward because no other acceptable housing is available. Meanwhile, the family-oriented population continues to seek and find its sites on the growing edge of the city.

The local associational structure of a population can be derived from such sociological characteristics as family-orientation, for contiguity indicates the likelihood of contact, homogeneity indicates the likelihood of similar interests, and

11. See the findings reported by Bell (in Dobriner, *op. cit.*) and by Richard Dewey in "Peripheral Expansion in Milwaukee County," *American Journal of Sociology*, 53 (May, 1948), pp. 417–422. Seventy-two per cent of Bell's respondents who had moved from Chicago into two middle-rank suburbs listed physical characteristics as a reason for moving to the suburbs; 50 per cent of their responses reflected improvement in privacy and geographical space. Dewey's respondents gave as reasons for their move, in order, "better for children," "less congested," "cleaner," and "larger lot," as the four most popular ones.

12. Schnore, *op. cit.* A polemical statement of the possibility is found in William H. Whyte, Jr., "Are Cities Un-American?" In Editors of *Fortune, The Exploding Metropolis*, Garden City, N.Y.: Doubleday, 1958.

population type indicates the specific content which may plausibly be inferred for those interests.[13] Thus the use of indexes which aggregate persons by geographical sub-areas implies contiguity and the relative homogeneity of the residential neighborhood. Specifically, the urbanism index developed by Shevky and Bell as a measure of average life-style yields social attributes of the geographically defined subpopulation, hypothesized here as crucial for spatially-based social interaction.[14] The less urban and more familistic the neighborhood, the more important is the dwelling unit as a site for everyday life, and for a particular kind of life.

The type and rate of interaction, however, is not specified in detail by this set of statements. All that is proposed, at this point in the argument, is that spatially defined interaction is related to the familistic character of the suburban population. In order to translate such interaction into social structure and political process, it is necessary to relate the gross variations in population type to a theory of spatially defined organization.

THE ORGANIZATIONAL STRUCTURE OF THE SUBURBS

The bifurcation of work and residence is sometimes taken as one of the defining characteristics of the suburban population.[15] But this bifurcation holds for most of the population in a metropolis; any local residential area is segmental in nature. Because a living area is the site for some, but not all, of the basic social activities of its residents, Janowitz calls it the "community of limited liability." [16] Such a community,

13. This argument is presented in another context by Wendell Bell in "A Probability Model for the Measurement of Ecological Segregation," *Social Forces*, 32 (May, 1954), pp. 357–364.
14. By relative homogeneity we mean no more than the probability that differences by a chosen criterion are greater between areas than is true within each area.
15. See, e.g., Martin, *op. cit.*
16. Morris Janowitz, *The Community Press in an Urban Setting*, Glencoe, Ill.: Free Press, 1952. See esp. Chapter 7, "The Social Dimensions of the Local Community."

however, encompasses some very crucial structures and therefore has constraining force—which allows the social scientist some predictive and explanatory power.

The definition of social organization used in the present discussion emphasizes functional interdependence. As the unit of analysis, we shall emphasize the spatially defined group. The locality group, or community, is thus viewed as a special case of the social form elsewhere defined as "an aggregate in a state of functional interdependence, from which emerges a flow of communication and a consequent ordering of behavior." [17]

Geographical contiguity, however, has no self-evident sociological meaning. It may become the basis for interdependence only when it constitutes a field for social action. We consider below three such fields, concentric in scope: the neighborhood, the local residential community, and the municipality. Using the definition of the group stated above, we ask three questions about each of these levels of organization: What constitutes the functional interdependence of the members? What are the channels of communication and the contents of the communication flow? What kind of ordered behavior results?

The Neighborhood. If the residents of a neighborhood consist of households with familistic ways of life (and consequently similar interests) existing in close proximity, there is a high probability of intersecting trajectories of action. Since surrounding households constitute important and inescapable parts of any given household's organizational environment, there emerge problems of social order, maintenance, and aid. Specifically, it is necessary to regulate the play of children, child-adult relations, and adult-adult relations to the degree that these represent possible blocks to the orderly performance of the household's way of life. To the

---

17. Scott Greer, *Social Organization,* New York: Random House, 1955. The spatially defined group and the changing nature of the urban sub-community are discussed in Chapters 4 and 5.

extent that contiguous sites overlap visually, aurally, and (sometimes) physically, it is also necessary to regulate the use of the sites. The unsightly yard, the noises of the night, the dangerously barricaded sidewalk may constitute such blocks. Finally, similarity of life routines indicates a probable similarity of equipment and tasks: thus the interchangeability of parts is possible. This may range from the traditional borrowing of a cup of bourbon to the baby-sitting pool.

To be sure, similar problems arise in the apartment house districts characterized by a highly urban way of life, but the structure of the neighborhood and the nature of the population result in different kinds of order. The lower rate of communication, due to lack of common or overlapping space, and the separation of routines in time, result in a greater dependence upon formal norms (rules of the building, laws of residency) and upon formal authorities. Thus the apartment house manager, or even the police, may be useful for the maintenance of order and the site. (Their utility, from household to *concierge* to police, is evident in the reliance placed upon such organizations by the state in various European countries.) In the suburbs, however, life-style and the relationships among the sites force inter-household communication.

Communication in the neighborhood may take place at many levels, but in viewing the suburban neighborhood as an organizational unit we shall emphasize casual interaction among those whose paths necessarily intersect. In the adjoining backyards, at bus stops, and local commercial facilities, considerable social interaction is well nigh unavoidable. This interaction may become elaborated into relatively permanent cliques—kaffeeklatsch groups, pools, and the like—and frequently results in a network of close friendships. These differ from "neighboring," or participation in the neighborhood organization, just as friendship within any organization differs from the ongoing structure of activity common to the aggregate.

The resulting patterns of behavior, the structured action, probably vary a good deal according to the type of neighborhood; however, the ubiquity of the phrase "the good neighbor" seems to indicate some generalized role system and normative structure.[18] Orderliness, accessibility in time of need, and cleanliness are salient characteristics rooted in the functional interdependence discussed above. Individual members conform to such norms (whether or not they love their neighbors) because the norms facilitate their ongoing household enterprises.

But the neighborhood is a microcosm. Nor is it the only spatially based social structure mediating between the household and the metropolis. The neighborhood then is a precipitate of interacting households; participation in it does not necessarily indicate a role in the larger local area as community or as political unit. The neighborhood produces, at the least, some order among the small enclave of residents, and communication relevant to the nearby scene.

The Local Residential Area. Neighbors in the suburbs tend to have similar interests, for their ways of life have similar prerequisites, while in the local residential area interdependence results when similar interests are transformed into common interests, based upon the common field in which they operate. Spatial aggregates are the distributing units for many goods and services—public schools, commercial services, and various governmental aids and are frequently available to the individual only through his residence in a geographically delimited aggregate. To the degree that this is true of vital resources, the population of a local residential area is functionally interdependent.[19] At the same time space, as the

18. The norms may vary of course by social rank and ethnicity; to simplify the argument the effects of these dimensions are considered irrelevant to the major hypotheses. Social rank is discussed in a later section.
19. The reader may question the existence of such "local areas" as social fact. However, scattered evidence indicates that the map of the city breaks down into sub-units for the residential population, whether or not these are congruent with ecologically defined "natural areas." The nature

site of common activities (street, sidewalk, park, playground), is a base of interdependence, as in the neighborhood.

The local residential community as here defined includes a number of neighborhoods. It may or may not be coterminous with a political unit. What is its minimal organizational structure? Communication relevant to the area ordinarily takes place through two channels, the community press and voluntary organizations. While each is a communication channel, we shall stress the communications function of the press and the action function of the voluntary organization.

The local community press in the suburbs, widely distributed and widely read, is a medium available to almost all residents of most local areas.[20] Its utility stems directly from the interdependence of activities within the local area; supported by local merchants, it provides support in turn for the various formal organizations which constitute the "community." To be sure, all areas are not now serviced by a community press, but so useful is the medium (and consequently, so lucrative) that it is rapidly "covering" the suburban areas of contemporary cities. As the press develops where there is a market for its services, this should occur most consistently and widely among the familistic populations.

---

and consequences of economic decentralization are explored by Foley, of social and economic decentralization by Janowitz. See Donald L. Foley, "The Use of Local Facilities in a Metropolis," *American Journal of Sociology*, 56 (November, 1950), pp. 238–246, and *Neighbors or Urbanites? The Study of a Rochester Residential District*, Rochester, N.Y.: University of Rochester, 1952; and Janowitz, *op. cit.* A more recent study reports a strong definition of sub-areas among residents of Boston. See Laurence Ross, *The Local Community in the Metropolis*, unpublished Ph.D. thesis, Harvard University, 1959. Furthermore, 98 per cent of the residents of suburban St. Louis County accept the notion and give a distinctive name to their residential area (unpublished research report, Metropolitan St. Louis Survey).

20. Thus 84 per cent of Janowitz's respondents were readers of their local press (*op. cit.*). Similar findings are reported for a Los Angeles suburban sample: of those who received the paper (85 per cent) over 92 per cent were regular readers; see Scott Greer and Ella Kube, *Urban Worlds: A Comparative Study of Four Los Angeles Areas*, Los Angeles: Laboratory in Urban Culture, 1955 (processed).

The suburban paper is quite similar to that described by Janowitz—parochial in its interests, reporting almost exclusively upon local happenings, translating metropolitan events into their effects on the local area, seldom reporting national events.[21] Such local personages as merchants, bureaucrats, and organizational leaders constitute the actors on this stage. Insofar as the local area is a social fact, the latter is reflected in the press and at the same time reinforced in the process of reflection, for the press in perpetuating lines of communication stabilizes norms and roles. If it is chiefly a merchandising mechanism in its economic function, it is also a public platform for the area in its social and political functions.

But what of the local area without a separate government? In this case, what kind of structured action is indicated as the third term in the definition of the area as a social structure? Noting again that spatially defined organization in the residential area is loose, unstructured, and does not engage all of the residents, here we emphasize participation in the local formal organizations. Such organizations are segmental in their membership and purposes; they include those residents who are dependent upon them for basic necessities to their way of life. Community-oriented organizations, improvement associations, child-centered organizations, some fraternal and service clubs are examples. They are particular to the area, their membership is largely limited to those living there, and they are instruments of persuasion and control with respect to various community problems, projects, and festivals. Furthermore, if there is no political structure they are the *only* existing structures through which an interdependence specific to the area (issuing in local problems), communicated through the press (as "community issues"), become manifested in social action.

The Suburban Municipality. The typical political struc-

21. Janowitz, *op. cit.*

ture of metropolitan suburbia viewed as a whole is a crazy-quilt of many small municipalities having various eccentric shapes and displaying little obvious order in their boundaries. It is likely, however, that many of these municipalities are roughly coterminous with one or more social communities of the kind discussed above. To the degree that this is the case, the seemingly arbitrary lines on the map may come to represent social communities. The congruence of municipal boundaries with a local residential community permits the translation of common interests into a polity. The common field of activity (and the various segmental interests sited in this field) is contained within a formal organizational structure having the power to control, within wide limits, some of the basic goods and services of the residents. Thus streets, parks, schools (and, to a degree, commercial and residential development) are not only sources of interdependence—their control is so structured as to allow effective action by the interdependent population. Furthermore, taxation, police power, and other governmental attributes are assigned to the local municipality.

Where such is the case, an additional level is added to the structured action which results from interdependence and the flow of communication within the residential community: political action, within a political community.[22] Communication now incorporates well defined political norms and roles, the latter including the governmental official, political leader, voter, local taxpayer, and so on. But this type of organizational structure does not displace the kinds of voluntary community organizations indicated earlier. Certain modes of action tend to become allocated to the governmental organization; others remain the functions of private and semi-private groups (including the neighborhoods).

22. This does not imply an automatic evolution which presumes that through time interdependence must result in communication and order. The precise processes by which organizational structures evolve are not spelled out here; they would be desirable but are not essential to the purposes of the present paper.

The organizational structure of suburbia may be summarized as follows: (1) The overlapping activities of households result in the neighborhoods, which exist as a kind of network spreading throughout the familistic population (for neighborhoods overlap among households, and the neighborhood structure of a metropolis frequently resembles St. Augustine's definition of God, an infinite circle whose center is everywhere and whose periphery is nowhere). (2) Larger residential areas with a degree of functional interdependence constitute "communities of limited liability." They exhibit communication through informal relations and the community press, and action through voluntary private and semi-private organizations. (3) In many cases, political units are roughly coterminous with, or include, one or more social communities. Neighborhoods are probably nearly omnipresent, though a network need not include all households; so are communities, but they vary widely in degree of organization; political communities may or may not exist. In the summary presented in Table 1, each analytical category is sketched in for each organizational level.

Relations Between Organizational Levels in Suburbia

The four types of organization discussed above—household, neighborhood, local residential area, municipality—are, generally, of ascending order as to size and descending order as to the probability of face-to-face or "primary" relations. They are also arranged in an order which indicates an increasing possibility of common "public" interest and action and, therefore, of policy relevance. Thus as formal policy becomes possible, representation rather than universal participation is a necessity.

The neighborhood, as the first level beyond the individual household, is very likely to generate interhousehold friendships and visiting patterns; neighboring then may be part of the informal communication flow of the area. The neighbor-

TABLE 1. SOCIAL-POLITICAL STRUCTURES OF SUBURBIA

	SOURCE OF INTERDEPENDENCE	CHANNELS OF COMMUNICATION	STRUCTURED ACTION
Neighborhood:	Overlapping field Similar interests	Informal interaction Casual visiting	Regulated interaction Maintenance of the site Mutual aid
Local Area:	Common field Common interests	Community press Local organizations Informal interaction	Segmental interests protection Diffuse community action (outside political structure)
Municipality:	Common field	Local governmental functions	Law-abiding (local), tax-paying
	Common interests	Local political organizations	Voting, holding office Attending meetings
	Common organizational structure coterminous with both	Local non-political organizations Community press Informal interaction	Use of bureaucratic structure for complaints and appeals Organization of electoral campaigns

hood, however, is not apt to form polity beyond the conventional "rules of the road," nor is it apt to be a representational unit for any larger collectivity. The social products of the neighborhood *per se* are small-scale order, mutual aid, and friendship. The lack of a formal structure oriented to the collective needs and problems of the inhabitants probably facilitates the performance of those minimal tasks discussed earlier: the informal and, indeed, often unspoken norms relevant to the group allow for considerable flexibility and effective control of deviation. But unformalized norms and unspecialized roles are suitable only for a given routine, and preferably one requiring little precision. The self-ordering of the neighborhood is an ordering of routine interaction, with wide limits of tolerance.

For these reasons, the neighborhood is not formally related to any other level of spatially based organization: it is too small to constitute an administrative sub-unit of a larger system and too informal to constitute a base for independent representation in a larger system. The interaction of households produces a luxuriant network of neighborhoods in the suburbs, but these have little direct significance for the polity.[23] Their chief contribution to other organizational systems is one of communication: they are a site for conversational ferment.

The household is related to the larger local area through formal organizations sited in the area. These include public and business structures and such "auxiliary" voluntary formal organizations as PTA and service club, as well as voluntary organizations built upon independent functional bases. In general, local organizations are concerned with common ac-

---

23. The reader will recall the widely reported relationship between the voting of respondents and their neighbors; however, the significant variables in the present discussion are quite different. Reference here is to *participation* (not direction of vote) in *local* elections, while neighbors are distinguished from friends (the latter is a sub-category). Near-dwelling friends may indeed influence voting in Presidential elections; this is *not* the proposition presented above.

tivities of specific segments of the residential population in the area.[24] The same household activities and interests which produce involvement in these area-wide segmental organizations also produce interest in the flow of local communication through informal relationships and the community press. Thus household members are differentially related to local formal organizations, while their reading of the press (and conversation with others) permits a familiarity with the organizations and actors of the local area as a whole.

In the present approach, the agencies of local government, although they possess distinctive political functions, are also viewed as segmental structures. For, despite its conventional identity with a geographical space and its population, local government has only limited powers and duties and affects only a small part of the residents' activities.

The non-governmental organizational structure of the local area is related to the suburban municipality through the congruence of fields of action (and convergence or conflict of interests) between voluntary organizations and governmental agencies. Possible interrelations of the two kinds of structures include, for example, the use of private organizations as representatives of community interests before the government, the overlapping leadership role within both government and private organizations, and the private organization as a political faction or party. Each of these would strengthen the argument that the local government is "truly representative of the community"; at the same time, each would have important consequences for the effectiveness of, and the constraints upon, local governmental agencies in dealing with problems and issues.

Thus, we should expect an overlapping membership between voluntary organizations and the municipal electorate. If the members of local organizations are exceptionally sen-

24. They may be coded as: child-centered, community-political, and fraternal-service, for those most intimately related to the affairs of the local residential area. The remaining voluntary organizations may be usefully coded as either work-related or church-related.

sitive to community news as reported in the press, and if at the same time the community press reports governmental affairs extensively and frequently, the persons most active in local voluntary organizations should be highly informed about the *dramatis personae* of community polity. Insofar as they are committed members of common interest organizations, they would be particularly aware of governmental decisions, for these frequently affect voluntary organizations. And, even though they do not read the local paper, they should be unusually aware of information concerning the local residential community through their organizational activities, neighboring, and local friendships.

In short, neighborhood structures involve a large proportion of the suburban population, are loosely related to the local area communication system, but are not formally related to larger organizational networks. The local residential community and the municipality both involve a smaller proportion of the population (and one that is largely composed of the same individuals), but their scale and functions are such that they "stand for" the total population with respect to many basic activities.

Types of Relationship to Community Organization

If there are predictable and orderly relationships between households, neighborhoods, residential communities, and municipalities, we can spell out the possible logical combinations, and can examine the distribution of community roles and the consequences for forms of behavior other than those built into the typology. In constructing types we emphasize neighborhood, local area, and governmental structure.

From the previous discussion may be deduced three levels of relationship to local social structure: (1) involvement in the small-scale system of the neighborhood, (2) a role in segmental structures based upon certain interests common to some people in the local area, and (3) a place in the flow of communication representing the local area "as a whole."

Dichotomizing each attribute for simplicity yields eight

logically possible combinations. Some of these, however, are inconsistent with the framework sketched out earlier. If we consider separately the possible relations between neighborhood interaction, community roles, and access to the communication flow, the theory, with its emphases upon the communication functions of neighboring and of the local press and the social consequences of roles in local organizations, leads to the conclusions that there are no necessary relationships between (1) neighboring and community roles and (2) neighboring and reading the local press, but that there *is* a necessary relationship between a community role and participation in the communication network, either through neighboring or the press or both. A person with a role in the local organizational network but who neither reads the paper nor visits with his neighbors behaves inconsistently with the general hypothesis.

Following the procedures and qualifications discussed above results in the "organizational types" presented in Table 2. The rubrics in the right-hand column of the table are something more than summaries and something less than fully explicated types. The local "isolate," on the one hand, and the "multi-level participator," on the other, are clearly extremes. "Neighborhood actors" have defined positions only within the neighborhood system (although they may read the paper for gossip and entertainment). "Voyeurs" read the papers only as spectators of the community; they do not hold positions in role-systems and are otherwise comparable to isolates. "Community actors" may avoid their neighbors but, through common commitments, may still participate in areawide formal organizations.

Population Type and Organizational Type. Certain associations are implied by the theory. Life style as the basis for similar interests at the neighborhood level and for common interests at the local area level should be a key variable in producing associational patterns. Thus, considering the urbanism dimension of the geographical sub-area as a rough measure of life style among contiguous populations, we expect neighbor-

TABLE 2. "ORGANIZATIONAL TYPES" IN SUBURBIA

	NEIGHBORHOOD INTERACTION	LOCAL COMMUNITY ROLE	ACCESS TO COMMUNICATION FLOW	TYPE
I.	Yes	Yes	Yes	Multi-level participator
II.	Yes	Yes	No	Community actor (A)
III.	No	Yes	Yes	Community actor (B)
IV.	Yes	No	Yes	Neighborhood actor (A)
V.	Yes	No	No	Neighborhood actor (B)
VI.	No	No	Yes	Voyeur
VII.	No	No	No	Isolate
VIII.	No	Yes	No	Error

ing to increase consistently as urbanism declines. Within a sample from neighborhoods at a given level of urbanism, however, variation in neighboring should be a result of variation in the life style of individual households: neighboring should increase with homeownership, number of children in the family, presence of wife in the household during the day. (The opposite extreme is the single person or childless couple with a working wife, who live in a rented apartment.)

One may object that the latter attributes of individual households would be a simpler and more reliable index than the urbanism of the geographical sub-area, clearly a possibility. However, neighborhoods are aggregates of persons in given sub-areas, and such aggregates cannot be inferred from a sample that is random with respect to neighborhood. If individual household attributes are the only data, we cannot allow for "the neighboring type of people" who live in areas where most women work, there are few children, and neighboring is difficult.[25] Contrariwise, considering only the average nature of the neighborhood, we lose the deviants

25. See Ch. 3, where we report a diminution in neighboring among non-working women, as the proportion of working women in a neighborhood increases. We explain this as a consequence of declining opportunities for neighboring.

within it. For these reasons, both aggregate and household attributes are significant.

The same logic should lead to similar relationships between the urbanism of the residential population and membership in local organizations. Commitment to the area, as measured by commitment to home, public schools, and other household investments, should increase as urbanism declines. Within the households residing in given types of area, however, those who are most concerned with the local residential area should be most apt to belong to formal organizations of a "community" nature.

The prediction of discrepancy between neighboring and activity in community organizations is based upon the hypothesis that in some familistic areas the neighborhood interaction system includes persons whose interests are deviant (for example, the post-parental couple, the non-family female), but that such interaction does not necessarily lead to a concern with broader community interests. And, *vice versa,* persons may be "good citizens" in the community at large although they are not involved with immediate neighbors. Thus urbanism should be related to both neighboring and community participation, but not necessarily through the identical group of actors.

Finally, the urbanism of the neighborhood should be associated with access to the local communication flow. The same variations in household commitment producing increased participation in neighborhood and local area organizational networks should increase the value of communication relevant to the residential community. As a consequence of these relationships, the constructed types of local "actors" (see Table 2) should vary with the urbanism of the neighborhood. Moving from urban districts towards familistic suburbs, we should find an increasing proportion of the adult population involved in the small-scale neighborhood and in the larger residential area as organizational systems—with isolates becoming a decreasing proportion.

A Note on Social Rank. A relationship is often postulated

between participation in formal community organizations and social rank (occupation, education, and income levels of the respondents or their neighborhoods or both). With social rank, however, as with age and sex, we are dealing with role variations which cut across the larger society, and these should have about the same effect *within* each type of neighborhood and, within the neighborhood, within each category of local actors. When social rank is controlled, therefore, community participational type should remain a major differentiator with respect to involvement and competence in the affairs of the local residential area.

Nevertheless, we would expect more community actors in upper-status neighborhoods, and among persons with more education, income, and with higher prestige occupations, for these persons may be expected to have more organizational memberships. At each level of social rank, however, the urbanism of the neighborhood should be salient, for it reflects the variations in life style relevant to spatially defined organization. Thus isolates should vary little by social rank, once the urbanism of the neighborhood is controlled. The chief effect of decreasing social rank would then be a decrease in community-level actors and an increase in neighborhood-level actors. Lower-status neighborhoods of low urbanism would be, not so much "massified and fragmented," as organized on the small-scale basis of the neighborhood. At each level of social rank, urbanism should make a major difference in the distribution of participational types.

This theory leads then to the proposition that urbanism *as such* has an independent predictive power for the identification of types of community actors because it indicates aspects of the population conducive to a greater or lesser generation of spatially defined groups. A corollary proposition is that type of community actor is a more powerful predictive instrument for many kinds of *local* organizational behavior than the social rank of the resident or his neighborhood and municipality.

Governmental Structure. It was indicated above that governmental structure adds another organizational level, provides a "mold" for community activity, a focus for the policy-oriented, and a set of roles for the actors on the stage of the local community press. As an additional segmental organization, local government is a voluntary formal organization in that it provides further opportunities for involvement in the residential area's affairs. Therefore, if residential sub-areas are classified by organizational and governmental structure, we should expect the following rank order of competence and involvement in local affairs: areas with (1) autonomous organizational and governmental structures, (2) autonomous organizational but not governmental structures, (3) autonomous governmental but not organizational structures, and (4) areas with neither structure. Type (1) would include the suburban municipality which is a "social fact" as well as a governmental artifact; (2) would include the "local communities" in the unincorporated suburbs; (3) would probably be found in the areas now surrounded by the central city but still retaining political autonomy or in the areas immediately contiguous to the more urban neighborhoods of the city; (4) would be found, for the most part, in the central city.

Such a scheme points up the probability that incorporation will tend to increase public communication and action within a familistic area, for government summarizes many segmental common interests. If we consider the further possibility of applying the organizational types presented earlier to the probabilities of interaction within the political system, the analysis becomes more pertinent to the general problem of relating political and non-political social systems.

Political System and Residential Community

Three general types of actors summarize the seven types presented in Table 2: isolates, neighborhood actors, and community actors. These terms are used below as shorthand for the description of organizational conditions and memberships producing each type.

With respect to the political and proto-political processes in suburbia, we may ask: To what degree does the suburban population participate in a local political system? Participation here refers to *competence* (the possession of adequate and accurate information on the political process) and *involvement* (including voting in local elections).

Interaction within the community-wide system is a clue to probable involvement in the polity (and, consequently, voting, electioneering, standing for office, and other manifestations). We assume that the action role is pursued only within a group context, and that the membership groups available in the suburbs are the various community-wide organizations. Such membership is thus considered a prerequisite to involvement in community politics; similarly involvement emerges from a functional commitment to the local area at other levels. Involvement, however, does not necessarily imply competence. We consider competence as the probable result of participation in the flow of communication *relevant to the community-wide system*. This may result from informal interaction (friendship or neighboring) or the community press or both. The general types of community actors should behave quite differently within the role system of the local municipality.—These hypotheses are suggested by the following tabular presentation:

	INVOLVEMENT	COMPETENCE
Isolates	Low	Low
Neighborhood actors	Higher	Higher
Community actors	Highest	Highest

The difference between political settings is crucial for testing the general hypothesis of organizational scale. If the three types of actors are further categorized by the political structure of their residential areas, isolates should differ little in their competence, whether they live in unincorporated or incorporated areas: they should be largely incompetent. Neighbors should be relatively incompetent in each area.

But community actors in the incorporated areas should have more knowledge about community organization, for there is more to know. For example, they should know a larger number of leaders, for their governmental structure provides such parochial leaders. When political leaders are subtracted from their knowledge, however, they should have a general backlog of information on local leadership quite similar to those who live in unincorporated areas: organization type should be a predictor when political structure is controlled.

Two implications may be drawn from this discussion which are relevant to the current controversy about metropolitan governmental reform. First, the areas in which a viable, small-scale, local governmental process is likely are those of familistic populations, within which there are many community actors and few isolates—whether or not such areas are now incorporated. Second, the strength of the resistance to the "merger" of the central city and the suburbs should be found concentrated in those areas with a strong organizational network involving a large proportion of the adults in the residential community. In fact, the rank order of opposition should be correlated with the rank order, stated above, of competence and involvement in local affairs by areal attributes. At the low end of the resulting continuum would be those who live in the highly urban neighborhoods of the central city, for whom the local residential community has little meaning—and these persons are usually strong supporters of metropolitan "integration."

Some Derived Hypotheses

Further applications of the theoretical scheme are possible and tempting. It is desirable at this point, however, to apply the theory to some derived observational requirements. The following hypotheses, implicit or explicit in the above discussion, merely illustrate a much larger number of possibilities. The hypotheses are stated briefly, but are consistent with the foregoing theoretical presentation.

Urbanism, Life-Style, and Organizational Participation.

Thirty-four specific hypotheses under this category may be presented as the following six propositions:

a. Despite the varying effects of social rank, ethnicity, and the characteristics of individual municipalities, urbanism is negatively related to neighboring, participation in formal organizations situated in the area, readership of the local press for local community news, and the incidence of community actors; urbanism is positively related to the incidence of isolates and voyeurs (hypotheses 1 through 6).

b. When urbanism is controlled, social rank is positively related to the incidence of community actors, and negatively related to the incidence of neighborhood actors (hypotheses 7 and 8).

c. Despite the varying effects of unit characteristics, the presence of children in the household is positively related to neighboring, participation in formal organizations situated in the area, and the incidence of community actors; it is negatively related to the incidence of isolates and voyeurs (hypotheses 8 through 11).

d. When the presence of children in the household is controlled (and despite the varying effects of other unit characteristics), urbanism continues to have discriminating power with respect to the six participational variables indicated in (a) above (hypotheses 12 through 17).

e. When the urbanism of the census tract of residence is controlled (and despite the varying effects of other unit characteristics), the presence of children in the household has discriminating power with respect to the participational variables indicated in (a) above (hypotheses 17 through 22).

f. Despite the varying effects of other unit variables, urbanism and the presence of children in the household are conducive to the same types of organizational participation. Specifically, extremely high participation rates characterize those who live in low urban areas and have children, with respect to neighboring, belonging to local organizations, and reading the local press; the opposite holds for those without children in highly urban areas. With respect to the constructed types, the most community actors and the fewest isolates and voyeurs inhabit low urban neighborhoods with children in the households; the opposite holds for high urban neighborhoods among childless households (hypotheses 23 through 34).

Organizational Participation and Political Behavior. Forty additional specific hypotheses are stated as the following seven more general formulations:

a. Because it indicates involvement in the local area as an organizational system, participation in local organizations is positively related to voting, naming local leaders, and knowing the electoral rules. Because it indicates participation in the flow of communication in the area, readership of the press is related to naming leaders and knowing the rules. This also holds for neighboring with respect to naming leaders and knowing the rules. Neither neighboring nor readership of the press has a strong relationship with voting when organizational membership and the other unit of the pair is controlled (hypotheses 35 through 43).

b. When the logically possible combinations are reduced to five, isolates (who neither read, neighbor, nor belong), voyeurs (who neither neighbor nor belong but who read the press), neighborhood actors (who neighbor but do not belong), deviants (who belong but neither neighbor nor read the press), and community actors (who belong and either neighbor, read, or do both), the following relative distributions result:

	COMPETENCE		INVOLVEMENT
TYPE	NAMES	KNOWS RULES	VOTES
Isolates	—	—	—
Voyeurs	+	+	—
Neighbors only	+	+	+
Community actors	+ +	+ +	+ +
Deviants	—	—	+

(Hypotheses 44 through 58).

c. When age, sex, and education (as an index of social rank) are controlled, each age, sex, and educational category will manifest the same variation by organization type (hypotheses 59 through 64).

d. If competence and involvement are considered simultaneously, those competent and not active should be concentrated among the voyeurs, those active and not competent among the deviants, those active and competent among the community actors, those neither active nor competent, among the isolates (hypotheses 65 through 68).

e. The rank order of the distribution of community actor types should be (1) local area coinciding with municipality, (2) local area without municipality, (3) municipality without local area, and (4) district with neither residential area organization nor political structure (hypothesis 69). This, in turn, should result in a similar rank order of ability to name leaders (hypothesis 70). The same rank order should hold for resistance to metropolitan integration movements (hypothesis 71).

f. With incorporation controlled, the organizational types should have similar ability to name local leaders (hypothesis 72).

g. If political office-holders and past office-holders are eliminated, organizational types in incorporated and unincorporated areas should have similar abilities to name local leaders, although a somewhat larger number should be able to do so in the incorporated areas. Therefore, naming of non-political leaders should be related to the urbanism of the area (hypotheses 73 and 74).

8

The Social Structure and Political Process of Suburbia II: An Empirical Test

The last article presented a systematic theory outlining the nature of suburban social structure conceived in organizational terms.[1] This structure was then related to (a) population types distributed in space and (b) the political process. The discussion concluded with a long list of specific hypotheses. This paper will present the results of empirical analysis based upon the theory and including most of the hypotheses.

THE RESEARCH DESIGN

In the spring of 1957 the author carried out an extensive sample survey to determine political participation and political opinion. The survey included a systematic areal random sample of the residents in St. Louis County—the suburban county to the west of the city of St. Louis. One randomly selected adult in every one-hundredth household in the county was interviewed. Interviewing was halted at the 86 per cent response level, and the final sample was 1,285 interviews.

1. Cf. Ch. 7.

St. Louis County includes most of the "suburbia" of the area. Analysis of census data, using the Shevky-Bell typology, indicates (1) that the county is overwhelmingly familistic, with very few census tracts above the 50 percentile on the Shevky-Bell urbanization index, (2) that tracts with a disproportionate concentration of nonwhite or foreign-born populations are very rare in the county, (3) that the county census tract populations range from near the bottom to the top in social rank.[2] Although there are large areas inhabited chiefly by well-paid and highly educated professionals and managers, there are also many areas housing clerical workers, craftsmen, and operatives.

The observations upon which the present analysis rests were produced by the sample survey. The schedule of questions includes a rough inventory of social participation, with particular emphasis upon the spatially defined social group on the one hand and suburban political processes on the other. Thus the existing social structure can be studied as it impinged upon and controlled the responses of the scattered sample: specific groups cannot be studied.

The strategy of analysis is based upon the use of constructed types which, as empirically defined, roughly approximate those mentioned above. These types simultaneously indicate (1) the ways people are involved in the structure and (2) the structure as evidenced in the behavior of a sample of people. The materials for constructing the types are those objective indicators logically related to organizational involvement and information at the various levels. Such a strategy aims at a high differentiation of behavior for highly specified types, and therefore a high degree of "prediction," even though a set of constructed types may stop far short of ex-

2. For a description of the metropolitan area in these terms, see The Metropolitan St. Louis Survey (8157 Delmar Blvd., University City, Mo.), *Background for Action, First Public Report of the Metropolitan St. Louis Survey,* 1957. For an explanation of the Shevky-Bell typology, see Eshref Shevky and Wendell Bell, *Social Area Analysis* (Stanford, Calif.: Stanford University Press, 1955).

hausting the *cases* in a sample. (For use in a more extensive kind of prediction, one develops grosser categories which demand less of the individual case and which will include all or most of a population—though with lower predictability in the main.)

Seven participational types and an error category were developed through logical permutation and combination of (1) neighborhood interaction, (2) a role in the organizational structure of the local community, and (3) access to the communication flow of the local community.[3]

The next step in the analysis was the construction of objective indicators for neighborhood interaction, local community role, and access to communication flow. At this point it was crucial that the indicators be developed independently of their use as a test of the theory, for the analysis aims at verification, rather than simply exploration. For this reason, the sample (after the elimination of 89 people who were ineligible to vote) was divided into a "laboratory sample" of 196 cases and a "testing sample" of 1,000 cases. The laboratory sample was analyzed by various possible indicators, and three were finally selected. Both the items selected and the discriminating categories of answers were determined with the small sample: they were not changed in the analysis of the testing sample. In short, a subsample was used as a pretest of the analysis; this sample was not allowed to contaminate the larger test sample.

The indicators finally selected were these: (1) for neighborhood interaction, those were defined as interactors who answered the question "How often do you visit with any of your neighbors? Is it once a week or more, a few times a month, once a month, a few times a year or less, or never?" by saying either "once a week or more" or "a few times a month"; (2) for local community role, those were defined as role players who answered the question "Which organizations

---

3. See Table 2, Ch. 7.

or clubs do you belong to?" by naming one or more voluntary organizations and, further, in answer to the question "And does that organization meet in (local community)?" indicated that one or more met locally; (3) for access to communication flow, those were defined as having access who, in answer to the question "Do you get any local community paper or shopping news?" said "Yes" and, to the further question, "What do you like best in it?" said "local community news."

Of the 196 in the laboratory sample, 44 per cent were neighborhood interactors, 49 per cent were local community role players, and 49 per cent had access to the local communication flow by these criteria. One's immediate suspicion is that there are the same persons in each case. This is far from true, however, as analysis indicates. To be sure, an association is evident between the three indexes, but those who belong to local organizations are about as likely *not* to neighbor as the reverse, and nearly half of those who read the local press for local news do not neighbor. Contrariwise, of those who do neighbor, 36 per cent do not belong to a local organization and 40 per cent do not read the local paper for local news.

The analysis thus justifies the use of the three indicators and would substantiate the notion that the organizational levels of suburbia are separate structures, with less overlap in personnel than one might have supposed. Neighborhoods include active members whose participation in the larger local community is negligible; vice versa, the local community system includes actors who do not neighbor at all intensively. It also includes a small number of those whom we have called "error" types.

The relationship of these levels to that of the political unit is apparent in Table 1. Here the typology is used as a predictor, with voting in local elections ("Have you ever voted for any local officials since you've been living here?") and ability to name local leaders ("In your opinion, who are the people who are leaders in [local community] and can get things done around here?") as the effect variables. The first generalization we can make is that the ability to name local leaders varies more consistently by participational type

TABLE 1. PERCENTAGE OF PARTICIPATIONAL TYPES WHO HAD VOTED IN MUNICIPAL ELECTIONS AND COULD NAME LOCAL LEADERS FOR THE LABORATORY SAMPLE

TYPES	% WHO HAD VOTED	NO. OF TYPE	% WHO NAMED LEADER	NO. OF TYPE
I. Multilevel Actor	77	31	71	38
II. Community Actor (A)	85	13	78	14
III. Community Actor (B)	86	14	72	18
IV. Neighborhood Actor (A)	42	12	46	13
V. Neighborhood Actor (B)	36	14	47	19
VI. Voyeur	45	20	37	24
VII. Isolate	45	31	22	40
VIII. Error	78	18	23	22
Total number		153*		188†

* Omitted are 8 persons who do not receive local paper and 35 persons who live in unincorporated areas and cannot vote in municipal election.
† Omitted are 8 persons who do not receive a local paper.

than does voting. (The latter, in fact, is high for the first three types and the last, and about the same for all others.) The second is that Multilevel Actors and the two types of Community Actors can be combined into one category since they behave in a similar fashion; the same is true of Neighborhood Actors on the one hand and Isolates and Voyeurs on the other. This simplifying scheme yields the types hypothesized previously and would seem to lose very little predictive power (the chief loss is the difference in knowledge between Voyeurs and Isolates). There is good reason for holding the "Error" category out; having a community role (as in the case of the Community Actors), these people are as apt to be local voters as any, but lacking access to the communication flow through either neighboring or readership of the papers, they are as uninformed as are the Isolates.

Their behavior, in fact, supports the separate importance of involvement and information.

A third generalization is simply that the typology has considerable predictive power. Extreme theoretical types (Isolates, Neighbors, and Multilevel Actors) vary sharply with respect to naming leaders, and the first two and the third differ sharply in their voting. An important question, however, must be answered before the typology is accepted: What is the independent predictive power of each level of organization as measured by these indicators? Tables 2 and 3 provide a partial answer.

TABLE 2. PERCENTAGE VOTING IN LOCAL ELECTIONS BY NEIGHBORING, BELONGING TO LOCAL ORGANIZATION, READING LOCAL PAPER $(N = 153)$*

	NEIGHBORS			DOES NOT NEIGHBOR		
% voting	64†			58		
Total no.	(70)			(83)		
	Reads local paper	Does not read local paper	Total	Reads local paper	Does not read local paper	Total
Belongs to local organizations:						
% voting	77	85	80	86	78	81
Total no.	(31)	(13)	(44)	(14)	(18)	(32)
Does not belong to local organizations:						
% voting	42	36	38	45	45	45
Total no.	(12)	(14)	(26)	(20)	(31)	(51)

* Omitted are 8 who do not receive local paper and 35 who did not live in an incorporated area.
† Percentages are of the basic N's (in parentheses) for each cell.

With respect to voting, the most striking association is that between belonging to local organizations and having voted. Neighboring is slightly related to voting, but the relationship disappears when controlled for membership in organ-

TABLE 3. PERCENTAGE NAMING LOCAL LEADERS BY NEIGHBORING,
BELONGING TO LOCAL ORGANIZATIONS, READING LOCAL PAPER
($N = 188$)*

	NEIGHBORS			DOES NOT NEIGHBOR		
% naming	62†			34		
Total no.	(84)			(104)		
	Reads local paper	Does not read local paper	Total	Reads local paper	Does not read local paper	Total
Belongs to local organizations:						
% naming	71	78	73	72	23	45
Total no.	(38)	(14)	(52)	(18)	(22)	(40)
Does not belong to local organizations:						
% naming	46	47	47	37	22	28
Total no.	(13)	(19)	(32)	(24)	(40)	(64)

* Omitted are 8 who did not receive local paper.
† Percentages are of the basic N's (in parentheses) for each cell.

izations. The same is true with respect to readership of the press. All in all, we might operate more efficiently through using membership in local organizations *only* to predict voting. (This is consistent with the earlier finding that the sample dichotomizes between Community Actors [and Errors] and all others with respect to voting.)

However, the story is different with respect to the naming of local leaders. Here each indicator has power. The theoretically extreme cases go from 62 versus 34 per cent, considering neighboring only, to 73 versus 28 per cent when organizational membership is added, and 71 versus 22 per cent when all three are considered simultaneously. Those who neighbor are, in all categories but one, more able to name leaders. Similarly, those who belong to organizations are, in all categories but one, more able. Those who read the paper, however, are no different from those who do not, *if* they both neighbor and belong to organizations.

These three exceptions, however, are easily derivable from

one of the earlier hypotheses, for neighboring and reading the local press are considered to be functional equivalents with respect to the local communications process. Therefore neighboring makes no difference in the ability of those who both belong to local organizations and read the local community press for local news. The one category in which belonging to an organization makes no difference in competence (those who neither read nor neighbor) is the one predictable from the hypothesis. Finally, if one neighbors intensively, the press is redundant; but if one does *not* neighbor, readership of the press makes a very striking difference, even among those who do not belong to organizations.

In summary: through the intensive analysis of the laboratory sample, a set of objective indicators was selected and used in the construction of eight analytical types. These types were then combined into grosser types, since a number of them seemed to fall into clusters, both empirically and theoretically. Thus the Multilevel Actor and the two types of Community Actor were combined in one category—hereafter to be called "Community Actors." Such Actors (1) belong to local organizations and (2) *either* neighbor, read the local paper, or both. The three options under (2) seemed to make little difference in relevant behavior. Similarly, the two types of Neighbors are combined into one category, with the assumption that, if they neighbor, reading the paper makes little difference. Finally, Isolates and Voyeurs are combined for convenience; though Voyeurs are somewhat more able to name leaders, they are a very small population in any sample. "Errors" are carried as a separate category, the "Deviants"; they cannot be logically combined with any of the three major types. Their status is, for the time being, that of a puzzle.

THE FINDINGS

The findings will be presented in this order: (1) the differential concentration of the organizational types in certain neighborhoods by average population type, (2) differential political behavior of the organizational types, (3) the effects of certain conventional controls upon the differential political behavior of the types, and (4) the relationship between political incorporation, local community, and political competence.

Since much of this analysis was preceded by analysis of the laboratory sample of 196 cases, the findings of the pilot analysis will also be presented. Although these analyses were the basis for decisions with respect to indicators, cutting points, and dichotomies, which were then used in the test sample of 1,000 cases, they constitute something of an independent verification of the findings in the latter. Further, comparison of the two sets of findings both reinforces certain conclusions and indicates some of the traps for the unwary when *post hoc* analysis of a small sample leads to large generalizations.

Population Type and Organizational Type. As noted above, the neighborhoods of suburban St. Louis County are predominantly familistic in character; few census tracts measure as much as the 50 percentile score of the Shevky-Bell index of urbanism. Nevertheless, there should be enough variation to influence (1) the predominance of given types of households and, consequently, (2) the type of spatially defined social organization which prevails. In dividing the sample, it seemed necessary to limit the use of the urbanism index to a dichotomy in order to protect the size of the more highly urban sample. Therefore the sample was divided into individuals living in census tracts with scores of 29 or lower on the urbanism index (this was about the middle of the range for most suburban tracts) and in tracts with higher scores. The results are presented in Table 4 (see the "Total" column). The salient finding is that Community Actors are more common in the low urban neighborhoods—47 as compared with 38 per cent—and Isolates more common in the more highly urban tracts—36 as compared with 27 per cent. (These differences are significant by chi-square test at the

TABLE 4. PERCENTAGE IN PARTICIPATIONAL TYPES BY TYPE OF NEIGHBORHOOD
AND HOUSEHOLDS WITH AND WITHOUT CHILDREN

PARTICIPATIONAL TYPES	1. LOW URBAN			2. HIGH URBAN			3. SAMPLE TOTAL
SAMPLE NO. 1	WITH CHILD	w/o CHILD	TOTAL	WITH CHILD	w/o CHILD	TOTAL	
(N = 188)							
I. Isolates	24	39	29	34	64	51	34
II. Neighbors	17	17	17	21	14	17	17
III. Community Actors	48	35	44	21	9	15	37
IV. Deviants	11	9	10	24	13	17	12
Total	100	100	100	100	100	100	100
	(86)	(56)	(142)	(24)	(22)	(46)	(188) *
SAMPLE NO. 2							
(N = 943)							
I. Isolates	20	40	27	29	43	36	29
II. Neighbors	17	20	18	13	23	18	18
III. Community Actors	55	30	47	50	26	38	44
IV. Deviants	8	10	8	8	8	8	9
Total	100	100	100	100	100	100	100
	(458)	(272)	(730)	(106)	(107)	(213)	(943) †

* Omitted are 8 persons who do not receive paper.

† Omitted are 57 persons who do not receive paper.

.05 level of confidence. All differences mentioned in the test in numerical terms are of similar reliability except as otherwise noted.) There is no variation in either Deviants or Neighbors. The census tract score, however, summarizes two aspects of "organizational preconditions." It tells the character and requirements of the average households in the area, and as such is an indirect indicator of individual household attributes, and it also indicates the nature of the *environment* for any household regardless of its particular attributes. The relative importance of the two is visible when we control for "children in the household," one of the major theoretically defined household attributes.

For households with and without children, there tend to

be more Community Actors and few Isolates in the low urban areas. There are thus grounds for speaking of an independent "areal attribute." However, the presence or absence of children is a much more powerful differentiator in the distribution of types; in low urban areas Isolates are twice as likely in the childless households (40 compared with 20 per cent), and Community Actors almost twice as common (55 versus 30 per cent). Although differences by urbanism of the area, with children in the household controlled, are in the predicted direction, they are not statistically significant. In the more highly urban neighborhood matters are similar. When household attributes and census tract attributes are taken together, however, there is even more differentiation. Actors from households with children in the low urban areas are Isolates in only 20 per cent of the cases; those from childless households in the more urbanized areas are Isolates in 43 per cent of the cases. And 55 per cent of the former are Community Actors, compared with only 26 per cent of the latter.

The results of the two samples are quite similar; it should be noted, however, that the smaller sample yielded more extreme differences. This is particularly true of the high urban category, where subsamples were very small. Finally, the reader should bear in mind the generally familistic nature of this sample: no truly "urbane" neighborhoods are included and the sample is loaded against the urbanism index. It still proves to be a very useful differentiator.

Participational Type and Political Behavior. It is clear from the earlier discussion that participational types, as first defined, have considerable discriminating power with respect to voting in local elections and ability to name local leaders. Table 5 presents the results of (1) combining the eight types into three, with the category of Deviants handled separately, and (2) using the analysis for the test sample of 1,000 cases (which dwindles to 763 when those ineligible to vote in municipal elections are omitted) .

TABLE 5. PERCENTAGE VOTING AND NAMING LOCAL LEADERS AMONG
PARTICIPATIONAL TYPES

ORGANIZATIONAL TYPE	VOTES IN MUNICIPAL ELECTIONS		NAMES LOCAL LEADERS	
SAMPLE NO. 1 (N = 188)	%	NO.	%	NO.
I. Isolates	46	(51)	34	(64)
II. Neighbors	40	(26)	44	(32)
III. Community Actors	81	(58)	75	(70)
IV. Deviants	80	(18)	17	(22)
Total number		(153)*		(188)*
SAMPLE NO. 2 (N = 763)				
I. Isolates	44	(208)	33	(279)
II. Neighbors	41	(153)	42	(174)
III. Community Actors	71	(343)	62	(417)
IV. Deviants	50	(59)	40	(73)
Total number		(763)†		(943)‡

* Omitted are those listed in the note to Table 4a.
† Omitted are 237 who either did not receive local paper or else lived in
unincorporated areas (or both).
‡ Omitted are 57 who did not receive local paper.

Community Actors are by far the most likely to have voted
in local elections (71 per cent) with Deviants next (50 per
cent) and Neighbors and Isolates about equally likely to
vote (41 and 44 per cent). Thus organizational membership
still seems to be the chief predictor of voting. With respect
to naming local leaders, however, there is a clear progression
from Isolate to Neighbor to Community Actor (33, 42, and
62 per cent could name leaders)—and the Deviants are no
more competent than Neighbors.

Once again, differences were more extreme in the smaller,
pilot sample. Community Actors, particularly, were far more
competent and substantially more apt to vote. Although the
over-all pattern is unchanged, theoretically extreme types
are less dramatic (there are differences of 35 per cent for
voting, compared with 27, and of 41 compared with 29 per
cent for naming leaders).

Controls—Background Variables and Participational Types. At this point the reader may suspect that the participational types conceal bundles of conventional sociological variables—that they are, in fact, spurious. The theory, however, prescribes that organizational participation is by far the most powerful differentiator in local political behavior. While background variables may affect the probability of a person's falling into a given participational type, once he has taken the requisite position he will tend to behave like others in the type.

Three variables are consistently important, across the society, in differentiating voters and nonvoters, the competent and the incompetent. These are age, sex, and social rank. Adults aged 30 or under are less apt to vote than older persons; women are less apt to vote than men; and the low-income, less-educated persons in the blue-collar labor force are less apt to vote than those with more income and education.[4]

When the sample is divided at these points, with education taken as an index of social rank (and the sample divided roughly into grammar school, high school, and college), the distributions presented in Table 6 result. The findings are very similar for both samples, with no difference as great as 10 per cent. Community Actors, as would be hypothesized, have fewer people under 30, fewer persons with an eighth-grade education or less, and more with college education than do the other categories. However, they are the category second most heavily weighted with women. (Here, perhaps, is some evidence for the proposition that the polity of suburbia is disproportionately matri-centered.) When Community Actors are compared with the remainder of the sample combined, they are of significantly higher age and education, but there is no significant difference by sex.

---

4. Cf. the author's extensive analyses of these variables, as related to participation in local elections, in John C. Bollens, ed., *Exploring the Metropolitan Community* (Berkeley: University of Calif. Press, 1961).

TABLE 6. DISTRIBUTION WITHIN PARTICIPATIONAL TYPES BY SELECTED
SOCIOECONOMIC ATTRIBUTES

	TYPE			
SOCIOECONOMIC ATTRIBUTE	I. ISOLATES	II. NEIGHBORS	III. COMMUNITY ACTORS	IV. DEVIANTS
Age: % 21–30				
Sample no. 1	14	25	10	13
Sample no. 2	16	24	10	14
Sex: % Female				
Sample no. 1	53	60	53	45
Sample no. 2	50	63	57	48
Education: % 0–8th grade				
Sample no. 1	35	25	17	32
Sample no. 2	34	32	22	34
9–12th grade				
Sample no. 1	44	49	46	50
Sample no. 2	46	52	46	42
13th grade+				
Sample no. 1	21	16	37	18
Sample no. 2	20	16	32	24
Total N:				
Sample no. 1 (N = 188)*	(64)	(32)	(70)	(22)
Sample no. 2 (N = 943)*	(279)	(174)	(417)	(73)

* Omitted are only those who do not receive local papers, 57 cases.

Isolates and Deviants are quite similar, having the next
lowest proportions of the young, having the lowest proportions of women (about half), but having the highest proportions of eighth graders and the next to highest proportions
of the college educated (after the Community Actors). Neighbors, like Community Actors, have a heavy weighting of
women (63 per cent); they have the largest proportion of
the young (24 per cent); and they have the highest proportion with a high school education and the lowest proportion
with a college education. These differences do not appear,

a priori, to account for the variation between participational types in their political behavior. First, they are not consistent in direction and, second, they are not nearly extreme enough to account for variations of 30 per cent and more.

When the sample is stratified by these control variables, the results presented in Tables 7 and 8 are obtained for voting and naming leaders, respectively. Younger persons consistently vote less in each participational category. With age controlled, however, the participational types discriminate *more consistently*. Thus, of those 31 and older, the percentage voting goes from 46 for Isolates to 58 for Neighbors and 73 for Community Actors. Furthermore, with age controlled Community Actors in each category are more likely to have voted than are the Deviants. While variation by age is somewhat greater than variation by participational type, the young are a small proportion of each category. And the young Community Actors are as likely to vote as the older Isolates.

Women who are Community Actors are more likely to vote than male Isolates or Deviants, and as likely as male Neighbors (though only the difference with male Isolates is significant). In general, differences by sex average about 15 per cent, with men more likely to vote in each case (significantly, the difference is least among Community Actors); the differences by participational types, however, at the theoretical extremes are 30 per cent for women and 20 per cent for men (Isolates as compared with Community Actors).

Education is a consistently important differentiator for Isolates and Community Actors; the proportion voting goes from 39 to 42 to 56, among the former, and from 59 to 66 to 82 among the latter. (The only significant differences are between the college educated and each of the other levels, however.) Education makes no consistent difference among either Neighbors or Deviants. And, at each educational level, participational type is a strong differentiator, with a variation range of about 20 per cent. Community Actors with an

TABLE 7. PARTICIPATIONAL TYPE AND VOTING IN MUNICIPAL ELECTIONS
CONTROLLED FOR AGE, SEX, AND EDUCATION

	% WHO HAVE VOTED BY CONTROL CATEGORY FOR:			
	TYPE I.	TYPE II.	TYPE III. COMMUNITY	TYPE IV.
	ISOLATES	NEIGHBORS	ACTORS	DEVIANTS
SAMPLE NO. 1 $(N = 153)$*				
Age:				
21–30	14	00	33	50
31+	50	55	86	82
Sex:				
Female	26	32	71	66
Male	66	46	93	88
Education:				
0–8	35	50	78	80
9–12	45	33	76	78
13+	58	40	87	75
Number	(51)	(26)	(58)	(18)
SAMPLE NO. 2 $(N = 763)$*				
Age:				
21–30	31	27	47	43
31+	46	58	73	52
Sex:				
Female	36	41	66	43
Male	52	66	77	58
Education:				
0–8	39	50	59	50
9–12	42	52	66	56
13+	56	50	82	43
Number	(208)	(153)	(343)	(59)

* Omitted are those ineligible to vote in municipal elections and those who do
not receive local papers.

eighth-grade education or less are more likely to have voted
than are any of the other three types with college educations.

Turning now to those who named local leaders in each
participational type, with similar controls exercised, we find

very similar results (Table 8). Age, however, is much less important than participational type in differentiating ability to name leaders. The average difference by age is about 10 per cent, but by participational type the range is from 23

TABLE 8. PARTICIPATIONAL TYPE AND NAMING OF LOCAL LEADERS, CONTROLLED FOR AGE, SEX, AND EDUCATION

	% WHO COULD NAME A LOCAL LEADER BY CONTROL CATEGORY FOR:			
	TYPE I. ISOLATES	TYPE II. NEIGHBORS	TYPE III. COMMUNITY ACTORS	TYPE IV. DEVIANTS
SAMPLE NO. 1 ($N = 188$)				
Age:				
21–30	22	50	70	00
31+	29	46	73	26
Sex:				
Female	23	42	62	30
Male	33	55	84	17
Education:				
0–8	14	60	66	28
9–12	43	44	69	18
13+	23	40	81	25
Number	(64)	(32)	(70)	(22)
SAMPLE NO. 2 ($N = 943$)*				
Age:				
21–30	23	37	48	33
31+	30	42	60	43
Sex:				
Female	22	35	60	31
Male	37	51	62	50
Education:				
0–8	28	32	51	52
9–12	34	45	57	31
13+	20	43	67	44
Number	(279)	(174)	(417)	(73)

* Omitted are those who do not receive a community paper, 57 cases.

to 48 per cent for the young, 30 to 60 per cent for those 31 and over. The same is true for sex, with a range (from Isolate to Community Actor) of 28 per cent for women, 25 per cent for men. And for this variable there is no important difference between the sexes in the Community Actor category. The results obtained after controlling for education show that there is no consistent difference in ability to name leaders except among Community Actors, where the proportion naming leaders goes from 51 to 57 to 67 per cent. (Only the difference between Isolates and Community Actors is significant.) Other differences are slight and inconsistent. Within each educational level, however, variation is striking, with a difference between Isolates and Community Actors of 23 per cent for the lower educational classes and 47 per cent for those with college education.

Young Community Actors are more competent than older persons in all other categories; female Community Actors are more competent than males in all other categories; Community Actors with grade-school educations are more competent than the college educated in all other categories.

Some Further Controls. The discussion thus far has presented the results of analysis of the test sample, based in every case upon prior analysis of the laboratory sample. In order to give more degrees of freedom to the data (and therefore require more of the theory) it was decided to select some independent measures of political action and information, as well as an independent measure of social rank. These were the variables selected:

1) For political action, voting in school board elections was selected; this is an electorate coterminous with the population sampled—all residents have a school district in which to vote.

2) For political information, reliance was placed upon a measure of ignorance of the electoral rules. In questioning the informant about voting in local elections, in order to minimize inflation of reported voting the following pro-

cedure was used: first, the individual was shown a card with a list of local governmental officials on it (officials in a city government, members of a school board, officials in a fire district, officials in a county government); second, he was asked, "Which of these officials can people vote for here?" A substantial proportion of the people living in the incorporated municipalities did not know people there voted for municipal officials, and another substantial proportion did not know whether they could vote for school board officials. (Only those who knew were asked if they had voted.) Those persons who could vote in either kind of election but either said they could not or they did not know were considered to be incompetent—or to have incomplete information.

3) For an independent control, individuals were divided into professionals, managers, proprietors and officials, clerical and sales workers (all termed white collar), and all others.

The results of these analyses are presented in Table 9 for the larger sample only.

With respect to voting in school board elections, the range is from 30 per cent for Isolates to 56 per cent for Community Actors; the range for the white-collar portion of the sample is from 25 to 57 per cent, for the blue-collar workers from 34 to 56 per cent. Thus the blue-collar Community Actors are more likely to vote than white-collar workers in the other three categories. The same is true with respect to correct knowledge of school board and municipal electorates: 21 per cent of the Community Actors are ignorant with respect to school board elections compared with 37 per cent of the Isolates, and 12 per cent are ignorant of municipal elections compared with 25 per cent of the Isolates. Although blue-collar workers are consistently more ignorant, the differences are slight compared with differences between participational types. In each occupational category Community Actors are significantly higher in competence than any other type. They are similarly more apt to vote—with the exception of Deviants—than any other.

In summary: not one of the standard background variables invalidates the importance of the participational types as predictors of political action and political information. In certain cases, controlling for background variables

TABLE 9. VOTING IN SCHOOL BOARD ELECTIONS AND INFORMATION
ON THE ELECTORAL PROCESS BY PARTICIPATIONAL TYPE,
CONTROLLED FOR OCCUPATION

PARTICIPATIONAL TYPE	% VOTING, SCHOOL BOARD ELECTION	% WITH INCORRECT INFORMATION FOR:	
		SCHOOL BD. ELECTION	MUNICIPAL ELECTION
I. Isolates (279)	30	37	25
White Collar	25	36	20
Blue Collar	34	38	29
II. Neighbors (174)	35	36	24
White Collar	39	37	19
Blue Collar	31	35	27
III. Community Actors (417)	56	21	12
White Collar	57	20	11
Blue Collar	56	24	16
IV. Deviants (73)	50	29	31
White Collar	51	27	21
Blue Collar	50	31	50

Total number = 943*

* Omitted are those who do not receive the local paper, 57 cases.

strengthens and clarifies the relationship between participational type and political behavior.

Social Community and Political Community. A large proportion of the St. Louis suburban area is unincorporated; that is, no municipal level of governmental organization exists. If the general theory here applied is correct, however, there should be a form of spatially defined social organization at both the neighborhood and the residential enclave (or local community) level. In order to test this proposition, the sample was divided into those living in incorporated and unincorporated areas. Distribution of participational types for the two kinds of local area are presented in Table 10.

There is only one striking difference between the two kinds of local areas; a significantly larger proportion of the population in the unincorporated areas is made up of Isolates, and a smaller proportion is made up of Neighbors. The proportions of Community Actors and of Deviants are, however, almost identical. This is strong evidence for the existence of a local community at the nonpolitical level.

In order to test the importance of this community, the following hypotheses were formulated: (1) there will be more people in the incorporated area who can name local leaders, for there are more organizational platforms upon which leaders can stand, (2) when, however, political leaders are differentiated from nonpolitical leaders, those in the unincorporated areas will be able to name the latter in as many cases as will persons living in municipalities, and (3) participational type will be an important differentiator of ability to name leaders in each kind of local area. The results of these analyses are presented in Table 11.

TABLE 10. DISTRIBUTION OF PARTICIPATIONAL TYPES BY POLITICAL
ORGANIZATION, INCORPORATED AND UNINCORPORATED

PARTICIPATIONAL TYPE	INCORPORATED AREAS		UNINCORPORATED AREAS	
	%	N	%	N
Type I Isolates	27	208	40	71
Type II Neighbors	20	153	12	21
Type III Community Actors	45	343	41	74
Type IV Deviants	8	59	7	14
Total* (943)	100	763	100	180

* Omitted are those who do not receive a local paper, 57 cases.

TABLE 11. Political Leaders and Community Leaders Named by Participational Type in Unincorporated and Incorporated Areas

PARTICIPATIONAL TYPE	UNINCORPORATED				INCORPORATED			
	% WHO NAMED:				% WHO NAMED:			
	ANY LEADER	POLITICAL LEADER	NON-POLITICAL LEADER	NO.	ANY LEADER	POLITICAL LEADER	NON-POLITICAL LEADER	NO.
I. Isolates	31	13	21	(71)	46	39	17	(208)
II. Neighbors	40	14	29	(21)	52	42	16	(153)
III. Community Actors	53	13	41	(74)	73	52	33	(343)
IV. Deviants	50	21	36	(14)	52	41	24	(59)
Total N*				(180)				(763)
(943)								

* Omitted are those who do not get a local paper, 57 cases.

There seems little doubt that persons in the incorporated areas are better able to name one or more local leaders. This was true for every class of actor. This is entirely accounted for, however, by the *political leaders* named. Persons living in the unincorporated areas were, in each category, more likely to be able to name nonpolitical leaders. Community Actors were far more likely to be able to name leaders in each type of area: 73 per cent could do so, compared with 46 per cent of the Isolates in the incorporated areas, 53 compared with 31 in the unincorporated areas. The same was true for political and nonpolitical leaders separately in the incorporated areas, but it only held for nonpolitical leaders in the unincorporated ones. There was such a paucity of leaders to name that there is no significant variation in the unincorporated areas by participational type.

CONCLUSIONS

The analysis has supported the major hypotheses derived from the general theory presented earlier.[5] It has, further, established some bench marks indicating the quantitative importance of the relations hypothesized—those between population type and household type and those between participational type and political behavior. It has, incidentally, indicated the utility of combining analysis of census data with analysis of sample survey data; the key operation in each case was aggregation by position in attribute space. The interposition of organizational theory between the regularities of mass data at the census tract level and of individual data at the sample survey level has resulted in a considerable increase of explanatory and predictive power.

However, differences between categories of 30 per cent or so certainly do not indicate that explanation is near completion. Further discrimination is necessary—at the level of theory and at the level of objective indicators. The latter

5. Ch. 7.

have been crude and simple, a first approximation, nor have the different explanatory levels been combined as they could be; the major purpose of this analysis has been to demonstrate the *chain* of relationships between social structure and politics. Further refinement and combination of the variables will result in much sharper discriminations (or predictions).

9

The Mass Society and the Parapolitical Structure*

(with PETER ORLEANS)

Observers of the social and political worlds of urban man have frequently presented a gloomy argument.[1] In the growth of modern large-scale society they have emphasized the rise of megalopolis, the mass city. In such a community no structured force is interposed between massive power and the isolated (and therefore vulnerable) person. Our urban communities, in this interpretation, show a weakness fatal to the preservation of democratic values and individual freedom, leading toward the totalitarian society

* This paper is a revised and extended version of one presented at the section on Urban Communities at the meetings of the Midwest Sociological Society, April 28, 1961. The writers wish to express their appreciation to the Graduate School of Northwestern University and to the Eagleton Institute of Politics which furnished funds enabling the execution of this analysis. The data were collected by the Metropolitan St. Louis Survey, a project supported by the Ford Foundation's Public Affairs Program, and the McDonnell Aircraft Charitable Trust.

1. Lewis Mumford, *The City in History: Its Origins, Its Transformations and Its Prospects*, New York: Harcourt Brace & World, 1961; Robert A. Nisbet, *The Quest for Community*, New York: Oxford University Press, 1953; and Emil Lederer, *State of the Masses*, New York: W. W. Norton & Company, 1940.

150

and administrative state. The widespread anxiety concerning the effects of rapid (and perhaps, eventually, near-total) urbanization upon the inherited norms of democratic government leads us to ask: how does democracy fare in a society dominated by giant formal organizations, the metropolis, and the nation-state?

The general theory of urban sociology does nothing to quiet such fears. Indeed, the work of Simmel, Tönnies, Park, Wirth, and others is remarkably congruent with such an interpretation.[2] The sociological picture of the city as culturally heterogeneous, dominated by bureaucratic structures and mass media, and destructive of smaller social units, is simply mass society viewed from a slightly different perspective.

However, sociologists have been busy for the past decade or so with the task of documenting the social structure of the city. The work of Janowitz, Axelrod, Bell and Boat, Wright and Hyman, and others, points toward a widespread and relatively stable associational structure in the contemporary American metropolis.[3] The network of kinship, friendship, and neighboring seems to be widely cast, involving a very large proportion of the population. Formal voluntary organizations exist in luxuriance among some populations of

2. Georg Simmel, "The Metropolis and Mental Life," in Paul K. Hatt and Albert J. Reiss, Jr., editors, *Cities and Society*, Glencoe, Ill.: The Free Press, 1951; Frederick Tönnies, *Fundamental Concepts of Sociology*, trans. by C. P. Loomis, New York: American Book Company, 1940; Robert E. Park, *Human Communities*, Glencoe, Ill.: The Free Press, 1952; and Louis Wirth, "Urbanism as a Way of Life," in Paul K. Hatt and Albert J. Reiss, Jr., editors, *Cities and Society*, Glencoe, Ill.: The Free Press, 1951.

3. Morris Janowitz, *The Community Press in an Urban Setting*, Glencoe, Ill.: The Free Press, 1952; Morris Axelrod, "Urban Structure and Social Participation," *American Sociological Review*, 21 (February, 1956), pp. 13–18; Wendell Bell and Marion D. Boat, "Urban Neighborhoods and Informal Social Relations," *American Journal of Sociology*, 62 (January, 1957), pp. 391–398; Charles R. Wright and Herbert H. Hyman, "Voluntary Association Memberships," *American Sociological Review*, 23 (June, 1958), pp. 284–294. Most of these studies and some others are summarized and discussed in Chapter 5, "Individual Participation in Mass Society."

the city, and even the extended family system has persisted in the urban milieu beyond our expectations. In short, the hypothesis that the city leads inescapably towards the state of the masses requires some re-thinking. The problem may be posed as follows: how does the associational structure disclosed by this research relate to the polity of the metropolis, and what implications does this have for the argument sketched in above?

A Theory of the Parapolitical and Some General Hypotheses

Durkheim, at the turn of the century (and, more recently, Lederer and Nisbet) emphasized the importance of "mediating organizations," groups which stand between the isolated individual and massive power.[4] All three see the plural organization of society as a precondition for individual choice and thus freedom. They consider such mediating organizations—the structural expression of a plural society—as effective because they can mobilize the population in such a way as to limit the administrative state. The groups they refer to range from B'nai Brith or the C.Y.O. to the garden and 4-H clubs, from the industrial association and labor union to the

---

4. Lederer, *op. cit.*, and Nisbet, *op. cit.* Durkheim discusses the relation of the individual to the state and the role of mediating organizations in *Professional Ethics and Civic Morals.* He suggests that the state, extending its influence over groups which mediate between itself and the individual, operates to secure the rights of individuals against the coercive repression of such groups. Durkheim visualizes a situation in which the forces of the state and the mediating groups are counter-balanced, thereby assuring the maximization of individual liberty. He states, for example, ". . . if that collective force, the State, is to be the liberator of the individual, it has itself need of some counter-balance; it must be restrained by other collective forces, that is, by . . . secondary groups. . . . It is not a good thing for the (secondary) groups to stand alone, nevertheless they have to exist. . . . Their usefulness is not merely to regulate and govern the interests they are meant to serve. They have a wider purpose; they form one of the conditions essential to the emancipation of the individual," p. 63. See Emile Durkheim, *Professional Ethics and Civic Morals,* Glencoe, Ill.: The Free Press, 1960, pp. 1–31.

philatelist or madrigal society.[5] They are on-going organizations, based on the routine of everyday life, which represent an area of autonomous social value, and *can* represent that value in political terms if necessary. Therefore, we shall call such voluntary formal organizations "parapolitical." Though not specifically oriented to politics in their major activities, they may become overtly political (as, for example, the Little Rock P.T.A. when it became a political machine committed to keeping the public schools open).

The parapolitical structure of a society allows the translation of norms, commitments, and interests, into political behavior. For the individual citizen, political information, influence, and identification require such a sub-set of organizations in which he may participate. His participation, in turn, allows him to be represented at the crux of decision-making. Thus parapolitical organizations are a precondition for the translation of individual "attitude" into social action. Though these organizational structures of everyday life may derive from a wide range of activities, important sources are the role in the world of work, the necessities of the household, and the consequences of ascribed ethnic identity. Each has salience for specific sub-populations, and each is the basis for strong social groups, since out of the interdependence entailed in such associations grow communication, norms, and constraint. They in turn allow a dependable structure for mobilizing political opinion and action.

Such organizations do not make a pluralistic polity inevitable. They may be dominated by the state or they may not be related to the polity in any meaningful sense. Yet, though they are not a sufficient condition for the development of a pluralistic polity, they are a necessary one. Thus it is possible

5. Durkheim, however, emphasized the importance of work-related secondary organizations (or occupational groups). See particularly "Some Notes on Occupational Groups," the preface to the second edition of *The Division of Labor*, Glencoe, Ill.: The Free Press, 1960, pp. 1–31.

to clarify, in some degree, the mass society hypothesis by ascertaining the patterns of membership in the parapolitical structure, and the relationship between parapolitical organizations and the political process.

AVAILABILITY OF AND ACCESS TO
SOCIAL OPPORTUNITIES

The contemporary metropolis consists of a variety of sub-areas which represent variations in the social concerns and commitments of resident populations, and, therefore, variations in opportunities for social interaction. In this sense the various sub-areas of the metropolis represent differentiated opportunity structures.[6] The social characteristics of individual residents are indicative of their potential for interaction (their access to the structure of social opportunities), whereas the aggregated social characteristics of spatially distinct sub-area populations denote the prevailing conditions for social interaction (the structure of available social opportunities).

It is our general hypothesis that variation in the structures of available social opportunities, as indicated by variation in the aggregated characteristics of sub-area populations, will be related to the parapolitical order and, through it, to the political process of the metropolis. Knowledge of the type of population residing in a given sub-area, then, should provide cues to the characteristics of the developing or extant parapolitical structure. Our research is therefore designed to analyze the interrelationship of sub-area population type and parapolitical structure with an eye to the way in which the co-variation of these two factors affects the political process.

Sub-Area Population Type. The contiguity and relative homogeneity of sub-populations in the metropolis enable and

---

6. The term "opportunity structure" as used here has the same denotation as when it is employed by Cloward in his discussion of deviant behavior (although it is not restricted to deviant behavior). Richard A. Cloward, "Illegitimate Means, Anomie, and Deviant Behavior," *American Sociological Review,* 24 (April, 1959), see particularly pp. 168–173.

justify the use of indices which aggregate persons by their residence in small sub-areas.[7] To this end the Shevky-Bell typology has been employed. The typology consists of a set of indices which allows one to differentiate sub-area populations according to their level of (1) urbanism (or familism), (2) social rank, and (3) enthnicity.[8] Each of these indices summarizes a set of attributes which have been hypothesized to indicate preconditions affecting the scale of spatially-based interaction[9] or, as suggested above, the developing or extant structure of social opportunities.[10]

The average "life style" of a sub-area population is reflected in the urbanism index which is based on measures of fertility, house type, and women in the labor force. The use of this index involves the assumption that the less urban a given sub-area population, the more important are the dwelling unit, the neighborhood, and the local community for everyday family-oriented life. With an increase in the urbanism of a sub-area population, the structure of available social opportunities should broaden out from its local base.

The social rank index, based on measures of education and occupation, operates as an indicator of the prevailing level of "cultural equipment" in a sub-area population, a level which limits the structure of available social opportunities.[11] The assumption involved in the use of this index is that with an increase in the social rank of a sub-area population there will be a wider structure of more varied social

7. By relative homogeneity we mean no more than the probability that differences by a chosen criterion are greater between areas than within each area.
8. Eshref Shevky and Wendell Bell, *Social Area Analysis*, Stanford, California: Stanford University Press, 1955. While we shall not in this paper be able to discuss the effects of ethnicity, we can indicate that its chief consequence, segregation, seems logically to define one kind of limitation on the scale of interaction in various sub-populations in the metropolis.
9. Eshref Shevky and Wendell Bell, *ibid.*, pp. 3–19.
10. Richard A. Cloward, *loc. cit.*
11. Axelrod among others has found, for instance, that formal group membership and participation, rather than being randomly distributed, are directly related to education, occupation and income. See Morris Axelrod, *op. cit.*

opportunities. Thus, for example, membership in voluntary organizations outside the local area should increase with increased social rank.

Parapolitical Structure. Although the indices of the Shevky-Bell typology may denote differentials in the structure of social opportunities available to differentiated sub-area populations, they cannot fully explicate the kind and rate of associated interaction. To indicate differentials in sub-area populations' access to available social opportunities, or in other words, to translate such interaction into social structure and political process, *it is necessary to relate gross variations in sub-area population type to a theory of spatially-based social organization.*[12] This has been done elsewhere.[13]

Briefly, it is asserted that geographical contiguity becomes the basis for sociologically meaningful interdependence only when it constitutes a field for social action. Three such fields —the neighborhood, the local community, and the municipality—delimit successively inclusive conditions for interaction. Variations in informal participation, access to the operative communication networks and affiliation with *local* voluntary organizations characterize participation in these

12. The differentiation of sub-populations, aggregated and categorized according to sub-area characteristics, enables the *description* of empirical regularities which may be viewed as structural or compositional effects as discussed by Blau and Davis in two recent articles. See Peter Blau, "Structural Effects," *American Sociological Review,* 25 (April, 1960), pp. 178–193, and James A. Davis, Joe L. Spaeth, and Carolyn Huson, "A Technique for Analyzing the Effects of Group Composition," *American Sociological Review,* 26 (April, 1961), pp. 215–225. However, it is to be noted that whereas behavioral variations from one to another differentiated sub-population may be a function of the location of each in conceptually distinct and distinctive social areas (or social contexts), an *explanation* of how and why these variations occur will depend upon an adequate theory of social organization. The discussion which follows, based on an earlier formulation (*vide infra,* note 13), is an attempt to set forth such a theory for residential areas. In it the consequences of compositional variation are taken as given and are conceptualized as differentials in available social opportunities. It is the specification of variations in the structure of access to these differentially available social opportunities which constitutes the elaboration.

13. Cf. Ch. 7 and Ch. 8.

fields of social interaction. Access to the structure of available social opportunities differs in the neighborhood and the local community. Therefore, these two fields of social interaction have been used to generate three types of social participators:

1. *Community Actors,* who are members of voluntary organizations based in the local community, and who are informed with respect to the affairs of the area;
2. *Neighbors,* who participate in the small world of the neighborhood, but who are not involved in the larger worlds of the local community; and
3. *Isolates,* who are involved at neither level. (Parenthetically, there is a non-type: *Deviants,* who are members of local organizations but are not a part of the local communication flow, via the local press or neighboring.)

Our analysis is based on the use of constructed types which, as empirically defined, roughly approximate the types of social participators described above. These types simultaneously indicate (1) the ways in which people are involved in the parapolitical structure, and (2) the parapolitical structure as evidenced in the behavior of a sample of people. Objective indicators, logically related to organizational involvement and information flow at various levels, were used to construct the types.[14] The types of social participators should be important predictors of political activity and competence, for they summarize involvement in and access to the communication flow of the parapolitical structure, and through it, we hypothesize, to the local polity.

Available social opportunities are assumed to vary with sub-area population type, whereas differential access to the structure of social opportunities is indicated by the various types of social participators. The relative incidence of one or another type of social participator is, in turn, assumed to

14. The indicators selected and the logic of the choice are discussed in Ch. 6.

depend upon sub-area population type; thus, given types of social participators will be disproportionately concentrated in different types of sub-area populations.

It is to be expected that the less urban (and therefore the more familistic) the sub-area population, the more extensive will be the involvement of the residents in the network of neighboring relations and local voluntary organizations. Therefore, with a decline in urbanism we expect an increase in the incidence of Community Actors and a decrease in the proportion of Isolates.

We expect these variations by urbanism at all levels of social rank, for we see variations in the social organization of the local areas of the metropolis as largely a result of variations in commitment to a familistic life style at whatever level of social rank. However, at each level of urbanism we expect variations in social rank to make an important difference. As social rank declines, we expect a larger proportion of the residents to be Neighbors, who participate only in the neighborhood, while a smaller proportion are expected to be involved in the larger residential community as Community Actors.

In summary, we conceive of urbanism and social rank as independently varying dimensions which delimit the available social opportunities characteristic of sub-area populations and, therefore, their existing social relations. Variation in the nature of the specific social relations of the residents, as indicated by the types of social participators, reflects differential access to the parapolitical structure. The parapolitical structure, in turn, is hypothesized to have important effects upon the polity.

Political Process. The metropolitan complex is both a mosaic of social worlds and a mosaic of political units. There is a dramatic dichotomy between the city districts and the suburban residential settlements. Disregarding for the moment the great variety within each of these, we may note a plausible assumption of the city-suburban dichotomy: the polity of the city, with its enormous budget and widespread news value, presents a very different arena for political action from the dwarf polities of the suburbs. In the latter, the government is small and personal; in the former, it is large and impersonal. The politics of the city have a broad significance, while those of the suburbs may very well appear trivial. In short, the city polity is of wider scale than are those of the suburbs. Its politics are mirrored in the metropolitan press, available "across the board" to all subpopulations in the metropolis.

We have suggested that the parapolitical structure will have a significant effect on political involvement. We have also suggested that available social opportunities will vary with the type of sub-area population. If the configuration of sub-area population types in the city differs from that in the suburbs, then the parapolitical structure will also vary and, with it, the incidence of the various types of social participators. Further, the difference in political involvement among types of participators in the parapolitical structure will change, as between the politics of central city and suburban municipality.

Involvement in the parapolitical structure is more diffuse (in the sense of being less tied to the specific local area) in the city. Municipal politics are also larger scale, encompassing a host of local residential communities. Therefore, we expect more of the local Isolates in the city than in the suburbs to be at least minimally involved (as opposed to being completely disinterested) in citywide politics. The structure of political and parapolitical opportunities available to the local Isolate in the city is not as restricted to the local area as is the case for his counterpart in the suburbs. In the city, to put it somewhat differently, political opportunities are available beyond the boundaries of the local area, whereas in the suburbs they tend to be coterminous with the village limits. Therefore the political and parapolitical structures are likely to be more disjunctive in the city and this would suggest a qualitative difference in the effects of the parapolitical structure on the polity.

By virtue of the same line of reasoning, we would expect Community Actors in the city districts to be less intensely involved in the local political process than those in the suburban municipalities. The major issues in the city are usually settled at the level of a centralized government, in whose decisions no single local area weighs very heavily. (The exception would be the case in which the policy of the centralized government is directed at a particular local area as, for example, in the case of land clearance for urban renewal.)

Basically, however, we expect continued involvement in local political affairs to be closely related to involvement in the parapolitical structure in both the central city and the suburbs. The role of the parapolitical structure might be altered in the larger scale polity, but its function is not likely to be obliterated. Controlling for parapolitical structure, then, we are able to see more clearly the effects of the *political unit* on involvement in politics. Controlling for political unit, we are able to estimate the constant effects of given population types on the parapolitical structure, and through it, the political process.

THE RESEARCH DESIGN

The data on which this research report is based were collected in an extensive sample survey carried out in the St. Louis Metropolitan Area during the spring of 1957. One randomly selected adult in every one hundredth household in the suburbs was interviewed. In the city, a $\frac{1}{4}\%$ sample was employed. Interviewing was halted at the 86% response level in the suburbs, and the final sample consisted of 1,285 interviews. Comparable figures for the city are 515 interviews or an 81% response level.[15]

15. Because of the difference in the intensity of the city and suburban samples, where percentages are based on combined samples the number of respondents in the suburban sample has been divided by four to obtain comparability.

We turn now to summary measures used to test the hypotheses. As noted earlier, sub-area population types are described by means of the Shevky-Bell indices. The parapolitical structure is identified through the typology of local social participators. Our final effect variables, local political involvement and competence were estimated as follows.

Political Participation. We have summarized four aspects of political involvement through a scale of participation in local government. The four indicators employed were: (1) voting in any (one or more) of six local government elections, (2) taking a position on local government issues, (3) trying to persuade others regarding local government issues, and (4) attending public meetings dealing with local government issues. These items, with responses dichotomized, follow the hypothesized Guttman pattern. Of 1,604 respondents, only 346 respondents had any error in scale score. A score of 0 indicates that the respondent did not participate at all in any of the four areas of local government, a score of 1 indicates that he voted, but was not sufficiently involved to take a position, persuade others, or attend local meetings. Scores of 2, 3, and 4, indicate that the respondent not only voted but was increasingly involved in the local political scene.

Political Competence. Ability of the respondent to name leaders in the local community was taken as an independent measure of the respondent's political competence. Scored as competent were those who named one or more local community leaders when asked: "In your opinion, who are the people who are leaders in (local community) and can get things done around here?"

HYPOTHESES AND FINDINGS

On the basis of the preceding theoretical discussion, hypotheses were formulated and tested. These refer to relations between (1) sub-area population type and the parapolitical structure, (2) the parapolitical structure and political process, and (3) sub-area population type and political process. The hypotheses, together with the findings, are discussed below.

Sub-Area Population Type and the Parapolitical Structure

H:1 The proportion of Isolates in a given sub-area will increase with an increase in urbanism.

H:2 The proportion of Neighbors in a given sub-area will decrease with an increase in urbanism.

H:3 The proportion of Community Actors in a given sub-area will decrease with an increase in urbanism.

H:4 The proportion of Isolates in a given sub-area will decrease with an increase in social rank.

H:5 The proportion of Neighbors in a given sub-area will decrease with an increase in social rank.

H:6 The proportion of Community Actors in a given sub-area will increase with an increase in social rank.

These hypotheses were tested through aggregating the sample by the social rank and urbanism scores of the neighborhoods of residence (see Tables 1a, 1b, and 2). The sampled

TABLE 1A. PERCENTAGE DISTRIBUTION OF FOUR TYPES OF SOCIAL PARTICIPATORS FOR FOUR CATEGORIES OF SOCIAL RANK
($N = 629$)

| | SOCIAL RANK | | | |
| | LOW | | | HIGH |
	1	2	3	4
Isolates	39	40	33	25
Neighbors	22	20	18	15
Community Actors	23	30	35	50
Deviants	16	10	14	10
Totals	100	100	100	100
Number	74	322	173	60

population of the St. Louis metropolitan area did not include enough households for certain sub-area population types to be represented. Therefore, the bivariate distribution in Table 2 includes no cells of the most highly urban sub-area populations, and only one cell of the sub-area populations lowest in social rank. Nine of the sixteen logically possible sub-area population types are represented. Our discussion can only apply to these types.

TABLE 1B. PERCENTAGE DISTRIBUTION OF FOUR TYPES OF SOCIAL
PARTICIPATORS FOR THREE CATEGORIES OF URBANISM
(N = 629)

	URBANISM			
	LOW A	B	C	HIGH D
Isolates	31	33	44	0
Neighbors	20	23	15	0
Community Actors	42	31	26	0
Deviants	7	13	15	0
Totals	100	100	100	0
Number	192	202	235	0

The first six hypotheses can be tested by examining the proportions found in Tables 1a and 1b. These tables record the shifting proportions of the various social participation types, as urbanism or social rank is increased. Comparing adjacent percentages in Table 1a (and excluding from consideration the Deviants), nine predictions were made with respect to the effects of social rank; all but one are borne out. (The proportions of Isolates are virtually identical for the two lowest quartiles, 39 and 40 per cent.) In Table 1b, comparing adjacent percentages (and excluding from consideration the Deviants), six predictions were made with respect to the effects of urbanism; again, all but one are sustained. (The proportion of Neighbors is slightly higher for the second quartile of urbanism than for the first, 23 as compared to 20 per cent.)

H:7 The relations stated in hypotheses 1–6 between social rank and social participation type should hold at each level of urbanism.

H:8 The relations stated in hypotheses 1–6 between urbanism and social participation type should hold at each level of social rank.

Here the findings are generally consistent with the hypotheses but, as Table 2 indicates, there are more exceptions. When social rank is controlled by means of sub-group com-

TABLE 2. PERCENTAGE DISTRIBUTION OF FOUR TYPES OF SOCIAL PARTICIPATORS BY SOCIAL AREA FOR THE METROPOLITAN ST. LOUIS COMBINED SAMPLE ($N = 629$)*

	high	1D	2D	3D	4D				
Urbanism		1C	2C	3C	4C	74	107	54	
		1B	2B	3B	4B		116	56	30
		1A	2A	3A	4A		99	63	30
	low				high	Number of Respondents			
			Social Rank						

39	50	40			22	12	14	
	34	28	36			26	20	16
	36	31	14			20	23	13
	Isolates					Neighbors		

23	26	28			16	12	18	
	30	37	39			10	15	9
	38	40	61			6	6	12
	Community Actors					Deviants		

* City and suburban respondents residing in segregated areas (as defined according to the Shevky-Bell Social Area index) have been deleted from the sample. In addition, 47 city respondents and 16 (weighted) suburban respondents in social areas 1A, 1B, 3D, 4C, and 4D have been deleted as the total n's for these social areas were too small to allow for computation of meaningful percentages. Of the sample arrayed above, all residents of the highest quartile on urbanism are in the city; all in the lowest quartile are in the suburbs. Combined marginals are given in Table 1a and Table 1b.

parison, the proportion of Community Actors decreases consistently with increasing urbanism. However, counter to hypothesis 7, the proportion of Isolates at the second level of urbanism is slightly lower in two cases than at the lowest level of urbanism, and the proportion of Neighbors at the second level of urbanism is slightly higher in two cases than at the lowest level of urbanism. When urbanism is similarly controlled, the effects of social rank are more erratic. The proportion of Community Actors increases consistently with increasing social rank, but the proportion of Neighbors also increases slightly with increasing social rank at both the highest and lowest levels of urbanism.

Comparing adjacent percentages in Table 2 (and excluding from consideration the Deviants), thirty-three predictions were made; twenty-five were borne out, eight were not. Five of these errors occurred at the second level of urbanism, where city and suburban neighborhoods are both represented. From other analyses one can infer a greater heterogeneity in these cells, which may account for the disruption in the predicted patterns. Five of the eight errors occurred in predicting relations between social rank and social participation type; three occurred with respect to urbanism and social participation type. Thus, with respect to hypotheses 7 and 8, Table 2 suggests that urbanism is a more consistent and powerful differentiator with respect to social participation types than is social rank.

Parapolitical Structure and Political Process. These hypotheses were tested through comparing types of social participators by scores on the scale described above, and by their political competence as indicated by their ability to name local community leaders.

H:9 Of those individuals classifiable as Isolates, Neighbors, or Community Actors, political involvement will be directly related to social participation type with Isolates being least involved and Community Actors being most involved. (This reflects involvement in the organization of the parapolitical system.)

From Table 3 it is clear that different types of social participators vary greatly in their political involvement. The proportion totally unpolitical ranges from a quarter of the Isolates to 11 per cent of the Community Actors in the City, and 29 per cent of the Isolates to 10 per cent of the Community Actors in the suburbs. At the other end of the scale, the proportion of social participation types with scale scores of 3 or 4 ranges from 14 per cent of the Isolates to 24 per cent of the Community Actors in the city, and from 14 per cent of the Isolates to 41 per cent of the Community Actors in the sub-

TABLE 3. PERCENTAGE DISTRIBUTION OF POLITICAL INVOLVEMENT SCALE SCORES FOR THREE TYPES OF SOCIAL PARTICIPATORS IN CITY AND SUBURBAN SAMPLES IN THE NON-SEGREGATED SOCIAL AREAS OF METROPOLITAN ST. LOUIS

CITY SAMPLE	TYPE OF SOCIAL PARTICIPATOR					
Political Involvement	Isolates		Neighbors		Community Actors	
	N	%	N	%	N	%
None (0)	40	25	17	25	11	11
Low (1–2)	96	61	42	61	62	65
High (3–4)	22	14	20	14	23	24
Total	158	100	69	100	96	100

$\chi^2 = 11.2 \; p < .05$

SUBURBAN SAMPLE	TYPE OF SOCIAL PARTICIPATOR					
Political Involvement	Isolates		Neighbors		Community Actors	
	N	%	N	%	N	%
None (0)	29	29	14	23	11	10
Low (1–2)	57	57	36	58	59	49
High (3–4)	14	14	12	20	49	41
Total	100	100	62	101	119	100

$\chi^2 = 27.8 \; p < .001$

urbs. Thus the hypothesized order holds in each part of the metropolis, but there is a stronger relationship between political involvement and the parapolitical system in the suburbs.

> H:10 Among those individuals classifiable as Isolates, Neighbors, or Community Actors, political competence will be directly related to social participation type with Isolates being least competent and Community Actors being most competent. (This reflects access to communications flow in the parapolitical system.)

The data relating to this hypothesis indicate that the predicted order holds in the city. There, 43 per cent of the Community Actors, 36 per cent of the Neighbors, and only 27 per cent of the Isolates are competent. In the suburbs, however, while Community Actors are more competent than suburban Isolates—59 per cent compared with 28 per cent—the proportion of competent suburban Neighbors exceeds that of the Community Actors by 6 per cent. (The size of the proportion of Neighbors who are informed is rather surprising when compared with Community Actors. The relationship between neighboring and competence is not. In constructing the types, neighboring was viewed as relevant to *communication,* not to organizational involvement.)

The percentage differences between Isolates and Community Actors are, for the city, 16 per cent, and for the suburbs, 51 per cent. The larger percentage difference in the suburbs, indicated in Table 4, is chiefly due to the difference in com-

TABLE 4. POLITICAL COMPETENCE AND SOCIAL PARTICIPATIONAL TYPE

| | PER CENT WHO NAMED LOCAL LEADERS IN: | | | |
| | CITY | | SUBURBS | |
TYPE OF SOCIAL PARTICIPATOR	N/base N	%	N/base N	%
Isolates	43/158	27	28/100	28
Neighbors	25/69	36	40/62	65
Community Actors	41/96	43	70/119	59
	$\chi^2 = 6.93 \, p < .05$		$\chi^2 = 21.35 \, p < .001$	

petence between Community Actors in the city and the suburbs.

Sub-Area Population Type and Political Process. It has been postulated that variations in the extent of political involvement of different types of sub-area populations might be expected. Since the city districts tend to be higher in urbanism and lower in social rank than the suburban settlements, it is to be expected that the level of involvement in local political affairs will vary with city-suburban residence. The extent to which each of the various types of social participators is politically involved may also be expected to vary from city to suburb inasmuch as the structure of available political opportunities, and access to that structure, is likely to vary with sub-area population type and governmental unit.

In line with this reasoning, the three hypotheses stated below
were formulated and tested.

> H:11 A larger proportion of the city residents than suburban
> residents will have a low level of political involvement
> in the local area; and a larger proportion of suburban
> residents than city residents will have a high level of
> political involvement in the local area.

The percentages of city and suburban residents completely
uninvolved politically in the local area are roughly comparable; 21 per cent for the city and 19 per cent for the suburbs.
Of the remaining city residents, 62 per cent have a low level
of involvement with local area politics and 17 per cent have a
high level of involvement with local area politics. The comparable percentages for the suburbs are 27 per cent highly involved and 54 per cent with low involvement. Of those city
residents who are involved in the local polity, 48 per cent
vote only, while the comparable percentage for the suburbs
is 39. It is interesting to note that, of those citizens who are
involved at all in the local polity, a majority do more than
just vote (although the percentage is greater in the suburbs,
61 per cent, than in the city, 52 per cent).

> H:12 A larger proportion of the city Isolates will be at least
> minimally involved in the local polity than will subur-
> ban Isolates. (The polity is more meaningful "across the
> board" but less clearly related to the parapolitical sys-
> tem.)

On the average, in the city 25 per cent of the Isolates are
not involved at all with the local polity, while 41 per cent of
all city Isolates do no more than vote. In the suburbs 29
per cent of the Isolates are not politically involved, but 36
per cent vote only.

> H:13 A smaller proportion of Community Actors in the city
> will be highly involved in the local polity than will

suburban Community Actors. (The disjunction in scale of parapolitical and political weakens the interrelation of the two.)

On the average, 50 per cent of the city Community Actors do more than just vote, whereas 64 per cent of the suburban Community Actors do more than just vote.

The evidence offered in support of these three hypotheses, while suggestive, is not statistically significant (by Chi-square tests). This may indicate that the constructed types, being derived from structural characteristics of local political *subdivisions* within the city, do not adequately account for some results of the large scale polity. Two kinds of evidence support this interpretation.

First, further analysis indicates that the politically involved city Isolates are significantly more apt to belong to *non-local* parapolitical organizations than the uninvolved city Isolates (44 compared to 27 per cent).[16] We take this as one indication of the existence of a larger scale parapolitical structure in the city, one which is relatively independent of the local political sub-divisions but which operates as an effective stimulus to political involvement in the polity.[17]

Second, city residents, regardless of participational type, prefer the mass media to specific people as sources of politically relevant information. Respondents were asked: "Which helps you most in making up your mind about local elections —talking with people, or things like radio, television, and the newspapers?" It was expected that, in the familistic neighborhoods and small scale polities of the suburbs, specific per-

---

16. This is consistent with the evidence reported by Wright and Hyman to the effect that, in their Denver sample, membership in voluntary organizations is related to political involvement. See Charles R. Wright and Herbert H. Hyman, *op. cit.*

17. Gusfield, in an article which explores how isolation from mass culture may actually accentuate local sources of extremist political response, notes that the lack of *local* attachments may result in attachments to *supra-local* institutions. See Joseph R. Gusfield, "Mass Society and Extremist Politics," *American Sociological Review*, 27 (February, 1962), p. 28.

sons would be more influential than mass media, whereas in the city, with its large scale polity and coverage by the mass media the reverse would be the case. As Table 5 shows, this is dramatically supported by the findings. In contrast to

TABLE 5. PREFERRED SOURCE FOR POLITICAL INFORMATION DESIGNATED BY POLITICALLY INVOLVED SOCIAL PARTICIPATORS

| | RESPONDENT PREFERS: | | | | | |
| | MASS MEDIA | | PERSONAL INFORMANT | | NO PREFERENCE | |
PARTICIPATIONAL TYPES	N	$\%$	N	$\%$	N	$\%$
Isolates						
City	64	54	33	28	21	18
Suburbs	25	35	40	56	6	8
$\chi^2 = 15.368\ p < .001$						
Community Actors						
City	51	60	30	35	4	5
Suburbs	28	26	74	69	5	5
$\chi^2 = 23.221\ p < .001$						

the city residents, suburbanites prefer specific people to the mass media. Thus, it appears that for the city resident the metropolitan daily, the radio and TV, with their city-wide orientations, serve as alternate sources of political information.

It is possible, then, that a spatially inclusive and diffuse parapolitical system in the city is effective in mediating local political participation for some of the electorate.

POLITICAL AND PARAPOLITICAL SYSTEMS IN CITY AND SUBURB

We have found that, regardless of city-suburban residence, a majority of the citizens involved in the local polity do more than just vote. We have offered evidence to support our contention that there is a differential in the structure of available political and parapolitical opportunities between the two parts of metropolitics which affects local area-based political activity. It seems appropriate at this juncture, therefore, to consider the consequences of the resultant socio-political organization for the competence of the affected citizenry, both as political actors and as social actors located in overlapping but non-congruent fields of action.

Of the city *Isolates* who are involved with political affairs in the local area, 54 per cent prefer the mass media to specific people as sources of relevant political information, but only 30 per cent are politically competent in the sense of being able to name leaders in the local political unit. For the suburbs, however, the comparable percentages are 35 per cent preferring the mass media with 35 per cent being politically competent. This is in contrast to *Community Actors* involved in local political concerns, of whom 60 per cent in the city prefer the mass media and 44 per cent are politically competent. In the suburbs, 26 per cent prefer the media but 62 per cent are competent.

It appears from these results that residents of suburban areas are (1) more apt to rely on other people for political information, and (2) are not only involved in political affairs, but are also involved at a higher level of competence. The reason for this, we suggest, is that the political and social (parapolitical) worlds of suburbia are roughly comparable, largely overlapping, and therefore mutually reinforcing. By contrast, in the city (where the mass media are in large part external to and more extensive than the wards), reliance on the media and non-local parapolitical organizations, although related to political involvement, does not appear to result in political competence with respect to the local area. The city dweller is likely to be more aware of leaders in the metropolitan government than at the precinct level. Nonetheless, the Community Actor in the city is involved in the local political area; perhaps as a reaction to the larger scale polity. In other words, he is something of a "displaced person," whose political involvement in the local area is weaker because there is no meaningful political structure which corresponds to the boundaries of the local parapolitical structure.

SUMMARY AND CONCLUSIONS

The theory of the mass society postulates an administrative state, a massified citizenry, and no mediating organizations between. We have discovered, in metropolitan St. Louis, that a widespread network of parapolitical organizations has consequences for the involvement and the competence of the citizenry with respect to local government.

However, the strength of the parapolitical varies widely among the sub-areas of the metropolis. This we have explained by the concept of variations in available social opportunities derived from sub-area population types. These, in turn, are based on differences in style of life and level of living.

This variation in sub-area population types is closely related to the city-suburban dichotomy. The city populations, on the average, are higher in urbanism and lower in social rank than those in the suburbs. Both variables work in the same direction: a higher degree of local isolation, a lower density of locally based parapolitical organization. However, differences in population type between city and suburbs are not dichotomous; many city neighborhoods are familistic and middle-class, while suburban enclaves may be working class and urbane. At the same time, the scale of the polity is much greater in the city, and it has therefore been necessary to partial by *both* population type and governmental dichotomy, in order to see the effects of each.

Involvement in central city politics takes three quite different forms: there are (1) those whose political actions are mediated by the local parapolitical structure, (2) those who are isolates from the local community but involved in a larger scale parapolitical structure, and (3) those who are not involved in any parapolitical structure but interact with the polity chiefly through the mass media. The last fit the image of the massified citizenry. They are far from a majority. In the suburbs the first type of engagement is the predominant one. The small scale polity fits the localized parapolitical structure like a glove. Such suburban populations we may well identify with the "localities" studied by Merton and Gouldner.[18] Their relationship to the polity of their suburban municipality is organizationally similar to the relationship Lipset, Trow, and Coleman discovered in the International Typographical Union, where politics was mediated by the "occupational community." [19]

The "cosmopolites" (or, more accurately, "metropolitanites"), on the other hand, are unengaged in the local area as a community. They may be involved in the non-local parapolitical structure, however, through organizations based upon occupational, class, and ethnic interests. Or they may be, in some cases, individuals who do not participate in either a local community or a geographically wider structure. The latter are casualties of increasing scale in metropolitan society.

In conclusion, we must caution against the over-interpretation of these findings. First, a study limited to a given metropolis is a case study, be the case ever so well documented. We believe the broad trends of increasing scale make them generalizable, but that remains to be determined by further research. Second, we have underlined the rather

---

18. Robert K. Merton, "Patterns of Influence: Local and Cosmopolitan Influentials," in Robert K. Merton, *Social Theory and Social Structure*, revised edition, Glencoe, Ill.: The Free Press, 1957, pp. 387–420; Alvin W. Gouldner, "Cosmopolitans and Locals: Toward an Analysis of Latent Social Roles—I," *Administrative Science Quarterly*, 2 (December, 1957), pp. 281–306; and Alvin W. Gouldner, "Cosmopolitans and Locals: Toward an Analysis of Latent Social Roles—II," *Administrative Science Quarterly*, 2 (March, 1958), pp. 444–480.
19. Seymour M. Lipset, Martin A. Trow, and James S. Coleman, *Union Democracy*, Glencoe, Ill.: The Free Press, 1956. More recently, Maccoby has corroborated the Lipset, *et al.*, findings in a community setting. He reports that members of a voluntary organization studied are more likely than non-members to be voters, to remain voters, and to become voters if they had been non-voters. See Herbert Maccoby, "The Differential Political Activity of Participants in a Voluntary Association," *American Sociological Review*, 23 (October, 1958), pp. 524–532.

rough and somewhat erratic distribution of social participational type when both urbanism and social rank are controlled. This may indicate some weakness in the sub-samples. It may reflect disrupting influences not included in the theory but perhaps necessary for increased empirical power; or it may simply indicate the crudity of the measures adopted.

It must also be borne in mind that the study says little about the content of political interest and information. The population types employed here have been shown to have considerable predictive power with respect to turnout and direction of vote in both Presidential and local elections. Several more recent studies indicate that the gap between the Community Actor and the Isolate is wide, with respect to knowledge and concern about metropolitan government, voting in a referendum election, and knowing the details of governmental machinery and the personnel of government in a suburban municipality.[20] Thus we have reason to believe that the generalizations tested here, in a rather formal manner, will be useful in studying specific public issues.

Finally, we wish to re-emphasize the limited degree to which these analyses test the theory of the mass society. We have shown that, for certain types of metropolitan sub-area populations, a parapolitical structure does exist; when this is true, it increases the likelihood that those involved in it will also be political actors, who are more politically informed than the average. We have not shown the consequences of their action for the local governors, nor the way in which this feeds back as change and adaptation in policy. These matters,

20. The voting study is reported in Walter C. Kaufman and Scott Greer, "Voting in a Metropolitan Community: An Application of Social Area Analysis," *Social Forces*, 38 (March, 1960), pp. 196–204. The evidence for the utility of the types of social participators in the referendum election will be published in *Metropolitics: A Study of Political Culture*, by Scott Greer with the advice and assistance of Norton E. Long (New York: John Wiley and Sons, 1963). The suburban study is reported in "Social and Political Participation in Winnetka," Northwestern University Center for Metropolitan Studies, 1960 (mimeographed).

at least, demand investigation before we can answer fully our earlier question: "how does democracy fare in a society dominated by giant formal organizations, the metropolis, and the nation-state?" We believe we have made a beginning.

III

MOVEMENTS
TO CHANGE THE CITY

10

Social Action Research: An Introduction

When I was invited to join a planning session for the newly created Metropolitan St. Louis Survey, to study the "metropolitan problem," I had never heard of either phenomenon. There was, however, a long history of general surveys of cities, dating back to Booth's great study of poverty in London. A survey was a large-scale description of a metropolis with an emphasis upon certain aspects which were considered social problems. In this case, the "problem" was that of governmental fragmentation of the metropolitan area and its population, and the survey was to focus on the governments, economy, and neighborhoods of St. Louis. Now I was not alone in my ignorance of "the metropolitan problem"; it was by no means an obvious one. One must ask the question: Why did they think it a problem?

It was believed that each of the two halves of the metropolis, city and suburbs, suffered major disadvantages which could be avoided only by their working together as a unit. The central city's plant was old and obsolete, its street system inadequate, its population disproportionately poor and segregated, its welfare bills rising. It had no land left for new starts, and reuse of urban land is very expensive. The suburbs, while newer and more prosperous, had heavy and increasing costs for public improvements, of which the greatest was education. The transportation system for the metropolis was inadequate and there was no land-use planning for the metropolis as a whole.

Thus the protagonists of governmental reform leaned towards governmental integration of the entire metropolis. They felt that creation of a new government would give the public interest a chance, even at the expense of various private interests, including those of the suburbanites who had moved to their present homes to escape the city. A metropolitan government would be able to plan transportation and land use to benefit the area as a whole, to assess property uniformly and fairly for taxation, to rescind "the segregation of resources from needs," as Wood calls it, which perpetuated poverty in the city and helter-skelter development of the new lands on the periphery.

In actuality the state of the metropolitan area was not nearly so parlous as the proponents of reform would have had it. While the central city did suffer losses in taxables, increases in welfare costs, substandard housing, and so on, the calculation of these trends was based on proportions of the central city population. When one considered them on a per capita basis for the entire metropolitan area, the metropolis as a whole was improving steadily. Thus one might say the city had serious problems because it was the specialized residence of the poor, the ethnic, and much of the working class, living in old structures in an obsolete street system. The suburbs had problems stemming from newness. The two sets of problems could be combined only if one assumed redistribution of income—that is, use of public monies from suburban areas to redress center-city ills.

Those who fought the campaign for the new Metropolitan District Plan tried to avoid this conclusion by speaking of the greater economic growth for the region as a whole which would follow planning. They also spoke of the need for overall control of land use, a uniform tax assessment, and other improvements in the machinery of government. Government would remain close to the people by leaving many municipal functions intact and all municipalities in existence, as well as all school districts. Caught between the suburban hegira and its reasons, on one hand, and the fierce independence of the central city mayor on the other, the Plan pleased nobody.

From the Metropolitan Survey results we had been very skeptical of its chances. People had expressed great satisfaction with existing government at all levels, with the exception of the single areawide government, the Metropolitan Sewerage District. They had identified government services they thought inadequate, but the most common complaints (about transportation) were made by only a minority. While they opted for a change, a more integrated government for the area, they also wanted small-scale government; while they wanted more governmental services, they wanted no increase in taxes.

The a priori argument for change had been: (1) there is poor and uneven government in the various municipalities; (2) it will call forth widespread discontent, which (3) will lead to the desire and will to change. What we found was that there was no relationship between the nature of government and dissatisfaction with it, but dissatisfied or not the citizens gave a mild yes vote to the idea of change.

These were confusing straws in very little wind, so far as being guides to the referendum campaign. How to sell the weak compromise plan that seemed to approximate what the citizens wanted was a problem never solved by the partisans of reform. Theirs was a newspaper and television campaign, with support from the various good government groups; it failed to stir the imaginations of the citizens. There was little reason for a strong campaign against it; it died of its own apathy. It could not shake the inertia of existing structures of government and thought. The measure was defeated by two to one in the City, three to one in the suburbs.

The consequences were not earth-shaking for the metropolitan area. Its economy continued to grow, with new plants preponderantly in the suburbs. It is now served by a massive system of expressways, largely financed by state and federal government. Much of the blighted area was rebuilt in apartment houses, sports arenas, and the like—again, largely with federal Urban Renewal aid. The citizens stayed close to governments which were, basically, caretaker governments; the major forces for change came from outside the local arena.

SOCIAL ACTION RESEARCH: URBAN REDEVELOPMENT AND RENEWAL

The Urban Renewal Program was very different from the movement to recentralize the city. It was national in its inspiration and federally funded; it did not threaten the economically and politically powerful but, quite the contrary, rewarded them; those whom it did threaten were the intrinsically powerless, the poor and ethnic. It became, despite considerable criticism, a very popular program.

When I was approached to conduct a critical study of Urban Renewal, I was as ignorant as I had been of metropolitan problems. I knew the goals,—to improve the physical structure of the city in a planned fashion and improve the housing of the poor at the same time. Like most adherents of the liberal-humanistic ideology, I assumed this was a good thing, the sort of thing government ought to do. Upon further acquaintance with the program as it existed in 1961–62 (and it has changed little in broad outline since), I had very serious doubts indeed.

Studying the metropolitan governmental problem, I had been impressed by the rigidity of governmental structures, their resistance to change; turning to Urban Renewal I saw this spelled out in greater detail, at every governmental level.

In the tug of war between public interest and private and that between local government and national government, the program was slow to act and often acted in ways that achieved something approximately 180 degrees away from the intentions of its creators. The poor were dehoused, the very core of the metropolitan area received subsidy, and the real growth was in the suburbs where neither local authorities nor the metropolitan community as a whole had the capability for long-range planning. The jobs of creating a comely city, of providing "decent, safe and sanitary housing for every American family," remain as incomplete as they were in 1949 when the program was begun.

11

Dilemmas of Action Research
on the "Metropolitan Problem"

During the year 1956–57, it was calculated that over 100 studies of "the metropolitan problem" were in progress, planned, or recently completed.

The purpose of this paper is to examine the "natural history" of one, the Metropolitan St. Louis Survey. This was an effort to improve the government of a great urban area. We will consider the origins, the results, and the way in which the former predetermines, or does not predetermine, the latter. In doing so, it will be necessary to discuss: (1) the origins of the Survey in public events and in the ideology which interprets those events, (2) the translation of ideology into research goals in the light of the demands of social action, (3) certain salient findings, (4) the implications of these latter for the ideology from which the Survey was launched, and (5) the dilemmas of action research in the social sciences.

This paper is thus an effort to relate the demands of ideology, action, and the scientific enterprise as they interacted within the framework of one specific research project.

Like any discussion of the social sciences which commences with their origins in the problems of the day, this may be read as damning criticism: it indicates that the roots of the social sciences are, today, in the world of common sense definition of problems. This is not, however, peculiar to the study of urban society: problem orientations are nearly universal in the fields and disciplines which make up the social sciences. The positive value of the Survey stands forth more clearly against the background from which it develops. Such enterprises, harboring difficult intellectual, moral, and operational problems, may yet yield a substantial theoretical pay-off from even a little controlled research, for they operate at the growing edge of both knowledge and public policy.

I. The St. Louis Survey in Historical Perspective

The Movement to Save the Cities. The Survey was, from its inception, a combination of applied and basic research. The first stated purpose of the Research Plan was "to prepare . . . alternative proposals for action designed to remedy some or all of the major ills arising out of the present pattern of government in St. Louis City and St. Louis County, and to provide ways and means to meet major metropolitan needs, present and future."

Such a formulation rests upon certain basic assumptions, which were stated as follows: "the governmental pattern . . . gravely impairs efficiency and dilutes responsibility . . . impedes the orderly and healthy development of the expanding community . . . (while) many major needs of the' people . . . which government is expected to meet are not being uniformly met and cannot be met adequately by uncoordinated, piecemeal local action."

These statements have a plausibility that results from their tendency to summarize whatever dissatisfactions one may have with an urban social complex. However, it is important to ask "Who has defined the 'major ills,' and what were their criteria?" The Survey movement is not a new one; the "metropolitan" adjective has been prefixed to an old noun. To understand the metropolitan surveys of the present it is necessary to recall the history of the "social movement" of which they are a part.

Cities, as dense agglomerations of population, are subject to ubiquitous and fertile problems, historically cumulative. We have, in urban areas, highly differentiated populations living in close proximity. Considering only the interdependence resulting from proximity, the following functional necessities result: (a) the location and movement of people and goods within the area must be ordered; (b) waste must be effectively disposed of; and (c) public safety and a degree of order must be maintained. These are minimal necessities: they are classic sources of urban problems.

Such necessities are functions of formal government in modern society, and approaches to them as problems are usually by way of the structure and functioning of urban government. This government, however, viewed as an institution of the culture and a segment of the society, is not fixed but is continually forming. Its structure, power, and access to resources are in a state of continual flux.

The rapid increase in the scale of modern western society has been reflected in the disproportionate increase of the urban portion of the population. Cities have increased in number, in absolute size, and in relative share of the population, and this has occurred much faster than appropriate changes in the legal definitions and powers of the "City." Consequently, a continual discrepancy results between the responsibility and power in the hands of the urban government.

The size and internal differentiation of the City's *electorate* increased even more rapidly than its population. When the political integration of this population is considered, together with the increase in functions resulting from continuous and rapid change, the sources of many public issues are laid bare. The legitimacy of power and the structure of government are inherited from the past; the field of function is continually changing as it emerges from the present.

Two kinds of problems were continually identified by the nineteenth-century publicists of the educated classes: "corruption" and "crime." Both reflected the differential administration of law and the suborning of the polity to the welfare of civic officials. Such causal breakdowns reflected both the inadequacy of the legal controls over the incumbents and the inadequacy of the older civic machinery as a supplier of essential services to the mushrooming cities. The resulting costs to important segments of the business class were immediate and tangible: the merchant is a classic source of loot for the banditti. There was, then, a social base in public indignation and in the interests of economically powerful persons for reform movements, intended to remove shame from the cities.

It is not necessary to recount the various battles and campaigns of this war. Suffice it to say that, with the aid of massive changes in the population (including the acculturation of ethnics, the increase in education and income, and the consequent decline of differentiation on these bases) the municipal government of urban America was made to approach considerably closer the norms acceptable to the economic interests and the moral preferences of the population.[1]

The ideology of the reform movement rested upon assumptions congenial to the business interests who were a main resource of reform campaigns. Adrian identifies two such assumptions, "(1) that the political party and politicians in general were not to be trusted and (2) that the principle of 'efficient business management' could and should be ap-

1. For this discussion I have relied principally upon Charles R. Adrian, *Governing Urban America*, New York: McGraw-Hill Book Company, 1955, particularly Chapters 3 and 4.

plied to the city government."² Minimizing conflicts of interest among the citizens, the ideology had the effect of masking those political processes allowing the resolution of real conflicts within a framework of legitimacy. Those accepting the ideology were committed to concern with the city, not as a pluralistic universe of interests and power, but as a corporation whose chief problems were those of "public administration." Overemphasis upon the analogy between business enterprise and municipality distracted attention from the great discrepancy between control systems in the two forms of organization and, at an extreme, even elided the fact that somewhere, somehow, basic policy must be made before there can be any administration. In this manner the social response to a plethora of conflicts was a definition of civic politics as a problem in "management."

The movement to save the cities emphasized rationality and accountability in management, economy and efficiency in operation, and the disinterested, non-political commitment proper to the bureaucrat: urban government in this definition approaches very closely to Max Weber's ideal type of bureaucracy. In the academic discipline of Political Science, a bureaucracy arose for the purpose of training bureaucrats for such structures, at the same time that its own ideology directed a further bureaucratization of government. The subject area of local and, particularly, municipal government became a near monopoly for the students of public administration; research was ordinarily applied to the problems as defined by administrators, and the literature of the field took this orientation. Applied political scientists took as their badge of expertise, their training in public administration.

The movement to remove the shame from the cities had its origins in the 1870's and had lost much of its original

2. *Ibid.,* 62. These assumptions were probably general in the urban society of the time, but they were far from being universal. It is necessary only to extrapolate a socialist position or a conflict-oriented syndicalist position in order to note the ideology's consonance with the thinking of Main Street.

force by the 1950's.[3] However, after World War II, a new target arose called "The Metropolitan Problem." The City, as a population complex, now tended to lie across numerous municipal, county, state, and even national boundaries; and to the old discrepancies between the responsibility of government and the power of government were added those due to spatial limitations in the scope of governmental control. Postulating interdependence between the elements of a real, or social City, the political fragmentation was defined as a set of limits upon the city's capacity to provide the minimal essentials in the way of governmental services. "The metropolitan problem" became a summarizing term for a series of problems, including "inadequate governmental structure," "service and regulatory defects," "financial inequalities and weaknesses," and "deficiencies in citizen controls." [4]

The increasing proportion of the population living in such metropolitan areas provided a dramatic argument for the urgency of study and action; if the United States is in the process of becoming a nation largely metropolitan in residence, then it is in the public interest to examine the implications of this change for governmental structure. At the same time the older move to improve the cities was carried over in the approach to metropolitanization. The definition of the subject as *"The* Metropolitan *Problem"* indicates the presence of value assumptions at the outset of the enterprise; and research projects in this field have usually been intellectually oriented toward the *improvement* of the cities through changes in governmental structure.

Within the framework of this intellectual tradition, the Metropolitan St. Louis Survey was conceived and launched.

The Immediate Origins of the Survey. In 1876, the City of St. Louis withdrew from St. Louis County and became at

3. For a spirited discussion of this development, see Lawrence J. R. Herson, "The Lost World of Municipal Government," in *The American Political Science Review,* 51 (June, 1957), 330–345.
4. *The States and the Metropolitan Problem,* prepared under the directorship of John C. Bollens, Council of State Governments, Chicago: 1956, 17–22.

once a city and a county, one of the most radical structural changes that had occurred in an American city up to the time. In the process, the boundaries of the City were enlarged to include 61 square miles (as against 18 square miles), an area which seemed adequate to the most imaginative boosters of the day. However, the unprecedented growth in world urbanization during the nineteenth and twentieth centuries was reflected in St. Louis and, by 1910, very substantial satellite settlements began to appear in the adjacent county (also known as St. Louis County, and hereafter to be called "the County"). The socio-economic complex of the metropolitan area spread rapidly outwards, until today the urban area includes parts of five counties, three in Missouri and two in Illinois; only 45 per cent of the population is to be found in the City of St. Louis. The proportion continues to decline, as the outlying areas absorb all of the population difference reflected in growth.[5]

The effects of consolidating municipal and county governments in the City of St. Louis were, ironically, to prevent further expansion of the City boundaries; thus they have been the same since 1876. In 1926 and in 1930, serious efforts were made to readjust the boundaries of City and County through popular referenda; both failed. The rapidly increasing population of the County, however, was not averse to municipal government as such; between 1945 and 1950 a total of 44 new municipalities were incorporated, ranging in size from a population of 57 to several thousand. This was largely due to fear of annexation by existing cities.

While the boom in suburban living and governing was indicative of growth in the City-County area, the City of St. Louis had ceased growing in population and was, in many areas, suffering structural decay. The population came to include a disproportionate share of the Negro residents and

5. This paper will deal only with the City-County Area which, however, includes the great majority of the Missouri portion of the metropolitan area. The Illinois side was not a subject of the Survey.

the poorer residents of the metropolitan area. The neighbor-hoods of highest social rank became almost wholly concentrated in St. Louis County, while the blighted areas were chiefly in St. Louis City. The political map of the City-County area which emerged was one containing 149 units of government: one large governmental unit at the municipal level (the City of St. Louis), two at the county level (the City of St. Louis and St. Louis County), ninety-six small municipalities, twenty-nine small school districts (and a large one for the City), numerous fire protection districts, and only one over-all government—a newly created metropolitan sewage disposal district. This maze of local governments lacked a structure having the power to legislate for the City-County area as a whole.

The immediate climate of opinion which fostered the Survey rested upon this history—a past unity, a dissolution of the social city into a multitude of political fragments, and sporadic efforts at reintegration. At the same time, there was a growing belief in the middle 1950's that St. Louis might be in the process of "rising from the dead." One concrete symbol was at hand in the impressive public housing developments rising on the sites of ancient slums. Another was the election of a reform mayor (a professional engineer who had ended air pollution while serving as Smoke Commissioner). His ability to secure the support of a small group of economically powerful citizens in "Civic Progress Incorporated" (again, a "non-partisan" group) and the success of a large capital bond issue in a referendum which this group sponsored, furthered the belief that leadership was available for a new era. Another augury of change was the success of a referendum on a Metropolitan Sewer District in 1954; with its establishment the District became the first governmental unit to include both central city and the urbanized part of the County since the separation of City and County in 1876.

The metropolitan daily newspapers were actively promoting belief in the need for a change and one ran a series called

"Progress or Decay" in which it was stated that the metropolitan area stood at the "crossroads of decision." National magazines of prestige carried major articles featuring the activities of Civic Progress, contrasting photographs of Negro slums with those of handsome public housing developments, and comparing the St. Louis "renaissance" with the rebirth of the Golden Triangle in Pittsburgh.

In this atmosphere a Citizens' Committee for City-County Coordination was organized with the avowed purpose of using a constitutional clause which permitted City and County to readjust their governmental relations. Like most such movements, this one reflected the interests of certain population segments and organizations, the ambitions of specific politicians, and the general excitement of a crusade. According to the Missouri Constitution, it was necessary only to file a small number of signatures from City and County to set in motion machinery which would lead to the drafting of a new constitution for the area. During 1955 and 1956, the signatures were gathered and considerable publicity, favorable and unfavorable, was showered upon the nascent movement.

The Missouri Constitution makes possible four changes in the relations between the City and the County; these are: (1) merger of the two in one City, (2) re-entry of the City of St. Louis into St. Louis County, (3) annexation of part of the County by the City, and (4) establishment of a new metropolitan district, similar to the Sewer District. The general lines of battle soon became defined in the press and in speeches by political leaders as "merger" versus "leave us alone." Merger seemed to be much more popular in the city, and *laissez faire* in the suburbs, judging by the public statements of influential residents.

The general situation was confused by imputations of private motives and bad faith, as usual, and the arguments pro and con suffered from a lack of documentation. As the situation progressed, certain civic-minded scholars began to feel that a question of considerable importance for local government in the area might be settled through default, confusion, and ignorance. In order to decrease the latter two conditions and to allow for a reorganization of the action campaign, these individuals drafted a proposal for a study of the situation by a team of objective social scientists. St. Louis University and Washington University, with the support of community leaders, submitted the proposal to the Ford Foundation whose support they won. This support was supplemented by a grant from the McDonnell Aircraft Charitable Trust.

The purposes of the project were first stated as follows:

1. To prepare, for consideration by a Board of Freeholders, alternative proposals for action designed to remedy some or all of the major ills arising out of the present pattern of government in St. Louis City and St. Louis County, and to provide ways and means to meet major metropolitan needs, present and future.

2. To provide, for consideration by citizens in other metropolitan centers:

    a. an evaluation of techniques used to gather information on typical metropolitan problems; and

    b. an analysis of attributes of residents in a metropolitan area, including their complaints and frustrations pertaining to governmental services and costs, and their reactions to suggested proposals for change; and

    c. an analysis of referendum campaign techniques and an assessment of their effectiveness.

3. To aid in the development of a systematic conceptual framework within which research in the general field of metropolitan government may be more meaningfully conducted.

4. To increase the supply of trained research workers in the general area of local government.

For these purposes, a time period of fifteen months was specified. This specification resulted from the pressure of the Citizens' Committee which indicated it would hold off formal action only this long. If the research results were to be of use in changing the form of government through the action of the Board of Freeholders, they had to be produced in this time period. The Metropolitan St. Louis Survey probably had the largest budget and most ambitious agenda for the shortest period of operating time ever allowed a study of metropolitan government.

II. Basic Assumptions of the Survey

As the Survey began work, its responsible administrators took every opportunity of saying publicly, "We have an open mind, and no preconceived notions as to what is best for the St. Louis Area." This statement, a response to the previous public image of the movement as one for merger of all local government into "one big city," was really an effort to define the Survey as essentially diagnostic and prescriptive. To understand the definition of the problem and the method of examination and prescription, we must remember that the Metropolitan St. Louis Survey emerged from both the ideology and lore concerning the improvement of cities and a specific action program to improve the St. Louis City-County area.

The goals were diffuse and contradictory, as is visible in the above quotation; however, that of constitution building quickly became dominant. The emphasis upon change led to concern with predicting the effects of planned change. The tradition of improving the cities led to the substantive goals of efficiency and order. In brief, the aim was to change the governmental pattern of the City-County area in these ways through drafting an outline of a new constitution which would be accepted by the voters in referenda.

The emphasis upon change had these general consequences: (1) it turned attention from the question, "How does government really function under the present circumstances?" toward the question of "How would it function under other circumstances?" (2) it emphasized the political consequences of any decision, since change could be effected only through persuasion. However, the change envisaged was notably *constitutional* change; it amounted to using the Missouri State Constitution's provisions to write a new charter and create a new government. This emphasis upon the provisions of the constitution led to the slighting of change which could not take place under that legal instrument (for example, it eliminated serious consideration of the half million residents of the metropolitan area in Illinois).

It also led to great emphasis upon public opinion, for the changes according to the Constitution could only be effected through a majority vote in two separate referenda (one in the City, one in the County). One positive consequence was a great concern to gauge the popularity of various changes; a negative consequence was the absence of major research investment in the study of the "power elite" of the metropolitan area. The concern with public opinion did encourage great sensitivity to the various citizens' groups and civic leaders who commented publicly on the Survey's purposes, reports, and recommendations.

Believing that governmental problems result from inefficient organization which allows irresponsibility and inaction in elected officials, the Survey concentrated upon formal governmental structure. Within this area, much attention was given the provision of services to the population. Fire protection, sewage disposal, police protection, and similar services were the "output" of government, with taxes the "input." The problem was defined as maximizing output for a given input. The Survey was also concerned that governmental output throughout the area reach an optimal level. (This level was very difficult to define clearly, for reasons to be considered later.)

The ideology caused an emphasis upon the organizing of

an adequate human machine; it leaned heavily upon the maxims developed for public administration. There was interest in the notion that control should be integrated under one authority to avoid duplication of services and conflicts in jurisdiction. There was also concern for the most economical size of unit and the economies of scale as applied to government. In this complex of goals, focus upon the administrator as provider of garbage disposal services or public order, rather than as representative of interest groups, is a logical outcome. Some traditional directives for achieving these goals are civil service, non-partisanship accounting and recording systems, and administration by "managers" rather than "leaders."

Another aspect of the ideology, however, emphasizes the responsiveness of government to the citizens, and the equity of the service-providing system with respect to costs and benefits. Here, received dogma is much more confused and the directives are frequently obscure and contradictory. *The bureaucrat should be accessible to the citizen, but the only known machinery making this possible for citizens at large, the political party, violates the image of the bureaucratic municipal government.* It is also frequently assumed that the smaller unit of government provides such accessibility, as compared with citizenship in a vast metropolitan governmental unit, but small cities cannot profit by the economies of scale postulated in the management approach. Furthermore, the responsibility of government to the people is one of the mechanisms for insuring "equity" in the citizen's cost benefit ratio in exchanges with his government, and equity was another value of basic importance to those who originated and defined the Survey's purposes. Doctrine is complex, and, again, the directives are confused.

It is implied in the Research Plan that persons should not receive governmental services for which they are not paying and should not pay for more services than they receive; at the same time the desirability of a minimal level for the entire area is emphasized. When, however, tax sources are based upon property, it is obvious that great inequality will result in services within a metropolitan area, unless there is equalization of services by governmental decision. However, the redistribution of income by government is an extremely complex issue of political and economic policy.

Finally, the ideology includes the assumption that government has an importance for the social and economic "health" of the metropolitan area beyond the immediate provision of certain basic services to the population. Economic growth and decline were felt to be both causes and consequences of governmental disorder in the St. Louis area; the changing population, composition, and distribution were also seen as related vitally to the problems of government and *vice versa*. With these questions, however, we reach the edge of the ideology; here it was incumbent upon the Survey to create its own frame of reference.

III. RESEARCH STRATEGY

The Metropolitan St. Louis Survey was designed and its "charter" written by political scientists who were relying upon the general approach of their discipline, with its strong emphasis upon public administration. At the same time, however, the Research Plan envisaged a much broader inquiry into the status of government as one part of a total metropolitan economic and social complex. The basic questions were formulated in terms of governmental policy, but the answers were to be sought in many aspects of the metropolis. It is important that the research directives be read with this in mind, and an effort has been made to present them in much the same form as their original statement in the Research Plan of the Survey. Thus, the following outlines reflect the questions that political scientists asked of sociologists and of themselves.[6]

The Government Survey Section. The scholars who con-

6. There was also an economic analysis but it is not central to this discussion.

centrated upon the study of local governmental units began work several months before the economics and sociology sections were in operation; their findings, in preliminary form, thus constituted the background for the other sections' work.

The first task was a simple but expensive one; as most of the various units of government do not have to report essential data to any central agency in Missouri, it was necessary to do a field study of more than 100 units of local government. Since the purposes of the Survey emphasized the governments as corporate service-providing agencies, concern was with (1) legal and constitutional structures, (2) fiscal procedures and resources, and (3) service-providing functions and structures. The first concern led to knowledge of the legal power to act and conditions of action in each governmental unit; the second, in general, showed the flow of resources into the system via taxes, borrowing, and licensing; and the third dealt with the amount and quality of services provided the citizens in the government's jurisdiction.

The rules of public administration and the goals of the movement to improve the cities lead to specific hypotheses. The unit of attention was an image of the City-County area as one large complex, and the general question was: "How well is this big structure performing its various functions?" This broke into several questions: (1) what is the minimal level of service being provided to all sections of the urban area, (2) how is this related to the present, fragmented political structure of the area, and (3) what are the inequities resulting? Thus governmental fragmentation was a key area of interest.

It was hypothesized that the *ad hoc* development of governmental units with little rational control would have these consequences: (1) great variation in the legal foundations and the real purposes of governmental units in the metropolitan area, even resulting in governmental legitimacy used chiefly to *prevent* integration, (2) overlap in the units of government providing the same or similar services, resulting in conflicts of authority and duplication of services, (3) great variation in the size of governmental units, resulting in an assignment of services (which must be provided the citizens according to the usual division of labor among local governmental units in America) utterly disproportional to the jurisdictional and fiscal resources of the governing unit.

It was further hypothesized that this congeries of heterogeneous and overlapping governmental units would produce these results: (1) great variation in output, or service levels, among the different units, (2) great variations in the efficiency, or cost benefit ratio, among the units, and (3) a generally low level of some services throughout the area, due to the deleterious effects of poor services in one governmental unit upon the services in other, interdependent units.

These are, in general, dysfunctional results in terms of the "input-output" model of local government. It was also hypothesized that certain inequities would result from the over-all pattern. (1) Persons in some parts of the metropolitan area would be taxed twice for the same services; (2) some persons would receive services for which they did not pay; and (3) there would be no reasonably constant relationship between the cost of government and the benefit from government among the various sub-areas of the metropolitan region. In other words, taxes would vary with idiosyncratic governmental variables unrelated to either the services provided or the type of neighborhood in which one lived or owned property.

Finally, it was hypothesized that size of governmental unit would have no relationship to the vitality of the local political process. Neither the proportion of offices for which there was active competition, nor the proportion of the electorate which voted for local officials, would be significantly related to the size of the unit. This hypothesis amounted to a tentative rejection of the notion that governmental fragmentation helps to "keep government close to the people."

This latter hypothesis has an obvious bearing on the community action programs for which the survey was conceived as a resource. Just as one argument for integrating smaller units into a large government is the putative efficiency of the larger unit, so one argument for the smaller unit of government is its "accessibility" to the citizens. The previous hypotheses are also directly relevant to the action program, in the following manner: (1) the present governmental structure produces inadequacies in service levels, inequities in services and in cost benefit ratio, lack of responsibility of government to citizen and thus of citizen confidence in government; (2) the result is, in general, dissatisfaction with existing government, particularly great in those areas where services are poorest and inequities greatest; (3) this, in turn, produces a widespread willingness to change the governmental pattern of the City-County area.

This complex implied a very rational model of political behavior in local government, one in which the citizen was seen as *primarily* a customer of a service-producing bureaucracy. He is envisaged as competent, concerned, and rational; he sees his government from a bookkeeper's perspective, and reacts much like a political scientist whose training has been in public administration.

These propositions were not initially stated as hypotheses; *their validity was assumed, for they were part of the over-all ideology of the movement to save the cities.* The Government section of the Survey could not test hypotheses (2) and (3) above: this remained for the Sociology section's work. However, a major part of the resources of the governmental section went into the assessments of services required to test hypothesis (1).

These several clusters of hypotheses lead to an intensive comparison of legal structure and history, fiscal resources, operating organization and service levels, and electoral statistics, for the 149 governmental units of the City and County. Some of the results will be noted later.

The Sociology Section. In the Research Plan, emphasis was placed upon the opinions and definitions held by the citizens of the metropolitan area. Although not stated as formal hypotheses, two important questions were asked: (a) What metropolitan problems are perceived, and how are they defined, by the population in the City and in the County? How do these perceptions and definitions vary among major geographical and socioeconomic segments of the metropolitan population? (b) What are the reactions of the citizens to proposals for change in the governmental structure of the area? A part of this project was the testing of the following hypotheses: (1) many citizens do not know what governmental agency is responsible for specific governmental services; (2) widespread criticism exists, among the citizens, with respect to the adequacy and/or cost of given services.

A second major need was the description and analysis of the metropolitan area's population. It was deemed important to answer these questions: (1) How is the socio-economic differentiation of the population related to governmental differentiation—what kinds of people live in different municipalities, counties, and so forth, in the metropolitan area, and, (2) what kinds of change, in the total population and in its spatial-governmental distribution, are taking place through time?

A third approach was the relation of population characteristics to voting behavior. In this study, particular attention was given the successful referendum for the Metropolitan Sewer District which, in 1954, had gained favorable majorities for the District in both City and County. The purpose of this study was to ascertain, if possible, the types of population aggregates which had supported the move to integrate the sewer districts of the City-County area. (It was hoped that such analysis would indicate the types of population most likely to favor integration of other governmental functions.)

The population of the City-County area was analyzed through the use of data from the 1950 decennial census. The population of each of the census tracts in the area was described in terms of sociological indexes of social rank, segregation, and urbanization (or urbanism).[7] The tract map, with the different social attributes indicated, thus constituted a "social mosaic" of the metropolitan area which could be compared with the political map.

When the social characteristics of City and County and the various subdivisions of each were measured for 1950 and preceding years, it was possible to indicate the changes in the nature and distribution of the population within political boundaries over time. And, when voting records were broken down to provide estimates of the vote within each census tract, the relationship between social characteristics and voting could be ascertained.

The questions dealing with citizen opinion and attitude were approached through a sample survey of the City-County area. A systematic random sample of households was drawn in City and County; one in each hundred dwelling units of the County was selected for the sample, and one in each four hundred units of the City. Altogether, the final sample amounted to 1800 interviews, 515 in the City and 1285 in the County.

The political opinions and reactions to governmental services were considered to be more than basic descriptive data, or even prognostic indicators for the state of health of the metropolitan area's government: they were also considered as *effect* variables, ultimately explicable in terms of sociological theory. Thus it was necessary to relate political behavior and opinions to (1) the over-all differentiation of the population by social class, ethnic background, and style of

7. The Shevky-Bell typology of urban areas was used as the method of analyzing populations. Cf. Eshref Shevky and Wendell Bell, *Social Area Analysis*, Stanford, California: Stanford University Press, 1955.

life, (2) the differentiation of neighborhoods and local communities as social systems, and (3) the differential participation of respondents in different kinds of social systems within the metropolitan environment. One of the most important kinds of social systems is, however, the political system of influence, communication, and overt social action. For these reasons, the interview schedule was much more than a set of opinion questions and standard questions about the socio-economic background of the respondent.

The point of departure was the classic survey question, "What is it really like at the grass roots?" What does local government mean as a social fact to the non-specialists in local government—as a political arena, as a provider of services and collector of taxes, as an image of a total community? What metropolitan problems are "real" at this level? And, closely connected with these questions, the policy question: "What conditions produce the massive resistance to metropolitan integration inevitably encountered by referenda on 'merger'?" How does a given *ad hoc* structure of government marshal the support among the voters which has repeatedly defeated efforts at metropolitan integration? A related question of importance was, "Who are the 'metropolitanites,' the citizens of the metropolitan area as a whole —or do they exist?" To what degree has functional interdependence of population within the metropolis resulted in anything resembling "community"?

IV. Some Salient Findings on Political Behavior

Three important congeries of ideas became hypotheses which were tested by the sample survey of citizen opinion in conjunction with research into governmental units. The first was the general notion that "widespread criticisms exist among the citizens with respect to the cost and/or adequacy of services." The second concerns the kinds of population and governmental unit most conducive to citizen participation in the governmental process. The final complex has been described earlier as the "rational model" of citizen-government relationships. This, it will be remembered, comprises assumptions that the citizen rationally evaluates governments by the services provided in relation to his needs and the cost of government; that his satisfaction with government results from such evaluation, and that his willingness to accept change is a direct function of his degree of dissatisfaction with present governmental services.

The Extent of Dissatisfaction. The Survey tended to bring over into its operations the rhetoric of the movement to save the cities by improving government. One important part of this rhetoric is the belief that, if governmental structure is *ad hoc* and irrational, the citizens will respond through general dissatisfaction and criticism. Though no quantitative estimates were made, it was believed that a large portion of the residents of the area were dissatisfied with *some* governmental service.

While a large proportion indicated some dissatisfaction (approximately 80 per cent had some suggestion for changes or improvements), there was very little consensus as to the improvements desired and there was no significant criticism of most major services of government. Thus, less than 10 per cent indicated they desired improvements in any of these services: police protection, fire protection, water supply, garbage, trash and sewage disposal, or pollution control. Schools, the subject of continual agitation, were identified as "problem areas" by less than 5 per cent of the subjects in the area. A miniscule proportion indicated a desire for lower taxes.

Certain service areas did elicit suggestions from substantial proportions of the respondents, however. Most important targets of criticism can be grouped around two aspects of urban life, (1) the neighborhood and (2) movement within the metropolitan area. Half of the respondents volunteered suggestions and criticisms concerned with the condition of their residential streets, 21 per cent were concerned with maintaining or improving the "character of the neighborhood" (slum clearance, slum prevention, rezoning, clean-up campaigns, and the like), and 12 per cent wanted improvements in parks and playground facilities. Thirty per cent indicated that they wanted improvement in traffic conditions and parking, and 10 per cent criticized public transportation.

Because the open-ended question indicates something about the "saliency" of a subject for the respondent, results are here given in some detail. However, a check list of structured questions, a "satisfaction inventory," elicited very similar responses. When asked how satisfied they were with each of a dozen major governmental services, the most dissatisfaction was expressed with those indicated above. In addition, a small proportion (15 per cent) indicated dissatisfaction with sewage disposal; these persons were almost all residents of the County. Another 15 per cent were dissatisfied with police protection and they were chiefly residents of the City.

From the complex welter of governmental services, only four elicited negative judgments from as many as 30 per cent of the residents in the metropolitan area. These were traffic, public transportation, the condition of residential streets, and parks and playgrounds.

A basic assumption of the ideology of the movement to improve local government in the metropolis is the belief that taxes are of great importance to the citizens and, as a corollary, that basic inequities in the value of services rendered as related to cost are an important source of dissatisfaction. As noted, almost none of the respondents suggested, in response to the open-ended question, that taxes should be lowered. Furthermore, when giving their reasons for wanting a change of governmental structure, less than 20 per cent indicated that "lower taxes" was an important reason for change. Finally, in response to a direct question on the equity of taxes in relation to services provided, only a minority (approximately 40 per cent) felt they were too high.[8]

In the study of government services provided in the various parts of the metropolitan area, considerable emphasis was placed upon the functionally and financially important services of police protection, fire protection, the schools, and the like. When, however, the citizen's perspective is examined it is evident that, for him, these services are not defined as "problems." There is no indication that any functional breakdown is imminent in local governments. Nor, on the other hand, were the respondents very concerned with what their governments were costing them. Instead, they were very interested indeed in the improvement of two aspects of urban living—facility of movement within the metropolitan area, and the upkeep and livability of their own immediate neighborhood. Government impinges on all citizens as a regulator of movement and upon many as a maintainer of residential streets and provider of parks and playground facilities. These latter services are not, traditionally, defined as the central "problems" of metropolitan government. If problems are to be ascertained by studying popular definitions, however, they are, together with traffic and transit, the major problems of the St. Louis area.

Participation in the Political Process. It was generally assumed that the smaller suburban municipalities had a definite superiority over the central City in making government interesting and accessible to the citizens—of "keeping government closer to the people." The approach of the Sociology

8. This item was adapted from one used by Morris Janowitz in studying perspectives toward the public bureaucracy in general. The results of the St. Louis study are practically identical with those reported by Janowitz for Detroit (the latter found that 41 per cent believed taxes to be too high); cf. Morris Janowitz, Deil Wright, and William Delany, *Public Administration and the Public—Perspectives Toward Government in a Metropolitan Community,* Michigan Governmental Studies No. 36, University of Michigan, Ann Arbor, 1958.

section investigated a similar hypothesis. The smaller size of the governmental units and the higher average social rank of the population, together with the "familistic" rather than "urban" way of life in the suburbs, were expected to work in the same direction: in brief, they were expected to result in more voting, more faith in the importance of local elections, and more effective access of the citizen to the local government officials.

The findings were not an unambiguous verification, nor did they support the null hypothesis that size of governmental unit made *no* difference. With respect to participation in the electoral process, a larger proportion of the City population had voted in each type of local election for which comparison was possible. Over 67 per cent of the City respondents had voted for municipal officials, compared with 57 per cent of those eligible in the County, and half the City respondents had voted in School Board elections, compared with 43 per cent in the County. Furthermore, the difference is largely accounted for by the much higher proportion of County residents who either didn't know they could vote or thought they *could not* do so. Thus the hypotheses must be reversed to account for these findings. Residents of suburban municipalities seem *less* competent and *less* involved.

Although County residents were less likely to have voted in local elections, they were much more convinced of the importance of such elections. When asked a question from Campbell's "Sense of Citizen Duty Scale," as follows: "A good many local elections aren't important enough to bother with. Do you agree or disagree?", 82 per cent of the County residents disagreed, but only 68 per cent did so in the City. Assent to the ideological importance of local elections is greater in the suburban populations, though the proportion who have voted is greater in the City.

In order to gain a picture of the citizens' relationship with the service-providing agencies of local government, a series of questions was asked which dealt with complaints made. The residents were asked if they had felt like complaining, and if so, whether they had complained, and if so, to *whom* had they complained.

The same percentage had felt like complaining in City and in the County—38 per cent. A majority of those who had felt like complaining did so in the County (54 per cent) but in the City only a minority did so (32 per cent). (Almost all complaints dealt with immediate necessities of the household—sanitation, utilities, street repairs, and the like.) There is an important difference in the "target" of the complaint. Forty-one per cent of those in the County complained to specific persons, compared with only 25 per cent in the City. And in the County 20 per cent had complained to *elected* officials, as compared with only 5 per cent in the City. The residents of the County municipalities do, in some ways, have greater access to the officialdom of local government. However, City residents are more apt to be members of the electorate for local government than the suburbanites. In short, the attitudes of the County residents are not implemented by their voting behavior.

Any explanation of the City-County differences in voting by distribution of population categories (social rank, urbanization, migration) also falls short, for the City-County differences persist for every major subsegment of the two areas. However, a clue to the difference is available through the study of voting for the County Government officials in the suburban municipalities. The vote for these officials is quite comparable in the total (and in most subsegments of the population) with that for City officials in St. Louis City. When it is realized that these elections are partisan elections for officials in large-scale government, while the suburban municipalities hold non-partisan elections for officials in very small-scale government, a hypothesis can be formulated which accounts for the difference as a result of political structure.

The fragmentation of suburbia into scores of municipalities and school districts might be said to have "trivialized" local elections. If the cake is cut into enough pieces, nobody gets a taste of either power, patronage, or glory. (It is significant that within the suburbs the proportion of offices contested increases consistently with the population of the municipalities.) As a corollary, large scale government is "news" for the metropolitan mass media. Finally, the "nonpartisanship" of local government in the suburbs (with the exception of the County government) is probably another way of trivializing the election campaigns.

Voting is not, however, the only measure of citizen response to local government. A much larger proportion of those with complaints about their services had approached the officials of the County municipalities. The very structure of local government in the suburbs, which takes the excitement and significance out of elections by breaking the units very small, also provides an army of elected officials. These officials (something over 600 in St. Louis County) perform a basic governmental function: they are accessible and they listen to the grievances of the population. However, they seem more comparable, in some ways, to union stewards than to the Mayor of St. Louis City.

The Rational Model of Citizen-Government Relationships. The research assumption of the Survey, within the context of its action orientation, implied an interconnected set of notions which we have called the "rational model" of citizen-government relationships. This model assumes that irrational governmental structure and its consequences for services and equity will result in dissatisfaction on the part of the citizens; this, in turn, provides the bases for change, for the citizens who are dissatisfied will accept proposals to improve the situation.

When the first hypothesis, that lack of services results in dissatisfaction with government, is tested, there is no very clear relationship between the two. Dissatisfaction is relatively rare for almost all governmental services, and where there is dissatisfaction it is, frequently, in just those areas where services are very good. Dissatisfaction with public schools is highest in the high rank, familistic areas of St. Louis County which have the best public schools in the metropolitan area.

At the same time, dissatisfaction with taxes in relationship to benefits from government is highest among those parts of the population which pay the lowest local taxes and whose governmental services are, in some interpretations, "subsidized" by the larger taxpayers. Concern with tax equity is more common in the County than in the City—but within each area the high rank neighborhoods with many homeowners are least apt to complain about their local tax bill.

Thus, on the basis of dissatisfaction with present services, there is no support for a broad movement in favor of governmental change. However, ironically, the second link in the chain is weaker than the first. The people of the City-County area, very satisfied with most governmental services, are at the same time overwhelmingly in favor of improving their governments through inter-government cooperation and many approve of some form of integration. Seventy-five per cent are, by any of several indicators, in favor of change as against the *status quo*. Their reasons for believing in change are not clear. However, when those who believed their community should co-operate with others in performing some governmental services were asked "in what way it would benefit their community," 80 per cent gave answers which can be summarized as "more and better services." Only a minority (18 per cent) emphasized tax reduction.

Still the rational structure is questionable indeed, for, when asked what services should be integrated, the only one mentioned by as many as 10 per cent of the respondents was police protection. This was mentioned by some 15 per cent, chiefly in the County. Yet the proportion of County residents who were dissatisfied with police protection was negligible.

In short, the citizens of the area are not dissatisfied with many governmental services. This is reinforced by their *very* favorable judgments of all local governments. No more than 10 per cent thought the relevant government was doing a "poor" job in City, County, or the County Municipalities. At the same time, a large majority is in favor of change, and less than one-fourth prefer to leave the governmental structure as it is. The reasons for this support of reform are, at the present stage of analysis, obscure.

Summary. These findings may appear to be chiefly negative. There is no really widespread criticism of most governmental service nor of the equity of the tax load. There is no more dissatisfaction in the smaller units of government than the larger. Nor, on the other hand, do these smaller units evoke more interest in local elections. There is no broad basis for reform in dissatisfaction rationally derived from the inadequacies of governmental structure as seen by political scientists.

However, deductive logic applied to the implicit empirical assumptions of the ideology of civic reform yields a wide selection of various and contradictory propositions about the nature of local government and the possibilities for change in any given metropolitan area. These findings here reported perform the very useful task of narrowing the range of possibilities. (Thus, it was on *a priori* grounds as plausible to expect a larger electorate in the suburbs as to expect what emerged from the research, e.g., a larger electorate in the City.) Through such tests the congeries of notions inherited from the movement to save the cities may be sifted and ordered, made internally coherent and more congruent with the nature of things.

By eliminating certain possibilities, the remaining assumptions are made to appear rather strange. Much more interesting questions than those derived from ideology begin to emerge as findings are compared with assumptions, and the latter emerged as discredited (or at least, unsupported) hypotheses. The lack of close relationship between dissatisfaction with present governments and willingness to accept change raises this question: what is the basis of the support for reform in metropolitan areas? Who are those who champion "merger," "one big city," a "metropolitan community?" On the other hand, who are the opposition? What, we must ask, provides the staying power of the "do nothing" suburban municipality? Why should the political process in the City involve a larger proportion of the potential electorate than in the suburb?

Our findings seem to indicate that the basis for governmental change in the St. Louis area does not rest upon the ancient cries of "Wolf" which were inherited from the movement to save the cities. Instead, the indications are that an economy of relative abundance has affected the kinds of demands made upon the local government by its citizens. When more citizens are interested in parks, playgrounds, and swimming pools, than in lowering taxes or improving police protection, one might venture to guess that some level acceptable to most citizens has been reached with traditional governmental services and that the *expansion* of governmental services is the real interest of a substantial proportion. There are, after all, certain goods which only government can supply and these include more than the "functional prerequisites" for the minimal functioning of the city; they include such articles of consumption as those mentioned earlier, as well as pleasant neighborhoods and clean air. It is not really likely that traffic conditions will ever "strangle" the economic life of a metropolitan area; however, our evidence indicates that they may come pretty close to strangling the individual resident in his capacity as a consumer of mobility.

V. Some Dilemmas of Action Research on
Metropolitan Problems

The Metropolitan St. Louis Survey was ambitious in its scope; the general aims were as broad as the "metropolitan problem." Financial resources were, for once, apparently adequate. However, as work began it became obvious that intellectual resources were not nearly adequate—not because of the personnel of the study, but because of the poverty of conceptual beginnings and systematic information concerning metropolitan government. Thus the Survey, although an exercise in the application of social science to a policy question, was forced to operate as an intellectual enterprise focused upon *basic* research.

There are certain hiatuses between the process of application and the process of basic research, particularly when they deal with the same empirical problems. As a method of simplifying this discussion, the effects of "action orientation" upon the intellectual enterprise of basic research will be discussed, followed by a discussion of the Survey as an action program.

Problems of Basic Research in an Action Framework. The resources and support for the Survey had been contingent upon an orientation toward improving government in the City-County area. The structure of control and the focus of research reflected this emphasis. Furthermore, the time schedule (15 months of field research during which two public reports were issued) was determined by the belief that the Survey would represent a kind of staff resource for the entire City-County area in its efforts to improve itself. This time schedule, as it turned out, was inadequate for the action program: the referenda were still far in the future.[9] The short period allowed for data gathering, and the subsequent dispersal of personnel, set a rigid limit on the research operations. There was every pressure for rapid application of known techniques and the translation of familiar concepts into tools for handling the given problems.

9. Ironically, the referendum for a new charter in the City of St. Louis occurred just at the end of the period of field work; this referendum could not be studied within the time period of the Survey, though such study would have yielded important findings. The new Charter was defeated by a very large margin.

The Survey was defined as diagnostic and prescriptive, an operation which was to determine the ills of the metropolitan governmental structure, and the cures for these ills. This involves two assumptions: (1) the value of the analogy to problems of physical health in the "metropolitan problem," and (2) a competence on the part of the Survey staff to take the pulse of the metropolis and prescribe.

These assumptions led to basic ambiguities. What, for example, are the bases upon which minimal "levels" of service—schools, transit, police protection—may be calculated? What is an equitable relationship between taxes and services provided by government? What is an acceptably "vital" political process at the level of the County, the municipality, the school district?

It has been indicated already that, by present standards of gauging public opinion, nothing like a crisis in governmental services existed. Nor was there any danger of organizational collapse; on the contrary, local government and its services are probably being slowly though steadily improved. Thus one basis for a diagnostic criterion, the probability that the structure will not be able to survive unless action is taken, was notably absent. The prognosis for metropolitan *health* must be based upon value assumptions and these cannot be derived from the procedures of empirical science, yet the role of the medicine man forces one to speak as a "scientist" concerning matters of illness and health, salvation and damnation. In the process, it is very easy to lose sight of value judgments made, previous to research, informing research, but neither proved nor disproved by the results.

Because of the Survey's role and the time limits, the extremely important enterprise of disentangling value theory from empirical theory, ordering each, and attempting to relate them as separate kinds of thought which interpenetrate in policy decisions, was given a second place in the work procedure. It was logically prior to any field work which could be done.

At the same time, concentration upon what should be—

what kind of government *should* handle what kind of services, what minimal level was required, what equity was desirable—led to a muting of the more basic problem—*What is the existing state of things?* and *How does it work?* Yet this is also logically prior to the question of bringing about desirable changes however determined. The results of basic research, which could have guided some of the policy decisions, were not available, for this research was being carried out coterminously with the drafting of a "plan of government" for the area. The physician was diagnosing heart ailments while attempting to test the proposition that the blood circulates.

Problems of Action in a Research Framework. The Survey was initiated with the hope that reform action would ensue; it will be judged by some on its action outcome. However, the personnel of the Survey were prohibited from taking any effective steps to initiate or guide a community movement. The legitimacy of the Survey as a public operation, and therefore its influence, depended upon the white mask of the scientific practitioner—one who "had an open mind and no preconceived notions." Furthermore, the Survey's status as a project supported by tax-free foundations meant that it could not engage in a local political campaign which would inevitably injure some interests in the community. The "action" program was curiously aim-inhibited.[10]

At the same time, the task of devising a new governmental structure for the metropolitan area meant, if taken seriously, a real attention to the conditions for the legitimizing of that government by referenda. If the plan of government were to be more than another "utopia," it had to take into account the probabilities of popular support in City and County separately.

As an action organization oriented to improving govern-

10. Professor Thomas Eliot, a member of the Board of Control of the Survey, has discussed these difficulties in some detail in "Dilemmas of Metropolitan Research," *The Midwest Journal of Political Science,* 2 (February, 1958), 26–39.

mental structure, forbidden to organize power in the community, though dependent upon referenda results for success, the Survey tended to mask any basic conflicts of interest, though such conflicts constitute the political process. The non-partisan, integrative mode of thought, inherited from the movement to improve the cities, became an important part of the assumptions about action. At the same time, much attention was given to the figments of popular comment about the City, the County, and possible relationship and conflicts between the two. Many more basic questions, such as, for example, the existence, strength, composition, and integration of a metropolitan power structure, were elided.

The net result was to give great weight to findings from the sample survey. The opinions of the 1800 citizens interviewed were allowed to stand for public opinion in the area, and little weighting could be given the organized groups which most assuredly would have a good deal to do with the outcome of any referenda on the issue of City-County integration. Furthermore, the opinion of the citizens was, necessarily, studied in a period when there was no active campaign to change the governments; thus the validity of the sample survey is confined to a period of calm when there is no official act in the offing.

Acting as staff to an entire metropolitan community, the Survey did discover a general willingness to consider governmental change. There was widespread dissatisfaction with certain functions as they are performed: one of these, the regulation of traffic within the metropolitan area, can only be improved through a solution which is areawide in its scope. This particular "problem area" is an object of dissatisfaction to many in all major segments of the population, and more salient among the suburban population than those of the City, the persons of high income than those of low, the "majority Americans" than those of "minority" ethnic status.

On other problems, however, the opinions of the experts in public administration and those of the public did not jibe.

There was little concern for inequities in public school facilities and budgets among the population as a whole, though these seem major to the experts. Even more basic, planning and zoning were of little concern to the public. However, there was much concern for parks and playgrounds among the residents of the area, although these did not seem to be basic metropolitan problems. In cases of this sort, the dilemma of policy becomes quite pressing. Should the social scientists urge a propaganda campaign to change the public definition of the "problems"? Upon what value premise, and with what right?

The dangers of premature application are great in an area where application has so far outrun basic theory and research.[11] The "metropolitan problem" has an obscure quality because its origins lie in a simple summarizing of the results of metropolitan growth. It is really many problems, defined in an *ad hoc* manner. This "problem solving" approach deserves some attention, for it dominates thinking in many quarters.

Developed as a logical extension from the expert's role as a diagnoser and prescriber for the ills of the metropolitan body politic, this approach leaves the most interesting nine-tenths of the iceberg, the concept of "health," under water. Values are implicit and "problems" are identified on a particularistic basis wherever implicit values are depreciated or contravened. Various levels of value are not related: the problem of responsibility of government to citizen is one problem; that of minimal service level is another. Thus, choices tend to be, essentially, rational with respect to a very limited area defined as problematic, but the effects of the solutions may be extremely dysfunctional for other values and, therefore, irrational as public policy.

Thus, the "problem solving" approach to local government eliminates policy, for it assumes a fixed policy which is never

11. Norton Long, "The Local Community as an Ecology of Games," *American Journal of Sociology*, 64 (1958), 251–261.

made explicit. In democratic society, however, substantive policy is never fixed; it is contingent upon a given balance of power, representing a given dominance of values. One cannot discuss the metropolitan problem until he has a framework in terms of which these *ad hoc* problems become aspects of policy. But in policy making, it is quite clear, "to choose is to reject." With very few exceptions, public policy making is always a readjustment of equity.

If this sketch of the problem-solving approach to the metropolis has any truth to life, then some of the needs of theory with respect to metropolitan governmental processes begin to emerge. Values must be made explicit, and their relation to the power and influence structure of the metropolis must be spelled out. They must be generalized at a level which will allow some economy of thought and, perhaps, theoretical elegance. It should then be possible to compare them in a common frame—to allow the interests of many to enter a common arena. In such an arena, choices can be made in terms of a common calculus, one which will emphasize the cost of a given benefit as *loss* of others. The "problem solver" will face *his* problems—somebody's ox is always being gored.

12

The Rational Model, the Sociological Model, and Metropolitan Reform

This is a post-mortem on a large-scale effort to use social science in the reform of metropolitan government. It deals with the work of the Metropolitan St. Louis Survey, with the campaign for the District Plan (a new charter that would have effectuated most recommendations of the Survey), and with the results of that campaign. As Chief Sociologist of the Survey, I had intimate knowledge of that operation; in 1959, I carried out a follow-up study of the electorate, immediately after the election on the plan.

THE RATIONAL MODEL OF REFORM

Most of us are aware of (if not obsessed by) the lack of rationality in political decision making. Nevertheless, any effort to use social science in application presumes rationality—at least in the strategy of action. And the logic of governmental reform in a democracy creates a heavy bias toward the assumption of reasonableness in the voter. Particularly when change requires affirmation in referendum, one must make assumptions concerning the voter's evaluation of the *status quo* and the changes he will accept.

The danger in such assumptions is a simple one, but it is grave. We tend to assume that the "folk rationality" of the actors we study is the same as the "skilled rationality" of the practitioners. Ignorance of this trap has led many a movement for reform to provide solutions for problems nobody saw, answers to questions nobody was asking. The avoidance of the trap is, however, more difficult than simply acknowledging its existence.

The directors of the Metropolitan St. Louis Survey tried to solve the problem by using the sample survey as the voice of the voters.[1] The results may be summarized briefly: (1) Considerable dissatisfaction was expressed with certain specific services, particularly traffic and transportation, but no service elicited such expression from over half the respondents; (2) analysis indicated little relation among objective conditions, dissatisfaction, and willingness to change; (3) willingness to accept greater coordination was expressed, and a split vote (near 50-50) in favor of each possible type of change was recorded—while a substantial majority rejected "no change" or the *status quo;* (4) a sharp polarization appeared to exist; about one-fifth of the voters chose all-out merger of local governments and most disliked the *status quo,* while another fifth chose the *status quo* and most disliked all-out merger.

The Survey directors, combining these results with those from extensive analysis of formal governmental structure, chose a middle way. They recommended a "federal system," leaving all municipalities in existence but creating a multi-purpose metropolitan district government. The district would have particular responsibility for traffic, transportation, and other services and amenities nominated by the voters in the sample survey, as well as some functions (such as tax assessment) recommended by the administrative experts. The recommenders hoped to mollify the extreme opponents of

---

1. For extensive reporting of these data, see John C. Bollens, editor, *Exploring the Metropolitan Community,* Berkeley, University of California Press, 1961.

change and those favoring extreme merger, and appeal to the middle of the range. They offered a carefully selected bunch of carrots which (1) required a metropolitan solution, and (2) deprived no existing government or official of much power or perquisite.

THE DISTRICT PLAN AND THE CAMPAIGN

A duly appointed Board of Freeholders sat for a year. It carried out in haphazard and amateur fashion research similar to that of the Survey, got similar and repeating results, and ended up deadlocked between central city respresentatives (who wanted all-out merger) and suburban representatives (who wanted a federal district). Although the Board of Freeholders superstitiously avoided using the research personnel of the Survey staff, feeling this would violate the purity of *vox populi,* the District Plan supported by the suburban representatives closely resembled the Survey's recommendations. It finally won out by a fluke.[2]

The District Plan was required to gain a separate majority in the city of St. Louis and in the suburban county. The political technology assumes a preexisting role system in the political community that can be activated in the given instant. Such a role system must provide an organized body of men who interpret alternatives with respect to the general norms shared by significant parts of the population and, finally, communicate with a significant body of the voters. This, they assume, will influence the voters to dispose of the proposition in a meaningful way. The campaign throughout a metropolis of over 1,500,000 people was organized and carried out by a few political leaders, the League of Women Voters, the Chambers of Commerce, and other civic groups. It neither engaged the regular party organization nor stimulated it to active opposition. The major symbols of civic virtue supported the plan (with one key exception—Raymond Tucker, Mayor of

2. Cf. Henry J. Schmandt *et al., Reform in St. Louis,* New York, Holt, Rinehart & Winston, 1961.

St. Louis); its opponents were organized in two *ad hoc* groups —one in .he central city supporting all-out merger, one in the suburbs (the "Citizens Committee for Self Government") that wanted no change at all.

The campaign for the plan was conducted through the mass media. It was assumed that the virtues of the plan in terms of the voters' desires could be broadcast over the heads of organizations, direct to the reasonable citizen. The campaign filled the daily newspapers, which were overwhelmingly in favor. In the last two weeks of the campaign, each major paper gave a daily average of over 50 column inches to the campaign. The campaign loomed large on local television and radio and was very important in the local community press, which vigorously opposed the plan. There was, however, almost no face-to-face solicitation of voters; the wards were inactive, and only the League of Women Voters mounted a telephone and buttonhole campaign. They were not very effective.[3]

Twenty-one per cent of the registered voters in the city of St. Louis voted, as did 40 per cent of those in the suburbs. The plan was overwhelmingly defeated, by 2 to 1 in the city and by 3 to 1 in the county. In the history of such efforts in the St. Louis area, this was the most overwhelming defeat ever suffered by the proponents of change. The District Plan carried only one ward in the city; it failed to carry a single township in the county.

THE FOLLOW-UP STUDY

Immediately after the election, the Center for Metropolitan Studies of Northwestern University carried out a sample survey of the residents.[4] Three hundred and twelve interviews

3. For a detailed description and analysis see Scott Greer (w'th the advice and assistance of Norton E. Long), *Metropolitics: A Study of Political Culture,* New York, Wiley, forthcoming.
4. The residents interviewed were a subsample from the 1957 survey's sampling frame of dwelling units. Wherever possible they were the same respondents; the rate of mobility, however, meant that only about two-thirds were the same. The sample we interviewed was, furthermore, limited to

were taken, 116 in the city and 196 in the county. While we took 66 interviews with residents who had moved in since the 1957 poll, their importance was, chiefly, in verifying our suspicion: such newcomers voted at a very low rate (6 per cent in the city, 16 per cent in the suburbs, compared with 30 and 60 per cent, respectively, of old residents). Omitting these newer residents, our sample included 165 suburban residents and 85 central city residents.

These two samples, drawn to exaggerate the politically alert and active, reveal the massive nature of opposition to the District Plan in city and county (see Table 1). First, if we

TABLE 1. PERCENTAGE VOTE AND PREFERENCE OF NONVOTERS
IN THE REFERENDUM

	VOTERS			NONVOTERS			NO OPINION	TOTAL
	PRO	REFUSED	CON	PRO	DIVIDED	CON		
City	7	3	20	6	10	13	41	100 (85)
County	14	1	41	6	11	11	16	100 (165)

assume that those who refused to answer were supporters of the plan (as would seem likely, since it was unpopular and an overwhelming loser), the division of the vote is very close to the over-all division of the electorate. Second, there is no evidence that the nonvoters with opinions were very different in their sentiments from the voters. Third, it is clear that massive opposition in the county was combined with massive indifference in the city (41 per cent of the city sample had no opinion *after* the election). One cannot imagine any turnout that would have changed the results.

What accounted for these results? (The answer to this question will rely on the suburban sample of 185; both its size and response rate give more confidence in the estimates.) About half the voters could recall some "good" arguments they had

those who had indicated in 1957 that they had voted in local elections: we took this as a fair estimate of registered voters. Comparison of voting in the sample and universe of registered voters indicates we were approximately correct.

heard for the District Plan. Most important was the plan's provisions for the solution of service problems (32 per cent named a specific service to be improved). Traffic and transit (16 per cent) and public safety (9 per cent) accounted for most responses. The major arguments remembered *against* the plan were its effect on taxes (36 per cent) and its weakening of local, suburban governments (15 per cent).

It is clear that those who supported the District Plan had no very effective way of reaching the voters. An overwhelming majority of the latter had not heard of the leaders who supported the plan (if they had, they did not know their positions or were wrong in their imputations), and if they knew the names of the supporting organizations they did not know they supported the plan. Knowledge of the plan was gained through two sources—the newspapers and personal interaction. The best arguments *for* the plan were heard through the media (28 per cent, or over half of those who could remember); the best arguments *opposed* were heard in personal confrontation (23 per cent, or half of those who remembered). But very little *knowledge* was gained by anyone: taking a checklist of major features of the plan (the services provided, the governance of the District, the taxes to be levied, and the effects on existing governments), we get some notion of what voters thought they were voting on.

Less than half the suburban sample could name any one service affected by the plan. Only two services were named by more than 12 per cent—traffic and transit, and police and civil defense. (The third most common response was naming a service *not* affected by the Plan.) It would appear that the suburban voters were deciding on a plan that was primarily a mechanism to improve traffic and transit and public safety. Taxes, a very hot issue in the election, were more mysterious: only 10 per cent of the suburban sample knew what the tax effects would be. About 13 per cent understood how the new district would be governed, and only 27 per cent got the very important message that no existing municipality would be abolished. Less than 60 per cent of the suburban respondents had voted, so that, even if we assume the competent were the voters, only a minority of voters *could* have understood, accurately, these major provisions.

Thus the rational model breaks down through sheer lack of information. Yet 56 per cent of these suburbanites had voted and overwhelmingly rejected the plan. One possible explanation is, simply, that they were opposed in principle to change. To check this, we returned to their responses in the sample survey of 1957 (see Table 2). At first glance, there appears to be no relationship between their opinions in 1957 and their position on the District Plan—certainly those who liked the "federal system" in 1957 were no more likely to vote "Yes" than anyone else. Yet there is one important regularity: the polarities are predictive. Those who chose *status quo* in 1957 voted "No" by 8 to 1 in 1959; those who chose *merger* turned the District Plan down by less than 2 to 1. Together, they made up about half the sample.

TABLE 2. 1957 PREFERENCE BY POSITION ON THE DISTRICT PLAN
(IN PER CENT)

| 1957 PREFERENCE | POSITION ON PLAN | | | | |
	PRO	NEUTRAL	CON	NO OPINION	TOTAL
1. Merger	24	13	43	20	100 (46)
2. One county	30	4	57	8	99 (23)
3. Federal system	13	8	60	21	102 (24)
4. Consolidation	30	15	50	5	100 (27)
5. *Status quo*	7	13	55	25	100 (40)
6. No opinion	20		40	40	100 (5)
					(165)

In summary, the civic organizations and civic leaders, speaking through the mass media, did not get their message to the citizens. The latter did not understand the District Plan. But willy-nilly they went out and voted it down. And yet, as the final joker, over two-thirds of the suburbanites who had just defeated the District Plan thought that some kind of metropolitan government reorganization was needed in the future. *This was about the same proportion as in the 1957 survey!*

A SOCIOLOGICAL MODEL

In previous work I have sketched out a sociological model for studying public influence in local areas of the metropolis.[5] Briefly, it postulates an organizational system in the locality (neighborhood, local residential community, and municipality) that provides three classes of roles. These are the Community Actor, the Neighbor, and the Isolate. They vary by access to organizational structure and communication flow, with the Community Actor most involved and informed, the Isolate least, and the Neighbor in between—more informed, through gossip, than the Isolate, less active than the Community Actor. The hypothesis is: key actors in local political activity will be preponderantly Community Actors—they will be best informed and most active.

The respondents of the 1959 sample were allocated to types on the basis of the participation patterns they reported in the 1957 study. This sample, "loaded" for the more politically active, broke into 53 per cent Community Actors, 17 per cent Neighbors, and 30 per cent Isolates (the usual proportions seem to be around 40-20-40, respectively). Their involvement in the campaign followed the hypothesized order pretty closely: 20 per cent of the Isolates, 25 per cent of the Neighbors, and 15 per cent of the Community Actors had no opinion; 40 per cent of the Isolates, 32 per cent of the Neighbors, and 18 per cent of the Community Actors had an opinion but did not vote; 40 per cent of the Isolates, 43 per cent of the Neighbors, and 67 per cent of the Community Actors had an opinion and voted. More important than these crude distributions, however, is the proportion of those with opinions who did vote: they were 80 per cent of the Community Ac-

5. Cf. Chs. 7, 8, 9.

tors, 60 per cent of the Neighbors, and only half the Isolates. This would be explained as a result of involvement in the nonpolitical, but politically relevant, social system of the suburban community.

Community Actors were better informed than Isolates (75 per cent knew at least one major provision of the Plan, compared with 58 per cent of the Isolates). They were not, however, significantly better informed than Neighbors. This would be explained by the importance of the conversational ferment in this campaign, and the exposure of the Neighbors to gossip. However, personal knowledge of the District Plan was not widely scattered: only a minority of each type (ranging from 21 to 28 per cent) knew two or more of the four key aspects of the plan discussed earlier. While Community Actors were disproportionately represented in the electorate that decided the fate of the District Plan (they were 65 per cent of the voters in the sample), they were no better informed than, and voted no differently from, the other categories. They participated vigorously, but they did not think rigorously. The typology predicts action, not direction.

There were some clues to direction, however. A majority of the sample had engaged in political conversation concerning the District Plan. They talked with kinfolk, work associates, friends, and neighbors in that order (47 to 27 per cent). About half of those who discussed the plan said they thought they had learned something from the conversations—either facts about the plan, or how others felt about it. The latter finding was overwhelmingly negative—two-thirds of those with opinions thought the talk was mostly negative, only 6 per cent thought it mostly favorable. This conversational ferment, and the tone of the conversation, was closely related to the position of the respondent with respect to the plan. For those who said they rely on people more than the media in political decision making, there was a consistent and striking association between position of the respondent and the tone of the conversations with kinfolk, neighbors, and friends.

With co-workers, there was no association. (For the minority who relied on the media in political decisions, there was a tendency for Isolates to rely on the central city dailies and favor the plan, while Community Actors relied on the local suburban press and opposed it.) These findings, though suggestive, are based on very small subsamples and should be considered only as clues. They seem to indicate that, for most suburbanites, conversations among relatives, friends, and kin were very important in transmitting influence: from other data it is clear that they carried little accurate information.

CONCLUSIONS

Marianne Moore has remarked that "one cannot love that which he does not understand." The peculiar requirements of democracy lead people who neither love nor understand politics to vote, and their vote has implications for our common fate. Ordinarily, indifference and ignorance are masked by the party system of representative democracy: in a referendum campaign they are laid bare.

In this campaign neither fact nor argument carried well. The noise seems only to have activated a set of mutually contradictory norms: "Big government is more efficient," but "Keep government close to the people"; "Increased services are a good thing," but "Beware of any rise in taxes." The District Plan, postulating a new and unknown government, did not lead people to investigate its characteristics. They cared, but not enough to learn what they cared about, and in the end they went by old rules of thumb: "Don't try anything new for the first time," and "Better the evil that is known." They favored increased coordination of government in general (much more so than in particular), but they wanted it without its price.

For those interested in metropolitan government the conclusions are sobering. They must (1) somehow mobilize a winning party to fight on partisan grounds for metropolitan government, or (2) so educate the voters at large that the questions will precede the answers and the problems the solutions, or (3) avoid the direct democracy of the referendum. The first is unlikely, owing to the Democratic preponderance in the central city and the Republican strongholds in suburbia. The second requires a radical change in our political culture—one that might take generations. The third is most likely—deviously, covertly, we shall achieve metropolitan government. It will probably come through temporary expedients grown old and sacred—special service districts, for example—and through Federal intervention completely circumventing the direct democracy of the local community.

13

Where Is
the Metropolitan Problem?

Two decades ago the "metropolitan problem" rose on the horizon of public concern. A large number of journalists on the "metropolitan beat" ran feature articles on local versions. Citizens' groups organized to consider it. The editors of *Fortune* published a lively and profitable book on the subject, and the entire enterprise was given the Good Housekeeping seal of approval—that is, many substantial foundation grants were made for the purpose of solving the problem. Eventually, the Public Administration Service published a survey of metropolitan surveys listing almost a hundred investigations of the problem.[1]

The question arises: what is this problem? The question may seem superfluous—most cities appear to be disorderly, schismatic, conflict-ridden, dirty, rackety, and not ordered the way a beneficent God or social system would order them. However, in this respect they differ not at all from many other aspects of our lives and works. What is peculiarly prob-

1. The Editors of *Fortune, The Exploding Metropolis,* New York: Doubleday, 1958; Governmental Affairs Foundation, *Metropolitan Surveys: A Digest,* Chicago: Public Administration Service, 1958.

lematic about the metropolis? As a first approach to the question, I will try to summarize, impressionistically, the kinds of concerns implicit in statements of the problem.

I

In 1957 the *St. Louis Post-Dispatch* published a cartoon of the St. Louis metropolitan area as Gulliver, bound flat on his back by the myriad tiny threads of diverse local governmental units. The implication is that the metropolis is organically united, but unable to act because of political fragmentation. The *Post* also published a cartoon showing Tweedledum and Tweedledee (two simpering fat boys) labelled as central city and suburbs. The implication is that halves of an identity have become split and separate. These cartoons correspond to the most common slogans of metropolitan governmental reform; both deplore "the crazy-quilt of local government in the metropolis," and "the Chinese wall between city and suburbs." Rift and fragmentation seen as vitiating the polity —this is one important element in the picture.

The division of government, in turn, is held accountable for many other losses and lacks. The policy power is divided with a resulting loss of communication and surveillance; land-use planning is impossible with 149 units as in St. Louis (or 1467, as in the New York area); development and maintenance of an adequate circulatory system is hamstrung by divided jurisdiction over roads; even the disposal of waste, sewage, garbage and noxious gases, is difficult when one watershed and one atmosphere are so divided, while such esoteric governmental tasks as preventive public medicine and standby organization for disaster control are all but impossible. And, as the argument goes, traffic, crime, disease and air pollution, tornadoes and hydrogen missiles, are no respecters of our divided jurisdictions.

A further argument might be called the local patriot's concern. "This is a great old City," remarked a leader in a recent metropolitan reform movement, "The only trouble is it's *dying.*" Newspapers hammer on the theme of "Progress or Decay," with the implication that the economic future of the area depends upon solving the problem of metropolitan government. As a variant of this, many are concerned with the very shape of the city . . . "the death of Downtown," the "sprawl of suburbia," the disappearance of surrounding countryside and forest, the decline of the central city as "symbol and hub of the metropolitan area" (in the words of Philadelphia's City Administrator). In short, the city is seen as changing, and in a direction which is foreboding.

Metropolitan surveys, varying in scope and resources, have tended to a common solution: governmental integration of the urbanized region. The consistency of such findings and recommendations may be evidence of convergence in our knowledge of the nature of things—that happy state of a mature science. It may, however, only bear witness to the weakness of our scientific tools, the uncontrolled nature of our inferences, and the consensus among us on certain values. For this reason it is important that we examine the thoughtways of the various actors involved. These include the rank and file citizens, the civic leaders of the area, the staff experts of local government, and social scientists.

A social problem has been usually defined, by sociologists, as a social situation departing from existing norms and therefore presenting a task to the actors. Thus, it is useful to ask, "What bothers different people about government in the metropolis?" There is a wide array of answers. For the general public, as reflected in sample surveys, it is the bread and butter issues—the amount and quality of consumption items provided by local government. Dissatisfaction clusters around such matters as the transport system, the maintenance of streets and sidewalks, parks and playgrounds, and the sewage-disposal system. Concrete and discrete items in the house keeping of the area form the typical agenda of discontent.[2]

2. *Exploring the Metropolitan Community,* John C. Bollens, ed., Berkeley and Los Angeles: University of California Press, 1959.

For the civic leaders who are involved, however, dissatisfaction focuses upon governmental structure. The various concrete items are seen as symptoms of a basic weakness, inefficiency, and disorder. Such leaders speak of the effects of government upon the good life of its citizens and, at another level, speak of the City's future, with an emphasis upon the economic losses caused by metropolitan fragmentation. These leaders, economic dominants, members of the Chamber of Commerce and Committee of 57, elected officials from the business or professional strata, assume responsibility for an area as a unit.

The staff experts of local government are earnestly committed, for the most part, to a particular and limited task in a functional segment of the society. The police administrator, public health officer, county school supervisor, traffic commissioner, head of the city plan commission—each, in his way, faces the consequences of metropolitanization. And the resulting problems are similar: to get hold of enough legal power, over a broad enough area, and enough money, to do the job at hand. In the main, such officials are in favor of extending jurisdictions and tax resources: they need them.

These positions coincide with the problem as seen by the social scientists, who might be defined as staff experts of the community as a whole. The social scientist, interested in metropolitan affairs, typically speaks of the disjuncture between social city and political city, or he emphasizes overlapping jurisdictions, waste, inefficiency, conflicting hierarchies of power, incompetent personnel, inadequate revenue, and unable government. Derived from the public administrative approach to local government, the definition focuses upon all those gaps in the system of control which should be filled in to produce an effective task-performing organization.

These are cogent arguments. However, if one steps back a moment and recalls some competing ideas, their plausibility suffers. While the people may be dissatisfied with some local services, they usually turn down proposals to right the wrongs done them. They vote against metropolitan government, they oppose annexation, they trim bond issues and tax levies, and they turn Urban Redevelopment programs into baseball lots for big league clubs. It is possible, of course, to simply say: The people are dumb.[3] This is a very damaging admission if one's argument for a problem's existence depends upon "widespread public discontent" (as in one foundation proposal). Furthermore, it is at least possible that the voters are committed to the present loose governmental congeries. In the central city, governmental autonomy may represent control of their own destiny by the working class and the ethnics, through the Democratic party. To those in the suburbs, their small neighborhood enclave bounded by governmental walls may be the "republic in miniature," offering some control over the collective fates of their treasures.[4] If such were the case, it would not negate dissatisfaction with governmental services, even those which seem to demand area wide control. Beyond the "bitch function" of the democratic sample survey may lie real dissatisfactions—endured, however, as the price of maintaining other normative structures.

Looking at the metropolitan problem as defined by experts and elites in the light of such considerations, leads one to question the validity of the approach. Estimates of the consumption norms for governmental goods may be correct; the discrepancy between what is and ought to be is indeed existent; weakness of governmental structure may even be an adequate explanation for this discrepancy. This weakness is not,

3. This definition is stated clearly in "Resistance to Unification in a Metropolitan Community" by Amos H. Hawley and Basil G. Zimmer, in *Community Political Systems, op. cit.*
4. An intensive study of one such campaign is Scott Greer (with the advice and assistance of Norton E. Long), *Metropolitus: A Study of Political Culture,* New York: John Wiley and Sons, 1963. Other relevant observations are found in "Decision Making on a Metropolitan Government Proposition: The Case of Cuyahoga County, Ohio, 1958–1959," by Matthew Holden, Jr., unpublished Ph.D. dissertation, Northwestern University. See also, Robert C. Wood, *Suburbia, Its People and Their Politics,* Boston: Houghton-Mifflin, 1959, and Scott Greer, "The Social Structure and Political Process of Suburbia," Ch. 7 above.

however, just a simple, accidental result of unplanned change; it also reflects interests, organized by ideology. These in turn grow out of the differentiation, stratification, and social organization of the metropolitan population.[5]

In a sense, all definitions of the "metropolitan problem" are folk-thought. Uncontrolled by systematic theory and unsupported by observation at the crucial points, they are forms of cautious utopianism masquerading as scientific analysis plus common sense.

II

We have identified the metropolitan problem by pointing. It would be more useful to identify it within the structure of sociological thought: this I will attempt in the remainder of the paper.

If the metropolitan situation is a problem, then it is an indeterminate situation to which the definer is committed, and one about which something basic is unknown. If it is, further, a *social* problem, it is one in which some aspect is socially indeterminate—i.e., the direction of social action is not clear. Typically arising as a discrepancy between what exists and what should exist, such indeterminacy may be of ends (what do we want?) or of means (how should we get it?).

Such problems imply questions about the nature of what is, and what should be, as well as interactions between them. The question of what is, the empirical nature of the situation, is formally simple—though practically very difficult, with anything as complicated as a metropolitan complex. What is required is a map of the way the thing lies and operates, tested at key points by logic and observation, grounded in a universal theory of human behavior. The question of what ought to be is the real difficulty. If, however, we focus

5. For a discussion of the consequences variable social position has for problem definitions, see Scott Greer, "Traffic, Transportation, and the Problems of the Metropolis," in Robert K. Merton and Robert A. Nisbet, eds., *Contemporary Social Problems*, New York: Harcourt-Brace and World, 1961.

upon the observable social world we can say that a *socially effective* definition of what ought to be is always an application of a norm—a groupwide consensus on what should be done.[6] Such norms are always specific to a social collective; in contrast to the various images flowing through a given nervous system, they are *social* fact.

To be sure, the occasional nonconformist may propose new normative concepts, importing them from outside the group discourse, or inventing them through logical extension and individual conception. In contemporary large-scale society, the introduction of new normative concepts to given groups is an everyday phenomenon. The sheer mixture of cultures and sub-cultures, as well as the emphasis upon cultural innovation (institutionalized in such organizations as university departments of planning and public administration), guarantees a wide range of concepts, while the winds of the mass media broadcast all kinds of seed in all directions. To take root and grow, however, they must be couched in the conceptual language of the group, which sieves individual conceptions through the flow of communication, limiting them to what may be understood. They will be effective only as they take a place within the organizational language of the group—the role system, and the normative system.

The available range of definitions of the metropolis and its problems is wide. There are those who think that what exists conforms to what ought to be. Then there are the deviants, the nonconformists who want more of the services provided and evaluate the system in these terms (the pragmatic reformers), and the nonconformists who want a new system. The latter compare their city with other cities—typically, the bright, new, rapidly growing cities. Or they compare their city with its own "golden age"—and derive radical proposals for change. In short, they contrast the Earthly City with the Heavenly City, and are dissatisfied. Many of their notions of what

6. This conceptual framework is spelled out in greater detail in Scott Greer, *Social Organization,* New York: Random House, 1955.

ought to be, and how to achieve it, are derived from what might be called the professional intellectuals of local government—the National Municipal League, the Public Administration Service, the professional planners, the political scientists, or columnists on the metropolitan beat. The new models for the city, growing within such circles, spread more widely through the public print. They are based upon such common norms as "efficiency," local patriotism, and boosterism. They imply a change in the structure of the polity.[7]

The basic effort then is revolutionary. But to make such an effort is to threaten a whole existing system, and resistance to change is one way we know there *is* a system. The intellectuals of local government, having made the existing order problematic through use of alternative norms, seek to make it objectively problematic for those who accept it. In the process they encounter violent counterattacks—from the Mayor and City Hall, the politicians and the unions, the Negroes and other ethnics of the central city; from the community press and elected officials, municipal attorneys and small businessmen, the tax payers leagues of the suburbs. Because the proponents of metropolitan government use a normative system derived from the intellectuals of local government, and because they frequently base their proposals upon a "scientific survey's recommendation," they seem to themselves to stand for the unvarnished, scientific truth. To their opponents, however, they may seem only irresponsible "do-gooders," or salesmen of "big government." It becomes clear in the heat of battle that the authority of social science is not adequate to convince opponents of metropolitan government.[8] It is my

---

7. For the Metropolitan St. Louis Survey, see "Dilemmas of Action Research on the 'Metropolitan Problem,'" above. I should also acknowledge a general debt to Karl Mannheim, for notions first clearly presented in *Ideology and Utopia*, International Library of Psychology, Philosophy and Scientific Method, 1936.
8. Our follow-up study of the referendum election in St. Louis indicated that voters on both sides of the issue categorized those who voted differently as "uninformed, incompetent, irresponsible, or immoral."

position that it should not. The reasons, I believe, go as deep as the roots of normative theory. To make the point clear, another brief detour is necessary.

By normative theory is meant the more or less systematic formulations of what ought to be in human society. Since what can be logically limits what ought to be in any practical sense, normative theory always subsumes a degree of empirical theory; it is constrained by notions of what is inexorable, but only within very broad limits. At the simplest level, if we inferred the normative order of a small group from observable behavior, we should particularly attend the sanctions used, and the inferred grounds for these sanctions we would designate as the construct "norm." The order internal to a collection of norms held by a specific group and effective in ordering behavior, we should call the "folk" normative theory of the group—something very similar to what anthropologists call "ideal culture." It is the effective consensus as to what ought to be done, given the nature of what is believed to be empirically true, as the complex is inferred and ordered by an observer.

The construction of a theory of the normative system in a group is an acknowledged task of social science. It is a construct; further, it is only a part of the explanatory apparatus of the social scientist. For example, he can foresee conflicts between what "is" and what "ought" to be, and he should be able to predict outcomes—modifications either of what is or what ought to be. Should he not command a theory larger than and inclusive of the normative order in the group, he is as culture-bound as the subjects he studies. Many experts in local government fall into this position; their recurring assumption of a rational voter, who remarkably resembles a public administrator, is one indicator of their endogenous relation to the system.[9]

What, however, of the claim for a scientific normative the-

9. On the irrational (or other-rational) approach of the voters, see Hawley and Zimmer, *op. cit.*

ory? Such claims have been made by classical political theorists, by neo-positivists in sociology, and by philosophers. The answer seems implicit in the above discussion of norms. If a normative theory is anything besides a dispassionate mapping of the notions of what ought to be in a specific collective's behavior, then it is simply a reflection of the social scientist's own role within a normative order. It may be more or less logically consistent, more or less possible in terms of known empirical limits. But if it has any social legitimacy, it rests upon the uniformity of response from other actors. As Wirth remarks, "there is no value apart from interest and no objectivity apart from agreement." [10] The objectivity of normative theory always rests upon shared interests and definitions; it can be extended only by persuasion, for the necessary assumptions are optional and have neither logical nor empirical coerciveness. They are given not by nature, but by the significant others who maintain the specific order.

The reason for the unauthoritative nature of the arguments for metropolitan government is clear. The authority in question was basically inappropriate to the subject. Normative theory, indicating "What kind of a city we ought to have," is not intellectually coercive, even when called scientific, for normative problems cannot be settled by scientific authority. Nor can they be *finally* settled by any authority. Normative theory is a means for group mobilization to achieve group ends. The area within which such ends are achieved is the polity. Indeed, this is the reason for the inescapable necessity of politics—there is no other means of resolving such questions.

Within the polity are forged the temporary validities of norms. The possible norms are limited as a control of behavior only by the nature of what is. Within these broad limits (for the flexibility of man, his collective opportunism, is notorious) the normative theory internal to a group can be

10. "Preface," *Ideology and Utopia* (Harcourt-Brace Harvest Books edition, undated), page xxv.

neither "true" nor "false." It can be dominant, declining, recessive—but not incorrect. As a social scientist, one can do no more than describe it, analyzing its antecedents, structure, and consequences. This task, of course, may be highly valued —but it does not, logically, dictate choice. We may be able to point out the costs of alternative means, in scarce values and in side-effects, but the rank order of cost-benefit ratios still remains a product of a polity.[11] Of course we may, as social actors with commitments to interests, groups, and norms, violently reject, tolerate, or vigorously espouse given normative concepts. Any member of the collective can do so with equal intellectual authority, however, for such choice is inherently political.

III

Returning then to the metropolitan problem, we may view it as a struggle among sub-units of a collective to formulate the normative system of urban life. Thus, it is clear that this normative system is, at least in part, problematic to some groups. Wherever such situations occur, we infer change in the normative or empirical order, or in both. The latter seems to be the case in contemporary settlements.

The empirical situation in our cities has shifted with broad trends in the total society. For example: (1) the space-time ratio within the city has altered radically, making a much wider geography available for action; (2) the way of life of the population has changed, with increasing social rank and

11. These uses have been stated unforgettably, for this writer, by Max Weber in "Science as a Vocation," in H. H. Gerth and C. Wright Mills, eds., *From Max Weber: Essays in Sociology*, London: Routledge and Kegan Paul Ltd., 1948, pp. 150–152. For a clear and useful recent discussion see W. H. Werkmeister, "Theory Construction and the Problem of Objectivity," in Llewellyn Gross, ed., *Symposium on Sociological Theory*, Evanston: Row, Peterson and Company, 1959. In a recent statement Merton is in substantial agreement, although his emphasis is upon the positive value of social scientific inquiry for normative theory (see "Social Problems and Sociological Theory," Robert K. Merton, in *Contemporary Social Problems, op. cit.*)

familism the trends; (3) from the interaction of these we have the rapid growth of familistic suburbs in the middle socio-economic range, and increasing segregation of working-class ethnics in the central city. For another example: (1) we have an increasing dominance of the local population by the national society, as the network of interdependence extends and communication and control follow; (2) we have a new use for municipal government as a barrier to invasion by certain aspects of the larger society, and a consequent reinforcement of the sacrosanct status of local units; (3) from the interaction of these, we have a conflict between the consumer norms for government, which require large-scale organization and finance, and the governmental norms which perpetuate the governmental enclaves—the villages, towns, cities, of suburbia.

These changes in the society as empirically determined are accompanied by changes in the normative order. The metropolis contains many functionally concentrated and/or segregated groups. Through interaction within groups and segregation between them, new concepts are formed, stabilized in the ongoing normative language of the group, and creating normative order within subsystems, diversity between them. Planners and architects, machine politicians, Negroes, suburban neighbors—these are specimen cases. Thus in some areas of the institutional order we have growing diversity. However, the mass media and mass education are powerful channels for broadcasting some norms to almost all 'groups. In other areas we observe growing similarity.[12]

Such a situation is conducive to throwing up new versions of old normative concepts, of pseudo-norms, ideologies, and utopias. Some ideologists are critics of what is, or what is projected to be, against the normative standards drawn from a golden age when the city was young; for them the central city

12. These arguments, presented in such a cursory fashion, are developed in an expanded and systematic form in *The Emerging City: Myth and Reality*, New York: Free Press, 1962.

is hallowed ground. Others find what is, is for the best, in the best possible world. Though concentrated in positions which benefit from the *status quo,* such persons find broad support among those whose slogan is "leave well enough alone" or "better the evil that is known." Still others are oriented toward an invented image of the future. Utopians struggle for the greenbelt principle, the shopping mall, the new concept in transport, the ideal size city. They are chiefly intellectuals of local government—planners, engineers, political scientists and that ilk, who wear the mantle of expertise and broadcast images of a city transformed. In short, the ordinary literate citizen has a plethora of normative theories to choose from.

There is little evidence that many citizens respond with enthusiasm to either ideology or utopia. For many, the response is profound apathy, hardly taking one to the polls; for others, it is a peripheral concern, leading to little light and less heat. It has been proposed that, over the long haul, discrepancies between what is and ought to be are resolved by change in one or the other. Looking at recent results of failure on the metropolitan front in St. Louis and Cleveland, it appears likely that the normative theories will change. Failure leaves, among the significant actors, acceptance of public disinterest as a limiting factor in any possibility for change. Thus, developments to be expected are those required to perpetuate the given system with less friction—*ad hoc* integration by administrative fiat where possible, the formation of *ad hoc* special district governments, the *ad hoc* extension of State and Federal aid.[13]

Meanwhile, it is possible that the very concept of a city has changed under our discourse for many of us. Instead of a centralized community with the Downtown as hub and symbol of

13. No adverse judgment of *ad hoc* structural development is implied. After all, the British government is a gigantic product of such social invention. Such piecemeal, experimental development might well be called "organic," "continuous," and other good things: it is, however, very different indeed from a master plan or a simultaneously conceived blueprint.

the metropolis, the picture is becoming one of a scattered, variegated set of low-density neighborhoods, looped together by freeways, which bind them also to the centers of production and distribution. Such a city would allow wide choice among residential areas with respect to location, house type, neighbors, governmental facilities, and price. It is a picture congruent with the new metropolis—that of the West Coast and the Southwest, but it can be found at the suburban growing edges of all our cities. If such is the new notion of a proper city, then the "metropolitan problem" is that of working out the details in the maintenance of that order. It is also the death rattle of an older normative theory.

14

The Political Side
of Urban Development
and Redevelopment

(with DAVID MINAR)

In a federal republic, the fate of planned urban development is largely dependent upon the political system. Too many people have a piece of the polity for any single actor to coerce all others; thus, however "intrinsically right" our plans may be, they are only plans until someone harnesses the wild horses of diverse polities to them. Since, however, any public development brings real change, on which some will suffer and some rejoice, this may be appropriate. There is, after all, no calculus which tells us who should suffer in such a way that all reasonable men must accept its results. Thus, all urban development is political in a double sense: it redistributes wealth by public action, and it is legitimate only when it is politically supported.

For this reason, our discussion will focus upon the political. We will describe the present state of the governmental complex in urban areas and the ways in which it influences and constrains planned urban development. We shall then indicate, briefly, the origins of this complex in the political culture of United States society. So coercive are the norms of this culture, so narrowly are they conceived, they probably make effective planning for urban development nearly impossible in *any* direction. Therefore we go on to consider the problem as one of political redevelopment. In the present impasse of the local polity lurk certain clues to effective change and experimentation. We select a few of these for examination in the light of the massive social trends which, willy-nilly, force us toward political decision.

One of the familiar and fundamental facts of the urban situation today is its political and governmental fragmentation. This fragmentation, as we shall try to show, has crucial consequences for redevelopment in the physical, social, and political senses. Before discussing consequences, however, we might profitably examine the dimensions of the fragmentation itself, particularly in the metropolitan complex, which, practically speaking, includes all significant urban phenomena.

The oldest and most fixed dimension of fragmentation is that created by the federal system, written deep into the American political culture and into the nation's constitutional ground rules. Its division of effective operating powers has always been a source of some difficulty, but, with the extension of scale, it has been even more a strait jacket on the processes of political response to social change. Urban problems have become national problems, and metropolitan social space has flowed over all sorts of geographic confinements. Still, the federal system is such that nation, states, and local governments remain as often rival and to some extent independent centers of problem identification and policy-making.

This is not to say, necessarily, that the federal system is obsolete. Many of the geographic, economic, political, and ideological reasons that made it seem a valid schema in an earlier age still pertain. But the point is that the barriers remain to impede accommodation. We do not get the kinds of action we come to want: integrated, unified, co-ordinated, innovative— these are the symbols of desire. They elude us because our problems are generated by relatively autonomous social forces and because our therapeutic techniques labor under the heavy hand of political tradition. And both techniques and problems search vainly for well-defined arenas of responsibility.

Accommodation does often come, of course; the system learns, usually painfully, to handle problems on the level where they occur, but the lag is likely to be long. The national government has a fair repertoire of techniques for dealing with the problems of an urbanized society, derived from the primitive constitutional powers to tax and spend, to regulate commerce, to assure equal protection and due process. But its weapons are still limited and, such as they are, they have been decades in growing. Much the same can be said for the action potential of the states. While their powers in local affairs are supposedly plenary, the traditions of home rule are so strong as to make state efforts to move on urban problems often look ridiculous, and this is to say nothing of the structural and political inhibitions to action built into our state governments.

A second type of fragmentation with similar consequences is that produced by the multiplication of local units of government, particularly evident in the metropolitan area. It takes no special knowledge to realize that the metropolis does not even fit together like a complicated jigsaw puzzle. It is nothing so rational. The very title of Robert Wood's study of government in the New York area, *1400 Governments,* tells a good part of the story of the condition of that metropolitan scene. The spot on which this article is written falls within nine governmental jurisdictions from the county level down. The Chicago standard metropolitan area has nearly a thousand such units. And this picture is duplicated not only in the great centers of population but in most of the smaller ones as well.

Here again the consequences have to do with abilities for action; here again the techniques are incommensurate with the problems. In the sphere of urban redevelopment as in others the difficulties introduced by fragmentation are manifest. Tradition ties action programs to the legal structures of municipalities while problems overrun jurisdictional boundaries. Supplies of leadership and revenue are distributed differently from the stock of urban problems, such as standard housing, crime, and intergroup tensions. Most often, the problems of physical and social decay are seen as the central city's problems, and, even when their broader implications are understood, long-standing legal and ideological boundaries prohibit all but the most feeble of broad-scale remedies. In many places the division of jurisdiction is not only spatial but also functional so that education and recreation and transit and sewage disposal and a host of other aspects of the urban development picture are charged to distinct units of government. Whatever the particular picture for a metropolitan area, its main blank spots are similar: no co-ordination, no power, no responsibility.

Even within jurisdictions fragmentation is a key feature of the political-governmental structure. Here the gross legal picture is one of unity, and, hence, it seems not unreasonable to expect integration of effort. Such integration is much rarer, however, than expectations would indicate. The reasons are several. One of these is simply the organizational difficulties encountered in mobilizing any complex structure for action. Another is the maze of "checks and balances" impressed upon governments at all levels in the interest of limiting authority. A third is the tradition of decision-making through bargaining, probably adopted from the private economy but often assumed to constitute the norm for the public business as well. It is probably accurate to say that our culture is anti-authority; as a result, a good deal of our political energies have gone to invent better ways of inhibiting the exercise of power at its formal and informal operating points.

Thus, mayors and governors have been hedged in with boards and commissions and with other elective officers doing quasi-executive functions. Civil service has been separated from "political" control, often meaning control by responsible administrators. Zoning and planning activities have often been made subject to extensive review procedures in which a variety of interests have their free shots at the "decision-makers'" programs. Even in systems that look symmetrical on organization charts, left hands do not know what right hands are doing and sometimes do not even care.

Out of this diffusion of power and dilution of responsibility comes a curious rigidity, not a rigidity of program but a rigidity of process that enervates program. Most of what we have discussed above involves mechanisms that in themselves or in their interactions make outcomes improbable. It is as though policy must follow an open road full of ruts and chuckholes, with hairpin curves and false crossroads to confuse the trip. But not only is the road itself difficult, the country is also filled with hostile tribes that may come out of the hills at any step of the way. If one but counts the veto groups that can snipe at public programs or confront them head-on in full battle dress, he may wonder if any program can negotiate the journey successfully. This is the way the system goes. In planning and formulation, in legislation and administration, in the courts and in the phase of popular approval, urban policy is exposed to the conflict of internal and external interests, to competing jurisdictions, competing subbureaucracies, and an endless array of interested private groups. Any one or combination of these may develop the power to revise, delay, obfuscate, or forbid action. This may simply be a way of saying that the urban political world is as complex and sensitive as the urban social world. In any case, its implications for innovation are apparent.

Despite the structural state of metropolitan government today, it has an enormous effect on our possibilities for action. It safeguards stasis. The pattern of delegation, from state to municipality, leaves the local polity as the only legitimate actor on many crucial issues. Though the towns, cities, villages, and special districts of a given metropolis may be completely unable to act effectively, they prevent action by their mere existence. At an extreme, they are governmental reservations, human zoos which keep government out and the animals safe from government.

These existing units of government have a degree of sacredness. This results not only from piety but from the fact that they are the arenas in which citizens may participate and, thus, the grounds for a legitimate delegation of responsibility. The representatives of the local polity, however denigrated in the local press and local gossip, are the only political actors of stature who take as their assignment the affairs of the local area. This dominance rests, in turn, upon a political culture which emphasizes local self-rule, fear of "big government," and the election of local representatives. Thus, consensus is strong on the *forms* of local government; this same consensus, however, prevents agreement on the substantive problems which face that government. Though the central city and suburbs can agree that they should each have their own government, they cannot agree upon the problems of the metropolis as a whole. Urban development, however, is a problem for the metropolis as a whole, and its present status is a result of this contretemps.

PROBLEMS OF URBAN REDEVELOPMENT

The only vigorous efforts to plan the physical development of cities in the United States have been the movement for city planning, the public housing program, and, lately, the urban-renewal program. The latter two are essentially redevelopment programs, aimed at undoing past land uses and creating new, planned uses. City planning, historically separate and preceding the others, has now been so closely linked with urban renewal that it seems useful to include them all under the rubric of "urban redevelopment." Planned development, through county zoning and subdivision control, is at present so new and sporadic that we shall devote most of our attention to efforts at redevelopment.

The redevelopment of our cities depends upon planned public action. The free market in land produces a haphazard order which rarely generates any corrective tendencies; having once developed a given space, the market value moves downward while new investment moves on to other, greener pastures. Planned public action, however, is dependent upon the organization of public powers in the urban area. Competition, conflict, and simple lack of organization characterize this "organization," but it is within such conditions that redevelopment must be carried out.

The present urban-renewal program is, historically, one of our most ambitious efforts to intervene with public power in community development. With its goals of decent housing for all American families, central business district redevelopment, and comprehensive planning for the metropolis, it is a radical program of urban reform. The logic of the program is simple. The police power is used to enforce housing codes, bringing the existing stock up to standard and destroying what cannot be profitably made standard; on the cleared land resulting, new development will replace the lost units. This is modified by the provision that standard structures can be acquired and destroyed if, in the eye of the redeveloper, the surrounding neighborhood is so poor that there is no chance of an upward surge.

The true shape of the program, as it works out in the hundreds of participating cities, is something again. Since the police power and the fisc are used to do the work, limitations upon them are reflected in the outcomes. These limitations include: (1) the dichotomy of public versus private control, (2) the tension between federal and municipal agencies, (3) the division of power among different federal agencies, and (4) the fragmentation of power at the local community level. Each is not so much a problem to solve as a powerful constraint to be "lived with," one that can distort the program beyond recognition in terms of its stated aims.

Although the urban-renewal program can acquire land, by

negotiation or eminent domain, displace the present owners and users and destroy existing structures, it cannot build any buildings except public facilities on the cleared land. Thus it is completely dependent upon the private market in real estate for its "renewal" effects. This means that the local public authority must either gamble on its knowledge of the private land market or prenegotiate sales. In either event, renewal occurs not where it might benefit the community directly but where it must do so indirectly through benefiting the private investors. This circumstance greatly limits the areas which can be redeveloped.

Urban renewal is also committed to the government of the local municipality. Because action can be taken only through a local public authority, it must be underwritten in terms of political and fiscal responsibility by the city government. While the federal agency has a veto power on the city's program, the city in turn may refuse to co-operate with the agency. Thus, many of the politically unpalatable aspects of the working program are honored in the breach: housing codes are enforced selectively or not at all, the local contribution in the shape of school buildings, street paving, and the like may be far out of phase with the urban-renewal efforts to improve neighborhoods, and a sudden revolt of the voters through referendum, initiative, or recall may throw out the entire program—in Springfield, Oregon, all three deities of the secular trinity were invoked: the referendum necessary to the program was lost, the housing code was repealed through initiative, and proponents of urban renewal in the city council had to face a recall election. Under the circumstances, the federal agency is notably chary about too rigid an insistence upon the letter of the law.

Many federal programs other than urban renewal have massive impacts on most of the cities where urban-renewal efforts are being made. Co-ordination among the federal agencies affecting a given city is almost nil; this may result from the use of the state as a middle-man, as in the case of the federal highway program, or it may result from simple lack of concern, as in the hiatus between the administration of Federal Housing Administration (FHA) mortgage insurance and the planners of urban renewal. In any event, urban renewal may be at the mercy of powerful federal agencies over which it has no control. The federal highway program may site a cloverleaf in the middle of the urban-renewal area, may displace thousands of householders and completely disrupt the urban-renewal relocation operations, and may hold up the sale of urban-renewal land for months while officials decide where access ramps should go. Meanwhile, FHA may co-operate with the highway program in stimulating dispersion to the suburbs while urban renewal struggles to revivify the central city.

At the metropolitan level, the multitude of jurisdictions—cities, towns, suburbs, special districts, counties, even states—makes any over-all planning of the city a farce. Weak as most planning commissions are in effecting development and redevelopment, their power is further curtailed by city boundaries; few of them exercise jurisdiction outside the municipality. And because there is no other local municipal body with power to underwrite the program, urban renewal is similarly limited—usually to a central city and, separately, one or two larger suburbs. The limitation of power is accompanied by a limitation of vision—the source of the "flight to the suburbs" may be not the declining structures of the central city but the patterns of development in the suburbs. Few urban-renewal programers take these matters seriously in their plans. Yet the governmental log jam at the local level, preventing *metropolitan* planning and development, results in serious distortions of the program. The central city-suburb schisms turn urban renewal into a holy war to recapture the suburban, white, middle class—a war the central city is doomed to lose—and distract attention from the major clientele of the central city: the working class, the ethnics, the disprivileged.

Thus, the implications of these various divisions of power for urban development and redevelopment are basic: they produce the dilemmas of the programs. Destructive as they seem to those committed to changing the shape of our cities, they are perfectly understandable in view of the political culture of Americans as it is now translated, through governmental structure, into the local polity. Indeed, many persons consider both that culture and that structure to be sacred —not destructive at all.

The Political Inheritance and the Redevelopment Process

Our problem at this point is twofold: to understand the culture out of which this urban tangle grows and to explore the alternatives for action it might permit. Both of these jobs are clearly too big for anything we might attempt here, but a look at the surface may suggest what lies underneath. Most of what we have described above rests squarely on a set of commitments that can roughly be equated with the Western liberal tradition. The commitments are not necessarily active items of detailed individual belief, but they are part of the cultural stock from which we draw rationalizations for our habituated practice. They go to a root individualism which holds (1) that power is evil and must be contained and (2) that its only legitimate exercise is based on common participation and consent.

Such are the themes that lurk in ideology and institution behind American political development. They may be found in the early codifications of the political culture, the Declaration of Independence, the federal Constitution, the original state organic laws. Though there is an element of logical— and often practical—tension between them, they have gone hand-in-hand to mold American practice. The interplay between ideology and institution provides mutual reinforcement which gives the entire structure a surprisingly durable quality, a quality the relative richness and isolation of the system have helped to preserve. Each helps to prop the other up, and both give shape to the prospects for public action.

Out of the former theme, the theme of constitutionalism, have come two kinds of political usages with an impact on the urban action potential. One is the simple negative imposed on authority by bills of rights and other abstract statements of limitation of power. In the redevelopment field, perhaps the most pertinent are restrictions on the power of eminent domain, but this, of course, is but one item from a lengthy catalogue. The other aspect of constitutionalism is structural, the aspect that has prompted us to separate, divide, check and countercheck governmental authority. The federal system itself and the idea of home rule are manifestations of this spirit of suspicion of power. Its premises, of course, are simple ones: authority that cannot be used cannot be used for ill, and society does not need much tending anyway. Hence, the unwieldy structures of local government, frequently multiplying the attempt to diffuse power by several times and in several directions, have fed on the main flow of American tradition. Further, the structures themselves— boards, commissions, loosely organized councils, lay administrators—were "natural" organs of authority in a predominantly rural, small-scale society.

The second theme of the tradition is the crux of democracy itself, the idea of consensus. This, too, has been taken as given, and, in effect, it has been interpreted to mean that authority must constantly be refreshed from the wells of popular participation. Its optimal institutional form was, of course, the town meeting, but that device could, over the longer run, serve only as a model to whose merits the representative system might hope to aspire. The career of local democracy in the United States need not be detailed here. We can note, however, that it has imposed burdens in several directions: on the local authority, an obligation to mirror an obscure voice of the people; on the people, an obligation to participate in an often ill-defined game; on the larger system, an obligation to devolve functions as near to the level of the "popular sovereignty" as possible. The principle of responsibility implicit in all this is clear in abstract but difficult in application. "The shame of the cities" has come at least as often from their stumbling over democratic procedures as from their failure to use them.

Two implications of this heritage for urban development merit brief exploration. One is that our classic model of good government supposes a kind of free market place of interests. To use the terms of the philosophical radicals, it assumes that most social conflicts can work themselves out through a natural harmonization and that only a residuum of conflicts must be left to the artificial devices of government. The latter in turn are subject to a similar pull and haul, on a different site; the brawl of interests is moved from the alley to the ring, with some Queensbury rules imposed. The interesting thing about this formulation is that it grants no initiative to the referee, political authority; at its extreme, it does not see the community-as-a-whole as a participant but only as a site, an arena. Innovation in public programs is thus an accident thrown up by the forces of nature. On the national level, practice has seldom conformed to the model; on the local level, it has come much closer. Tradition has thus served as a brake on energetic local public participation in social change.

A second implication lies in the force the tradition has given to localism. The locality, especially the small-scale place, has obvious virtues from the standpoint that would minimize authority and maximize consensus. Its interests are fewer, its life routines more visible, its problems more familiar. Presumably, then, it demands less of authority and knows more about it when it is summoned. So strong is the identification of the local place with the central tenets of the tradition that localism has come to be regarded as a good in itself. Its derivatives include distrust of the big city as an "unnatural," perhaps even an "un-American" place and a "we-they" perspective on national government. Probably to most Americans "the government" means that bunch of people and structures in Washington, D.C., an object of some loyalty and much suspicion. The consequences for innovation, responsibility, and organization in the society of growing scale are evident.

This account has emphasized the rigidity-inducing aspects of the American political culture, the strains that stultify action and inhibit change; yet the system has been a viable one. It has endured the transition from an underdeveloped, small-scale society to the complex society of today, adapting itself to internal socioeconomic revolution and resisting external threats. Certainly part of the reason for the system's persistence may be charged to our capacity for waste. Our endowment of resources has been so rich as to permit us much leeway.

There is, however, another side of our political culture that helps explain what has happened and suggests potentials for the future. This is an ideological capacity for experimentation, an ability to take risks and make bets on the future. Whether this is a unique characteristic of the American culture may be doubted, but that is not the point. Its sources are open to speculation; perhaps it derives from the coincidence of the nation's early development with the bloom of modern science, perhaps it is part of the perspective of a nation of adventurer immigrants. Its manifestations are evident in technological development and economic life, in political organization, even in formal philosophy. The political side is, of course, what chiefly interests us here.

Again we must be content with scattered examples where an exhaustive discussion would serve us better. The history of American politics is full of instances of experimentation, particularly with organizational forms. Often, indeed, the nation has turned with almost mystic faith to tinkering with institutions. The framing of constitutions, federal and state, may be regarded as collective acts of societies willing to try innovation. If their products combined forms and ideas handed to them by tradition, many of the combinations and some of the forms were novel, even brave. Federalism, separation of powers, the presidential institution, judicial review, these are some of the relatively untested devices the nation has committed itself to in spectacular fashion.

The propensity and sometimes the opportunity to experiment have been even more evident at the state and local levels. Because much of what we have been discussing in this section is in some important sense our Jeffersonian heritage, we might remind ourselves of Jefferson's own urgings in the experimental direction, particularly in the local governmental sphere. Jefferson is often and correctly regarded as the patron political saint of the local-self-rule idea, but we are less likely to see his proposals for organizational innovation as pleas for experimentation. Twice when Virginia revised her constitution, however, he suggested extensive revision of the political framework of the locality. It was in this setting that he developed his well-known proposal to divide the country into small nearly autonomous wards, each to be like a "tiny republic unto itself."

Following Jefferson, the nation has continued to try a great variety of local and state organizational modes, to the point where it is possible to see these units as "laboratories for political experimentation." Some devices have succeeded, others have failed. The standards for testing have been undefined and controversial. But the catalogue of attempts is impressive enough to assure us that innovation is a possibility: consider, for example, cumulative voting, proportional representation, initiative, referendum, and recall, various primary nomination systems, unicameralism, commission forms, civil service and merit systems. All of these and others have been put to trial in political practice, and all relate directly to the problem of our political system: How can we make democracy work in the society of expanding scale?

SOME KEYS TO CHANGE

The tradition thus hands us both rigidities and flexibilities. Our problem is to find the workable mix for the urban area. One thing seems certain: we will not be permitted to transgress the culture's long-term image of legitimacy founded on consensus. Whatever paths to action we find, they will be paths that lead through the perils of democratic procedure. To put the point in another way, this means simply that urban redevelopment must continue to do whatever it does in the setting of a politics. The kind of politics, however, is up to us to determine.

Perhaps the answer to our dilemmas lies in further institutional alterations, particularly in the consensus mobilization area and in the matter of fixing responsibility. Innovation for urban action probably needs to take greater account than it has of the functioning of the mediating devices and mechanisms of the society. It needs to decide what its proper publics are and what questions they are asking. And it needs to free some parts of the system—institutions, agencies, people, define them as you will—for the tasks of creation. This implies, at least, the selection of visible and responsible representatives of the major corporate interests—the metropolitan press, the ethnic groups, the business enterprises, and the labor unions. Too frequently, the public for government action is limited before the act, indiscriminately expanded afterward. Equally important, the local polity needs an expansion of competent staff among the interests capable of evaluating change. While genuine conflicts of interest are frequent in the local polity, spurious conflicts are probably more common.

The problem of innovation is not simply a matter of whether there is freedom to do but whether anyone has the time, the insight, and the responsibility for doing. In part, the matter is simply organizational, simply a question of setting aside the slots and filling them with people. In part, too, it is a question of training and recruiting people whose intellectual backgrounds make it possible for them to undertake the rather unique role and functions involved. This is where a live and adventurous social science might come in, for social science can serve not only to show us the conditions and costs of the possible, it can also provide the yeast that can make the organizational loaf ferment. The potential should be a challenge to the academic and practical imagination.

Any change, however, is going to require some adjustments in perspective, some visions of order that transcend those we commonly hold. Perhaps the basic need involves our notion of community, of the fundamental unit for political activity. Much of what we have been saying amounts to propositions about the inadequacy of the community basis for our ongoing political activity. The concept of consensus implies the question of consensus *among whom,* the question of the relevant community public. Our units of community have probably become too small; clearly, they are irrational in terms of patterns of social structure. It is not, however, sufficient to seek community on a broader basis. We should also be prepared to think through the grounds on which community is defined.

Ironically, the cultural heritage itself has given us potentials that we have to a large degree discarded, particularly the repository of state power. The state is seldom a "natural" community, but it affords certain ready opportunities for broader scale planning and action. It is not the paucity of authority but our reluctance to use it that has made of the state a bypassed, neglected unit in the political system. While it may be foolishly optimistic to hope for such development, the state seems to be the most promising organizational lever to break the urban log jam. Among the side effects of vitalizing state power would be the bringing of the hinterlands into proper focus in their relationships with the urban system.

If such vitalization were accomplished, the broader public of the relevant community might be content with exercising its consensual power on such questions as what kind of society it wants to create rather than self-hypnotism with policy details. If so, authority would be freed from its concern with problems that should not be problems, and the state could assume the role of steward for the general interests of the society, including its local components. This may be a dream; as a dream, it suggests ways of harnessing tradition to current needs.

POSSIBILITIES AND LIMITS

Our discussion has emphasized two seemingly contradictory aspects of the situation: the rigidity and massive resistance of our political system to innovation, and the wide range of possible changes in that system. These possibilities do not rest upon basic changes in political norms so much as *experimentation in their application*—experiments appropriate to the changing world of mid-twentieth-century America. This society of enormous and rapidly increasing societal scale *demands* change in the polity appropriate to massive change generated elsewhere. The network of interdependence increases daily, in its extension and its intensity: we are whorled inevitably together in one community, the nation-state. Never before have so many been so interdependent with so many others. This is made both necessary and possible by our enormous energy resources, producing fantastic wealth and possible freedom.

Increasing wealth is evident in real income, in educational levels, and in the phasing out of brute labor. Even the central-city population shows a steady increase in social wealth. This means, for the urban population as a whole, increasing surpluses of money, of time, and of access to communications. No occupational levels of the United States have to be poorly educated or poorly rewarded, when compared to the past or to any other nation on earth.

Freedom from economic anxiety, from intellectual inability, and from parochialism, taken together, amount to major resources for the task of governmental experimentation and change. It should be increasingly possible to educate the people about their public affairs, instead of hypnotizing them with technological vocabularies or bilking them with promises of something for nothing. This is due not only to the mass adult education carried on through the media but also to the flood of new high school and university graduates entering the status of adult and citizen. In a very few decades, half the adult population will have had at least some college experience. This could mean an increasing receptivity to political change as well as a more realistic grasp of our basic political norms and their significance for the quality of our life.

But increasing scale has also meant increasing freedom of location. The space-time ratio, the cost of moving in terms of time and other scarce resources, has shifted radically. With speed of transport and communication, it is possible for us to be a single community in a wide variety of ways. But, while the national order demands such freedom of movement, this freedom is destructive of many older orders: one is the local community. Today the boundaries of all local units are permeable: residents, stores, factories move with ease outside the city—carrying with them all sorts of resources for the municipal corporation. As this occurs, some struggle to reconstitute the city-state; it is a losing struggle, for the nation-state guarantees freedom of movement, and nothing requires continued commitment. Thus, the question arises: Could we, or should we, try to reconstitute the older style of spatially defined community?

Certainly, work on the physical structure of the urban areas, alone, cannot bring it about. The primitive theory of urban renewal, which assumes that land once used will be reused, that centrality equals community, is irrelevant to the broader questions we have raised. Even governmental integration and expanded governmental powers can do no more than refurbish the horizontal and rapidly expanding urban texture.

In truth, community applies to limited, exclusive groups, organized around shared activities. They come together, partially and fortuitously, in the urban scene. And, in that scene, the only encompassing organization is the *political* community—marginal to many, unconsciously accepted by most, an object of passionate striving for a few. It is inescapable, for only the city as a political form guarantees public order and public action. Whether we can make it an arena for significant participation and, in Hannah Arendt's sense, "social action" remains to be seen.

IV
SOME FUTURES

15

Ideology and Utopia: The Intellectual Politics of Urban Redevelopment

The changing nature of the programs to redevelop the cities reflects, in part, the changes in our intellectual politics. In expanding this proposition I will first detail and evaluate the assumptions about the nature of cities and American society underlying this programmatic thinking. I will then attempt to interpret these assumptions in terms of broad *Weltanschauungen,* socially grounded perspectives and differences in perspectives. Finally, I will adumbrate processes which might free us from the societal solipsisms, the irrealisms in our policies, which I see as the greatest constraints upon planned social change of any sort.

The program to redevelop the cities began with the housing program of 1937, which was intended to replace poor housing with public housing and to finance housing for those who could afford to pay but could not raise capital.[1] It was a sensible program, but the advent of World War II prevented

1. This discussion of programs to redevelop cities is brief and somewhat oversimplified. For a fuller treatment see Scott Greer, *Urban Renewal and American Cities: The Dilemma of Democratic Intervention* (Indianapolis: Bobbs-Merrill and Company, 1965).

our testing it to its limits. In 1949, in a period of great housing shortage, a bill was passed to continue public housing and mortgage guarantees for new house-buyers, and it included a proviso for redeveloping areas of the city with federal help. This was the germ of Urban Renewal. It allowed acquisition of land, clearance, and resale to new users. In 1954 it was extended to include more non-residential renewal, as well as programs to conserve and upgrade areas which, while not total losses, appeared to be going in that direction. In 1961 the Kennedy administration extended focus of the program from "projects" to the total community, requiring Community Renewal Plans of participating cities. And under the Johnson administration the "model cities" approach was used, which proposed a wide array of tactics to renew the cities *and* improve the economic base of their population.

The program was thus consistently expanded in its aims. From replacing slums with new housing, it grew to include improving neighborhoods. The reason given was that slum removal was not keeping up with slum creation. From improving residential neighborhoods it expanded to include non-residential areas, for the two were seen as interconnected. Its focus expanded (via the Community Renewal Plan) from areas or projects to urban communities as wholes. Finally, with the Model Cities Program, it expanded from a consideration of housing and land-use planning to a concern with the entire range of problems found among the urban poor—economic, medical, legal, *et al.*

Undergirding the original housing program were these assumptions: (1) slums could be destroyed if the very poor were subsidized through public housing, and the less poor by mortgage guarantees which allowed the building of new single-family structures, while the houses of the latter (presumably better than slums) would "trickle down" and increase the supply of cheaper housing; (2) an ailing (if not moribund) housing industry could begin to contribute to the faltering economy.

However, this scheme, which seemed basically sound (and which appealed to a wide array of interest groups), was hampered by the extremely slow recovery of the economy and the building industry from the Depression. Before recovery, of course, World War II diverted most of the new construction to military needs: the cities built few houses but accumulated huge unsatisfied demands for housing. In the postwar atmosphere of affluence, demand, and scarcity the great concentration was on building what is now called "suburbia" with the aid of mortgage guarantees, leaving the inner city as it stood.

As a result, slums grew at a great rate in the city, while the slum *clearance* program lost ground. Instead of concentration on slum clearance, the trend was towards expanding suburbia while the slums expanded. The Housing Act of 1949 was an effort to change this course through major investment in public housing: it took years to get it through, with every major trade organization engaged in producing, financing, or dealing with residential property violently opposed. One of the bill's selling points, however, was a radical program for "urban redevelopment," whereby the private market was to be used for slum clearance. Government agencies would buy and clear land; private developers could then buy it (at a fair price) and build.

The basic assumptions here were that: (1) there was a great pent-up demand for land in the inner city; (2) such land was not available in large parcels for redevelopment; (3) major redevelopment required large areas; and (4) if, therefore, the government could buy and aggregate land, it would lead to massive rebuilding in the central city. These assumptions were congruent with the Chicago ecology school's theory of city growth as well as with the folk beliefs of realtors. However, between the time of the city studied by the early ecologists and the city of 1949 had come the truck and the car, depreciating the value of centrality for many activities. Indeed, with the demand for horizontal housing and plants, large undeveloped areas on the peripheries were clearly preferable to older areas at the center in both price and convenience. The "zone of transition" around the central business district, where residential areas supposedly turn into commercial and industrial areas, was now in competition with the expanding suburbs: in many cities it became a "zone of stagnation." Incidentally, the effort to improve housing had now become an effort to improve cities generally, though over half the acreage cleared still had to be used for residential purposes.

The 1949 program was criticized from many directions. It dehoused the very poor in a time of housing shortage; it allowed no federal control over housing code enforcement; housing continued to decline and commercial strips to blight; there was no overall plan for the city. In 1954 the Eisenhower administration had another try at putting the private and public sectors in double harness for public purposes: it was called Urban Renewal.

Briefly, within the framework of a comprehensive plan, the city was to be analyzed into major uses—industrial, commercial, residential, transportation, public facilities. Residential neighborhoods were to be classified as conservation, rehabilitation, or redevelopment districts, depending on their degree of "substandardness." The first were to be kept viable through enforcement of housing codes, loans for improvement, and improved public services; the second, through these tactics plus "spot removal" (analogous to pulling bad teeth); while the redevelopment areas were to be cleared and put on the market for private development. The program was to provide standard housing for the displaced persons, with cash to assist in the move. Public participation was to be organized through official Citizen's Advisory Boards. This was the so-called "Workable Program," to be agreed upon jointly by the federal renewal agency and each city applying for Urban Renewal. It was not very workable; it assumed too much that was not correct.

It is easy enough to get agreement on comprehensive plans; after all, nobody uses them. They are a mixture of description of what is, extrapolation (straight-line) of what will be, and a few public dreams by private persons. They are honored, if at all, in the breach. But the classification of neighborhoods by degrees of blight is a touchy and ambiguous enterprise; we do not all agree on what blight is. When the consequence is destruction of houses, businesses, and neighborhoods and eviction of voters, the political system responds. Enforcement of housing codes suffers the same handicap: nobody wants to walk into a house, judge, and command its owner to shape up. (The rigidity of the codes, which ignored differences between owner-occupied and rental units, single-family and multiple-family units, increased the difficulties of enforcement.) Relocation of displaced persons in standard housing was usually impossible, with public housing oversubscribed and most cheap alternatives clearly substandard (and higher priced, as the cheap housing supply dwindled). As for the Citizen's Advisory Committees, they were often coopted by the agency, boycotted by the astute, and generally of little importance. Most serious, perhaps, the land did not sell fast: it sometimes took a decade to rebuild an area, and since it was a buyer's market, the redevelopment plan had to accommodate the desires of those willing to redevelop. To be sure, *some* provisions were honestly carried out in most cities, but the logic of the plan required them all: destroying cheap housing without uniform code enforcement is a sure recipe for extending slums.

The Kennedy administration's response to this mixed situation was to impose a new requirement on the cities: the Comprehensive Renewal Plan. It had to include four dimensions—since planners had noticed that cities go on through time, with resulting changes in nature, possibilities, politics, and goals. The plan also had to include all relevant populations and sites.

However, a key factor in our present situation is the fragmentation of both information and power in the metropolitan areas. There is no single authority for the metropolis as a whole, and only the bare beginnings of data banks for the total of relevant units. Planning and renewal have, perforce, been carried on in terms of a single municipal corporation's boundaries and powers. These are limited by surrounding governments, as well as by the "higher" agencies of state and federal government. The divisions are real, representing more than perspectival variance: they are based upon conflicts of interest, zero-sum games. Downtown competes with suburban shopping plaza, central city housing with tract developments, mass transit with the expressway system. The Comprehensive Renewal Plan must be viewed as a statement of human aspiration, not as a technique for control.

Finally, the Model Cities program was initiated by the Johnson administration. It amounts to "total therapy" for selected cities, with massive attention to both physical decline and poverty; it envisions physical and social planning, public and private cooperation, local and regional and national cooperation. It assumes great fiscal capacity, great political agreement on goals and cooperation, great intellectual capacity to analyze, prescribe, and execute, and great cultural capacity to absorb such radical innovations.

However, the fiscal capacity has not been forthcoming; I think we can see why. The New York City Planning Commission's program of renewal presented a few years ago would have cost $52 billion at a time when the military budget had precedence over all else. Indeed, during the Vietnam war the Department of Housing and Urban Development's dollars seem to have turned into pennies. Even with funding available for one or two cities, however, the political will was not there: every Congressman wanted some for his district, and the Model Cities idea was thoroughly lost in a program that has a little bit for everyone and not enough for anyone, thus neatly inverting the basic concept.

Such a program, concerned with everything from poverty

to parking, police to citizen participation, also strains our cultural resources. Who sees the metropolis as a whole? Most citizens do not carry maps in their heads; they travel itineraries through the urban region. Few see any great proportion of Chicago or New York in a lifetime of living there. Then too, the political culture, while advocating citizen participation, is hardly at home with such ventures as Community Action programs, which deliberately create poor, often black, political groups independent of the administrative machinery. At another level, that culture is very ambivalent with respect to racial schism—integration is no longer the generally voiced ideal, while separatism gains in popularity among the extremes of black and white alike. We can no longer assume value consensus on the matter even among blacks and liberals. Nor, for that matter, can we do so with respect to most of the dichotomies I have noted.

Thus the *program* ideals, which had begun with a limited goal, replacing worn-out housing with public housing and increasing the production of new units, grew to enormous proportions. From a house to a neighborhood to a city to a metropolitan area, in time and space; and many other dimensions were added, from mental health to the political to the economic, while the older goals of housing adequacy and aesthetic amenity were retained. It seems that the response to program failure was always an extension in responsibility without much extension in power.

At the root of failure lay false assumptions about the nature of our cities. How could serious and intelligent men make such obvious mistakes? Why did they not realize slums would grow proportionately to the remainder of the urban texture in the absence of income redistribution? Why did they believe the destruction of cheap housing would automatically result in a supply of standard housing in its place, one which could be paid for by the ex-tenants of the destroyed neighborhoods? Why above all did they believe that Americans basically wanted to live, work, and trade in the older center of the city, when all the evidence showed just the opposite? I believe these questions may be amenable to analysis in terms of thought and value patterns, ideologies and utopias.

A. SOCIOLOGY OF KNOWLEDGE APPROACH

Karl Mannheim is usually associated with the ideology-utopia dichotomy of thoughtways.[2] It is important, however, to remember that he identified several distinctive modes of thought, each an outcome of a group's interest in action, and each having both an ideological and a utopian version. For our purposes, three are important: the conservative, the liberal-humanistic, and the chiliastic.

The conservative thinker is oriented towards the past; that is where his touchstones for truth and value lie. He is, in Mannheim's terms, a "morphological" thinker—that is, he uses *Gestalten* already extant as definitive of possibility. (In critical terms, he is fond of unanalyzed abstractions.) His thought is cognate with his interests: he wants things to remain the same, and if possible more so. The liberal-humanistic thinker, for Mannheim a descendant of the philosophes, is oriented towards the future. He expects and demands the emergent, and his thinking is analytical. He takes things apart intellectually because he wants to change them, to put them together in different combinations. The chiliastic thinker is extremely present-oriented; he thinks intuitively, emotionally, introspectively, relying for communication on the evocation of shared interest. His concern is to insulate the valued group, vision, experience from the corruption of the outside world. (It should be noted that Mannheim has a fourth

2. For a fuller, less clear, but more profound investigation of these matters, see Karl Mannheim, *Ideology and Utopia*, translated from the German by Louis Wirth and Edward Shils (New York: Anchor Editions, n.d.). See particularly Ch. IV, "The Utopian Mentality," pp. 192–263. I may have done some violence to the concepts by taking them out of their context and reapplying them to one quite different; however, Mannheim does not spell out the rules of application (or "interpretation") of his theory, so one does what seems sensible and useful.

group, the anomic, who are either confused, indifferent, or in transit from one style to another.)

For each style an ideology and a utopia are possible. The ideologist assumes what is, and his thought is a defence of it; in a strict sense, he rationalizes it as the best possible in a less than perfect world. The utopian, however, criticizes and often rejects what is in the name of what could be better. In the process he forces the ideologist to become specific and logical—if possible—so we might say that the *Ur*-thoughtways of men are implicit conservative ideologies, but with the rise of disgruntled utopians a dialectic is set in motion.

If we cross these two sets of categories we have the following types: the conservative ideologist, the conservative utopian; the liberal ideologist and the liberal utopian; the chiliastic ideologist and the chiliastic utopian. Let us see what use these categories may have for understanding the intellectual politics of urban renewal in its first thirty-three years.

B. Application to Cities and Urban Renewal

The approaches that have characterized the conflict and resolution of most public issues in the United States are variants of the conservative and the liberal. The chiliastic, which Mannheim sees as a group analogue to Weber's charismatic leader, has been important chiefly as a pressure on one or the other intellectual faction or as a catalyst for mobilizing the anomic. Thus the varieties of conservative and liberal thought with respect to the city are in the first order of priority.

1. The Conservative Ideologists. These believe that the city is fundamentally all right; if there is trouble it is due to imperfect application of what we know, or deviancy and failure of groups and individuals, or, at the paranoiac fringe, a dark conspiracy to destroy. They tend to take the free market in land and housing as given, as well as those municipal corporations which happen to exist. Indeed, they concretize these matters and believe a given suburb, say Winnetka, to be a real entity, a general government, a necessary part of the world. But even for conservative ideologists error and failure *are* possible: thus Senator Taft, by no means a liberal, knew there is no money to be made in housing the poor. He believed in the free market, but due to its imperfections saw government as a last resort.

2. *The Conservative Utopians.* These people believe that the concrete good city is still in evidence, but is being eroded by various mistakes and evils and (in contrast to Senator Taft) believe this should be corrected. At one time they believed the rural life to be the only one fit for man, the city an evil. Today, they remain fixated on the past, but it is now the dense, polyethnic, centralized city of the railroad age. They wish to return us to that city, chiefly by limiting our freedom to exploit opportunities for new kinds of cities and forcing a regathering of the tribe. Many central city mayors, along with Jane Jacobs, would have us regard the suburbs as epiphenomena created by escapists. (As the suburbs become a population majority in urban America, the fallacy of the position should be obvious.) Many movements to reintegrate the metropolitan areas in single, centralized governments were sparked by such people.

3. *The Liberal Ideologists.* A large proportion of the actors believe that the winds of change on the city are good; that the decentralization of people and workplaces, the declining dominance of the center, the increasing differentiation by ethnicity in the city's politics, are trends allowing a better future. They believe that we must analyze the processes involved, capitalize on new opportunities to maximize choice, and take care of the victims. Such a position assumes that democratic choice is critical, and that urbanites get their choice through the market in housing and neighborhoods; the key problem is to reincorporate the poor and segregated, the victims of social change, in the productive

and rewarding part of the economy so that they also may have a choice. Many suburban liberals, including the ex-Undersecretary of HUD for Urban Renewal, Robert Wood, share this position. They like the suburbs, as they are, "the best possible in an imperfect world." Yet they have no anti-central city bias. They want to *include* change in the existing system.

4. The Liberal Utopians. These are the true intellectual radicals of the city, with such thinkers as Goodman and Mumford in the vanguard. They envisage new towns, a national urban policy which would incorporate a whole new concept of human community. Arguing that the particular synthesis of technology which created our present "megalopolis" is no longer inevitable (or even viable), they argue for controlled city size, the phasing out of the obsolete inner city, and a wild variety of new patterns, from isolated towers (single-building cities) to completely encapsulated towns with controlled atmosphere and weather as well as land use. A double economy (market and subsistence), segregation by resulting life-styles and age—such are some of the more original notions generated by liberal utopians.

A note on chiliastic movements in the city. Ideological chiliasm is a quietistic, pietistic movement; it is essentially a withdrawal. It is visible in the quiet majority of blacks who remain anchored to life through religion. The slogan is keep yourself to yourself, enrich the ghetto and make your world; separate. The utopian version speaks of power to the people, attacking the system, destroying to create. Other groups unequally included in the society develop similar positions—with the middle-class young this might distinguish between hippie and yippie.

C. THE PROGRAM FROM THIS PERSPECTIVE

The Urban Renewal program is the result of varying weights being given to these various perspectives over time.

Until 1952 the program was basically that of liberal-humanitarian ideologists; change was needed and sparked within an unchanging framework of policy and politics. There was FHA, then VA, mortgage insurance for those who could buy, while public housing was provided for some of those who could not afford decent housing as administratively defined. This was the old coalition of the New Deal, providing something for all—poor southerners of both colors, center-city ethnics, suburbanites and would-be suburbanites, the building trades.

The Eisenhower administration, with a conservative ideology, attempted to use scarce public funds to attract private capital. The general belief was that the market *would* work if it were given a chance through central-city clearance; the ordinary man would work in upgrading his home if given a loan. This was the genesis of Urban Renewal. And the unkind critic could say, "Is the private market to rescue us from the situation created by the private market?" But never mind: new things, plausible or no, were tried.

Since 1960 liberal utopian views have come to the fore, at least in stated policy. The Community Renewal Plan, Model Cities and total therapy, new towns—a spate of utopian ideas have become "policy," at least on paper. This has been accompanied by the rise of the chiliastic views, both separatist and activist, ideology and utopia. This movement is represented by neither political party, but indicates trends among spatially defined, concentrated, repressed and excluded groups: the blacks and Puerto Ricans, Mexicans and Indians, and the hippies, yippies, new leftists and acid-heads of the campuses. (Those who might once have been allies have been coopted: labor, white ethnics, farmers.) Thus, utopian chiliasm is an unknown quantity, though I would guess its effect will be to strengthen the ideologies, conservative and liberal.

My picture is far too simple. To begin with, there is seldom unanimity among those enacting a program. In my studies of urban renewal in specific cities, I identified at least two groups: the "housers," generally liberal ideologists from the 30s and 40s, and the "planners," liberal utopians of the 50s and 60s. Given cities chose one program or the other, as much due to intellectual politics of the staff as to the *Realpolitik* of the elected officials. Nor was there much in the way of a better guideline: we were all woefully ignorant of what we wanted and how to get it. With resources scarce both intellectually and financially, we waffled around.[3] Rationales were 180 degrees from actions; policies and effects had little known relationship. I do not think this unusual when we attempt a serious program of amelioration or radical social change; I am concerned as to how we might have clearer choices. Roosevelt and Truman subsidized suburbia and gutted the central city; Eisenhower further impoverished the poor and segregated the segregated. I doubt that any of these gentlemen intended these results.

Of course political pressures, based on economic interest, influenced policy. However, my point is that nobody could demonstrate the relationship between the cost of an action to the objective of a program and its cost to the political base of the relevant officials. I believe the goals of the program would frequently have been the overriding consideration, if it could have been proven politically popular or at least not too costly. Political leaders, whether or not more committed to the good, true, and beautiful than you or I, certainly at least match us for vanity. Nobody wants to be remembered as incompetent on one hand, a consistent loser on the other.

And, while we are all in the grip of our own thoughtways, we can still, if forced to, recognize unpleasant truth. Let me postulate empirically valid propositions about the relevant field of action, which can be triangulated from a number of utopian and ideological positions: they are "points of resistance" to uncontrolled speculation. A simple one would

3. Greer, *op. cit.* See also above, Part II, Ch. 14, "The Political Side of Urban Development and Redevelopment."

be the relationship between housing supply and the possibility of relocating dehoused families; a complex one, the relationship between size, growth, and the decentralization of a city's population and enterprise.

I am not suggesting that we can make these propositions with any great confidence. I note that, after starting programs in hundreds of cities, we still have no coercive evidence of the constraints and possibilities of Urban Renewal. I think there *is* a way to collect hard data and generalize from it, to make of reform an experiment upon which further reform may be carried out. By this I mean a true experiment —not a quasi-experiment, an evaluation study, or an ex post facto design. I mean experiment in the only way we know how to when we cannot specify relevant parameters which must be controlled—random sampling for treatment and control groups. My colleague Donald Campbell has argued this persuasively in a well-known article.[4] His pragmatic argument is persuasive: if you have scarce resources it *may* be possible to assign them at random, since this is the most democratic way. (He adduces the first experiments with the Salk vaccine.) One can also gain legitimacy by dubbing them "pilot projects"—an initial notion in the Model Cities program. With such an approach, we might learn under what conditions and to what degree Urban Renewal makes *any difference at all to a city*. We do not, as of now, know.

For cities vary over time, though about the mean, for almost any quality. This is why "matching" will not work. If you took Chicago in a moment of weakness, say under Kenelly, you had a city formally and practically without centralized control; with Los Angeles under Bowron at one point in time you had a city with centralized leadership.

---

4. Donald T. Campbell, "Reforms as Experiments," *American Psychologist*, 1969, 24:409–29. See a similar argument applied to a different problem in Donald T. Campbell and Albert Erlebacher, 'How Regression Artifacts in Quasi-Experimental Evaluations Can Mistakenly Make Compensatory Education Look Harmful," in *Compensatory Education: a National Debate*, Vol. III of *The Disadvantaged Child* (New York: Brunner/Mazel, 1970).

Within a short period Chicago resumed its course as a controlled town; L.A. fell apart as usual. Thus, given our ignorance of relevant parameters (I have not mentioned interaction effects), the simplest solution is by far the best one. If urban renewal is to rain on the just and unjust alike, as it does, let it do so in a neatly random fashion so we can learn what effects, if any, it has.

To conclude with a further paraphrase of Campbell's work: I think I can tell an Urban Renewal executive how to succeed. First, remember there is often a lag between new development and the demand potential. So, pick an "underbuilt town." Little Rock, Arkansas, in the late 1950s, was excellent; it was at a great lag in building from where its economic potential lay. It had also suffered the "Faubus effect," which had resulted in a moratorium on new corporate investment in the urban area for three years. Furthermore, most citizens knew this. Consequently, when conflict was resolved the lag was reduced abruptly: an explosion of new development occurred and the Urban Renewal program was an all-around success. Thus the cynical use of the regression effect is: choose the fuzziest part of the bivariate distribution (in this case, between existing downtown buildings and the market for such buildings), choose a town from this set of towns, and wait for the real relationship between growth potential and growth to assert itself. Publicize your program and take the credit for downtown growth. Then, of course, get out of town at the peak of the "success."

16
Urbanization and Social Character

All of us are aware of the immense increase in the proportion of the population living in cities. Indeed, if we have paid attention to the literature on urbanization we have probably memorized the figures by now, realizing that the United States is over 70 percent urban, that the 64,000,000 new citizens expected by 1980 will be urban dwellers, and 80 percent of them suburbanites.[1] But the importance of this piling up of people in cities is by no means clear and the whole concept of "urbanization" obscures as much as it reveals the nature of our society. For our urbanization is not the dense concentration of the nineteenth century factory city—its growing edges are the open neighborhoods of suburbia. Nor is the way of urban man sharply dichotomized from that of his relative in the country—often he has moved directly from a village to a suburb, visually and socially little different from his previous home. "Urbanization" is a loose summary word, absorbing many meanings and pointing to

1. Philip M. Hauser, *Population Perspectives* (New Brunswick, N.J.; Rutgers Univ. Press, 1960), Ch. 4.

different things. Let us see how it can be made into a working tool.

Cities are possible because of a geographical division of
labor. Briefly, urban dwellers have not extracted the raw
materials from the soil; they have bought, stolen, or taxed
these resources from countrymen. Thus cities depend upon
the agricultural hinterland. In the past they were never dominant, for the countrymen could not produce enough surplus;
urbanites were a small class released from bondage to soil
and the seasons by the work of their rural cousins. Our enormously increased urban population today rests upon the increased productivity of the extractive industries; this has allowed us to reverse, in less than one hundred years, the proportion of the American population dwelling in cities.

The building of cities does not, in itself, change the basic
structure of human life.[2] It is change in the basic political
economy of the society which allows—indeed forces—the
creation and growth of cities. Two meanings wrapped up in
the term "urbanization" can be separated in view of this
fact: the first is simply the "concentration of people in cities."
The second, and more basic, is the social transformation that
releases manpower from an agriculture which remains adequate to sustain large and growing urban centers.

The release of labor from extractive industries is made
possible by two intertwined developments. The first is the
use of nonhuman energies harnessed to machines as substi-
tutes for the human beast of burden. The second is the coordination of human behavior in larger and larger networks
of interdependence. The two interact. Nonhuman energy
makes possible the release of men from manual work and,
equally important, the constraints of distance: it allows rapid
communication and the coordination of behavior over greater
spans than was possible before. This, in turn, allows for the

2. Scott Greer, *The Emerging City* (New York: The Free Press of Glencoe,
1962).

development of giant armies, corporations, nations, and other functional groups. The latter hasten the tendency to exploit nonhuman energy and the machine. Thus, the two developments of technology, physical and social, result in an extension of the network of interdependence, the social interdependence of large groups cemented by a common dependence upon the man-machine-resource nexus sustaining the entire society. So close is this dependence that none of our great cities could survive more than a few weeks without the national market, while few (and deviant) are the individuals who could get a bare subsistence from the earth on their own.

These radical transformations of society have been given the summary name, "increase in societal scale." [3] They have two major consequences for the ordinary citizen: they increase his dependence upon a large-scale system and they free him to a large degree from dependence upon the near-at-hand, the neighbors and neighborhood and parish of his immediate surroundings. But his freedom is not from the boundaries of social groups per se; it is simply a shift from the constraints of Main Street and the neighbors to the control system of the bureaucracy. For, with increasing scale the major work of the society is delegated to large task forces. These, formally organized and rationally oriented towards production, distribution, and survival, uniformly take the shape of bureaucracies. In them the citizen holds office, affirms norms, receives punishment and rewards, and achieves (or fails) his destiny. Upon them he is dependent.

Thus, underlying the process which concentrates people in cities is the major process of *organizational transformation*. This is a process which can best be measured by its effects upon a total society: cities and hinterlands are equally affected in the process. In setting the conditions within which one can earn a living, enjoy citizenship, procreate and be

3. Godfrey Wilson and Monica Wilson, *The Analysis of Social Change* (London: Cambridge Univ. Press, 1945).

protected, the organizational structure is a major clue to the way people will behave. From interdependence among ourselves we learn to organize our actions, controlling ourselves and each other. The organizational system tells us, in short, what men must do if they are to hold a job in the society.[4] (Thus we require of American workers a rigorous attention to chronological time, to efficiency, to the subtle cues of interpersonal blandishment and bargaining, with a weather eye to the "rules.") But beyond the requirements made upon the individual citizen are other constraints derived from our social organization: the mutual dependence of the economy, the polity and the family system, separately and interacting, set the limits of what we can and must do *collectively*. The Great Depression indicated the force the polity will exert upon the economy when unemployment grows to disastrous proportions, while the present "war on poverty" indicates the ways in which the economy *forces* issues upon the polity. At the juncture of the great organizational segments of the society, where the President treats with the directors of big steel and the United Steelworkers of America, the interdependence of giant organizations (and our common dependence on their coordination) is dramatic and clear.

Urbanization stands, then, for the concentration of people in cities and the processes which lead them there. Concealed in the term, however, and frequently assumed without being made explicit, is another meaning—a certain kind and quality of living which we call "urbanity." Derived from the same linguistic roots, "urbanity" indicates a life-style which was once automatically associated with the dwellers in cities. It meant that those who dwell in cities become more sophisticated, accustomed to variety and wont to see the world in a larger perspective. Contrasted with the peasant or countryman, the urbanite was free from the automatic demands of custom and habit, the brute pressure of "the nuzzling herd

4. Scott Greer, *Social Organization* (New York: Random House, 1955).

society of the village." Literate and exposed to literature, he was both more "rootless" and more "cosmopolitan" than the yokel. Urbanism, in this perspective, is the cultural parallel of increasing scale: the urbanite was envisioned as a citizen of a larger universe because he lived at the meeting place of many disparate and distant worlds.

In societies of the past, energy-poor and dependent upon the peasant village for surplus, the three meanings implied in "urbanization" were closely related in the empirical instant. The concentration of people in cities required a sufficient scale of organization and surplus energy to provide dependable fodder for Caesar's herds, and the people of the cities (the "urbs") did indeed become different in their culture and point of view from the daemonical universe of the peasant villager. They worked at the structure of controlling the larger area of city state or empire through the army, the state bureaucracy, the church, and the market. Their cities rose and collapsed with their varying success in controlling the peasants. But meanwhile, everywhere underlying the urban society, was the vast majority of mankind still chained to village, province, *latafundia*—a low energy source but the *sine qua non* for the entire system.

Today the matter is otherwise. As new sources of energy surplus have been harnessed to our machines, farming has become our most highly mechanized industry. The number of people actually working at agriculture is about the same as the number of the unemployed in the United States today, and only a small minority of the workforce stands for the tradition of village and country. The massive mode of the society is the employee of some exclusive membership organization, living in a giant metropolitan area and moving (or hoping to move) his residence towards its outskirts. We cannot define his way of life as "urbanity," for his country kin live in very much the same fashion as he does. All we can say is that the culture of urban man is radically transformed. All men are exposed to the communication flows of the urban society, a necessity flowing from their dependence upon the market and the state. Thus the city is no longer either the source of increasing societal scale, nor a prime shaper of the dominant culture. It is part of the more inclusive national system, and we must bear in mind its limits within, and its dependence upon, that system.

SOCIAL CHANGE AND SOCIAL CHARACTER

The culture of urban man is a major clue to his social character. For culture, that general agreement within a group concerning what the world is and what should be done in it, limits and determines the vocabulary in which he can communicate with others and formulate his own course of action. Its sources as diverse as dreams, images, logic, and misunderstanding, culture is a set of definitions which can be expressed symbolically with a common meaning among men. Of all the traits which could enter into the common storehouses, various and exotic as the findings of the anthropologists, only some can be accepted and used in any given cultural group. That which is accepted will pass through a history of natural selection. Favored by its resemblance to the existing culture, it will survive insofar as it is useful to the members of the group in playing their inescapable roles. As new traits are incorporated into the common culture, they add to the bases for communication and the ordering of individual behavior oriented to the rewards and punishments provided by the group; they become new limits.

The individual's character as a social actor will be intimately related to this preexisting common culture. For social character is nothing more than the probable behavior of an individual when confronted with a given kind of life situation. The Balinese go to sleep in the presence of overwhelming danger; the crew of the Texas City refineries remained at their station to maximize control for the common safety, though their entire environment might explode at any moment; the Hindu prays before the bayonet. However intertwined in the life and nervous system of the individual, each of these courses of action is a learned response to a kind of social situation, a statement of fact and of moral imperatives. Thus social character reflects the common culture, and can best be identified through social behavior, including verbal behavior. It is always a constructed pattern inferred from observations over time—as abstract as the id and as concrete as the prejudices which limit and frustrate our aims.

The basic importance of social character to the collective and its fortunes is this: it is one set of limits upon what men can understand and find it necessary to do. This means that the average social character of an aggregate tells us what can be assumed as common before clustered people form into a structured group. It provides the beads which can be strung on many different sorts of organizational wire. Social characters tolerating or condemning the game of gossip are major considerations in forming the kaffeeklatch groups of Levittown, while the most scientific public administration practices fail in a society of feudal sheiks, whose nepotism is morally prescribed. Moore and Feldman have recently dramatized the consequences for economic development of a social character "uncommitted to labor" while those attempting to change fertility rates in traditional societies are well aware of the characterological barriers to sterility. Social character is a "lurking variable," an old palimpsest on the supposed tabula rasa which frequently makes nonsense of our efforts to rationalize the snarled affairs of a society.

While social character is a major basis for commonality in a social collective, it is more. Unlike the common culture, it points to patterns of *individual variation* in definitions and goals. In any collective large enough to be called a society there will be variation in the common culture, hence the character, of the important subgroups. Even in hunting and gathering societies the differences by age and sex are marked: the general unifying culture is subtly modified as it applies to the warrior, the old woman, the child. That which is accepted as general social fact and that which is a categorical imperative for action separate: the latter is specific oftentimes to the role. Thus a woman in New Guinea or the Tennessee hill country may know that blood revenge is required in a certain situation without feeling any compulsion to execute it. Social character varies enormously within a society—by one's subgroup, and by one's role within that subgroup.

This variation is a major resource for the society, for it supplies an array of alternative possibilities for social action. Small group research projects have made clear the variation in social types which take leadership roles under routine as against crisis conditions, while Pareto and Machiavelli speak of Lions versus the Foxes. And from another perspective, Levy points out the brilliant coup of the modernizing Japanese, who enrolled the Samurai estate, en masse, in the police force. This preexisting social character fit nicely the requirements of the function, and the dangerous Samurai had a job in modern Japan.

Beyond the differentiation of social character brought on by variations in group and role, there are other processes tending to differentiate. It is important to remember that we have defined social character as the probability of an individual's acting a certain way *in a certain situation*. But the social situations any actor faces will vary enormously, and what holds for one in a given situation may not hold for another. Thus the "role-set," as Merton has called. it, may include for an individual the roles of leader, follower, father, son, provider and client, ally and competitor—the list is nearly endless. Under the circumstances, there are many opportunities for error if the roles are not clearly defined and the situations clearly identified. The literature of the American frontier is replete with the pioneer father who treated his household as a factor of production, while Hughes underlines the temptation for French-Canadian foremen to treat their kinsmen as kin and *not* as factors of production.[5] The interaction of roles in the life-space of the same person may result in all kinds of "sports," while his effort to organize behavior with consistency from situation to situation may be still another dynamic. Fundamentalist in politics and religion, the small businessman is often the victim of consistency in his business policies, harvesting his marginal existence in the form of bankruptcy.

These are, then, some of the causes of variation in social character. As societies increase in scale, variation increases. The different kinds of work, of life-style, of ethnic background, tend to maximize the number and variety of subgroups which interact intensely among themselves and have little to do with other such groups. Massive migration into the larger society and within it, the fractionation of the job structure (from a few dozen titles to 40,000) and increasing choice resulting from leisure, wealth, and education, allow immense opportunities for variation in social character. At the same time, however, the increasing inclusion of the entire population in a large-scale national state and national market increases the uniformity of communications via the mass media and mass education. From variation among small groups segregated by region, class, race, and religion, we move to variations among segments of one integrated system. Integration is important; it is the necessary condition for the persistence of the entire social system.

THE DISTANCE FROM PAST TO PRESENT

Robinson Jeffers says in one of his poems that he would have men keep apart from each other in small groups, so that occasional madness would not infect the whole. And for most of mankind, during most of its career on earth, this has been the pattern. The hunting and gathering societies

5. Everett Hughes, *French Canada in Transition* (Chicago: University of Chicago Press, 1943).

that have dominated our history perforce had to stay apart; grazers, they literally lived from hand to mouth. With an energy source providing much less than one percent of that available to the average American today, they stayed in motion most of the time; like hummingbirds, metabolism was their master. Only with the agricultural revolution of a few millenia past was it possible for man to settle down with a modicum of security and the resources to develop, eventually, city-states and empires.

It is important, therefore, to remember that most men, through most of our recent history, have spent their lives in what Turner calls "the daemonic world of the peasant village." They had, in a sense, a long childhood. Tied to the soil, illiterate, receiving the common culture by word of mouth from the older members, the individual was born, lived and died in a tiny circle of earth. With powerful traditions and a frozen technology suited to little more than a subsistence economy, he acted with fatalism, piety, and a superstitious fear of the unknown which hovered around him. Investing the world with magic powers, he believed implicitly in immament justice—the automatic punishment of transgression by the very nature of things. When his limited expectations were fulfilled he was, presumably, content. When famine, war, and plague descended he accommodated, to persist or to perish.

To be sure, empires were erected upon the economy which the peasant maintained. Armies marched and counter-marched, cities were built and looted, and high cultures were developed within their walls. But this involved only a few persons, at the most perhaps one out of ten. For most men the capital city was as far away as the moon. Neither the literate world of the high culture nor the role of responsible citizen and leader meant much to the traditional peasant villager. His character was to maintain the older traditions of work and family, and to accept, with piety or fatalism, the hardships imposed by armed men, believing it beyond his powers to control or destroy them. His religion justified some of the world's way with him.[6]

This state of affairs persisted, with minor variations, among all the "higher civilizations" until a few hundred years ago. It is still the norm in much of the world—the 60,000,000 Indian villagers who live on no road are the thing itself, as are millions of others in Africa, Spain, South Asia, and Latin America. But in certain parts of the world nonhuman energy resources of enormous surplus, the fossil fuels, were discovered and harnessed to machines. Increased power allowed for the rapid extension of networks of interdependence; social organization increased in its extent and the intensity of control; the modern world emerged in western Europe and America. As it did so, the common culture changed from that of the peasant village to that of the rational, productive, society.

From the peasant village to industrial society the distance was, for the ordinary man, probably as great as that from the Shoshone Indians to Imperial Rome. Among the western European nations where the change has been best documented, we see the complete destruction of the earlier world in a period of less than two hundred years. Beginning with the creation of national markets and the rationalization of agriculture, the "great transformation" destroyed the subsistence economies of the peasants through improvements in production which drove them from the land. Arriving in the cities, they provided immense pools of cheap labor useful for the rapidly developing factory and market system. The products of the latter, in turn, were traded back to the hinterland, joining city and country in an indissoluble link of economic interdependence. The bifurcated society of city and village was fused in a national whole.

The peasant villager was poorly prepared for this transi-

6. Ralph E. Turner, *The Great Cultural Traditions* (New York: McGraw-Hill, 1941), especially Vol. 2, Ch. 20.

tion. It is doubtful that anything less violent than hunger could have driven so many into the chaotic social world of the cities, for that world took an immense toll of life, family security, health, and happiness. The casualties provide Marx's most vivid documentation of capital and its evils. But the destruction of the village as a social security system forced the peasantry to make their "great leap forward" into the world of rational production. It forced them to subsidize, through their weak bargaining position, the rapid expansion of European and American industrial society.

In the process the social character of the average man was forced to change, for he had to learn the common culture of city and factory in order to survive. He learned that work was instrumental, negotiable, and contractual. Beyond the bargain he had no protection. He learned that the public order was problematic; in the stews and sinks of London he learned to take account of the law and of that peculiarly urban social form, the police. (Not that he worried so much about lack of police protection; like the bottom dogs of our contemporary cities, his was the opposite need—protection *from* the police.) He learned to focus upon the market and its prices; his home, livelihood, family, and future depended upon the prices for labor and commodities.

In short, men became rational producers. The process of rationalization is, in this context, the separation of means from ends which allows one to estimate the fit between the two. Men moved from traditional, habit-bound, time-honored acts which guaranteed a livelihood, to rationally designed and prescribed acts which had an end reward—a paycheck. The reward of pleasure in the act itself frequently disappeared; what could be gotten from a tense and near-hysterical fourteen hour day of loom operation except the end reward, the paycheck? [7] This separation of the task into disvalued means and split ends was the source of Marx's concept of

7. Lawrence K. Frank, *Society as the Patient* (New Brunswick, N.J.: Rutgers University Press, 1948).

alienation, for it left the worker without pride or satisfaction in his work. From Durkheim's point of view, the rationalization of factory labor had another consequence; in destroying the value of the task as action in and for itself, rationalization destroyed the norms for behavior. "Anomie" means, precisely, the "lack of norms," or limits. The limits that remained were not visible in the rules for behavior during the performance of the task; they could only be inferred through foresight and planning. The net result was the devaluation of work as a good thing in itself and the definition of work as a *means* to an *end*.

The resulting social character of industrial man was one which fit the task forces of production and a life in the city maze. From the functional requirement that men be coordinated in production developed the limited work role, the job. This required self-control, for one must be at work on time, must carry out his role on time and at given levels of accuracy, and must remain at work while the steam shafts rotate. From the requirement of balancing labor market and commodity market developed the household budget: week by week and year by year the necessary costs and income must be balanced on pain of hunger, disease, or the debtor's prison. And from the generally low level of income (one which rose little or not at all for decades) came the most rigid requirement of all, the necessity for parsimony. The norm of efficiency deified in mechanical production was thus translated into the everyday working rules of the household, exalting the cheapest articles of consumption. In brief, the social character of early industrial man was one emphasizing self-control and abnegation.

Much, however, did not really change. There is, after all, more to life than the acts of producing and consuming, the major spheres where new learning and a new character were required. There remained such various realms as public affairs, religion, the high culture, kinship, and social class.

In these matters the social character of the peasant villager could and did persist in many ways.

Urbanization of his residence and mechanization of his job did not elevate the political role of the ordinary citizen. Illiterate and accustomed to compliance, he merely learned the self-controls necessary to avoid trouble with the police, the army, the wealthy, and others who dominated the urban scene. Having no tradition of public responsibility or participation, he became only a consumer of spectacles and a spectator of consumption. Nor was he able to participate in the high culture of the society. Uneducated, without security or leisure, he found his high culture in religion, where he was a poor consumer. Only in the deviant sects and cults did he find an opportunity and reward for active participation, and the reward was less intellectual than social. With his family he remained traditional and authoritarian, struggling to maintain the older kinship norms even though the network of kin was attenuated by migration and child labor. Nevertheless, his escape from the village probably facilitated his conservative authoritarianism in many ways, for he was free from the pressure of a close community and its public opinion.

The foregoing is a highly simplified view of social character in the early phases of industrial society. Emphasizing the mode, it does not do justice to the increasing differentiation of the population which followed upon the increasingly complex division of labor—a differentiation which resulted in the proliferation of social types. The peasants remained, a dwindling minority oriented to traditional, noncontractual, and habitual social roles, along with their reciprocal types, the landed gentry and the rentiers. In the cities the free professional man, expert and small businessman at once, became important, along with the salaried professional of government and private business. But cutting across all roles were the dominant concerns of the dominant organizations, the rapidly expanding empires of production and the market.[8]

The norms of production—self-control and enterprise—had some surprising consequences for the behavior of the workers drafted from farm to factory. Segregated in the working-class slums, thrown together in the factories, sharing a common lot and a common fate, the urban working class in every industrializing country began to experiment with organization and collective bargaining. The very demands of rational production encouraged such a development, for literacy and technical competence, organization and organizational skills, were taught in the processes of work. The new common culture of working-class man was thus created, to be articulated by the emerging working-class leaders, the craftsmen of physical and social organization. It was a culture which incorporated the norms of self-control, parsimony, planning: it accompanied a social character oriented towards work, security, and equality. Its consequences were apparent in the increasing control the workers exerted over the conditions of production. Out of common fate had evolved a common culture; with common enemies came the creation of a social class. All of the differences in life situation came together under the generalizing term "the working class," and Victorian polemics are studded with references to the "labor problem." Economic weakness, common enemies, the life of factory and slum provided the organizational leverage; a family culture based upon traditional kinship, religion, and thrift provided common folk values; individual weakness and inability to play public roles provided the basis for a corporate protest.[9]

The effects of the emerging industrial working-class culture were not confined to the situation on the job. As the

8. Raymond Williams, *Culture and Society, 1780–1950* (Garden City, N.Y.: 1960, Doubleday Anchor Edition).
9. Selig Perlman and Philip Taft, *Labor Movements* (New York: Macmillan, 1935).

society was increasingly committed to the complex interdependence of the urban factory and the urban market, it became increasingly dependent upon the orderly performance of tasks by the workers. Their technological monopoly was translated into political pressure through the strike; their organizations, resting on common fate, brought increasing pressure on the party organizations. They fought for two resources beyond trade unionism: formal education and the vote.

In their victory they achieved the most important social revolution of all time. They forced the society to treat them as citizens, through their achievement of the political franchise; and to treat them as responsible actors, through their achievement of the intellectual franchise, universal education. But their success was complementary to the inexorable demands of developing industrial society, a society that could not be operated without the assurance of proper behavior from its vast work force of manual workers whom the political franchise involved organically in the status quo. Nor were illiterate workmen capable of the increasingly complex work roles that the productive system kept throwing up; mass education was a necessary working tool for the entire economy.

The end result was a vast increase in the "internal inclusiveness of the society," as noted by Wendell Bell.[10] The various forms of partial citizenship decreased in their actual distribution and were condemned in principle, though they persisted in the differential handicaps of the poor, the illiterate, the rural, and the ethnic. At the same time, other blessings and burdens of citizenship were more widely distributed. Universal manhood conscription may not seem an increase in citizenship—until one remembers how many regimes could never have dared trust weapons in the hands of the entire male citizenry. Universal taxation is another ambig-

10. Wendell Bell, editor, *The Democratic Revolution in the West Indies* (Cambridge, Mass.: Schenkman Publishing Company, Inc., 1967).

uous gain, yet it forces the political beneficiary to look at the price of benefits—just as it ties the taxing power more closely to the consent of the citizens.

These immense changes were hastened along by crises in the overall structure of the large-scale societies. In the twentieth century, modern warfare twice demonstrated the intricate interdependence of the polity and the economy, increasing that interdependence in the process. The great economic collapse of the 1930's made clear to all the political vulnerability of a large-scale society which could not provide economic security for its population. The Full Employment Bill of 1946 was a major symbolic act, for it stated authoritatively the principle that every worker had a right to a job, the basis for economic citizenship. The trend is clear, from the struggle for popular education and the franchise back in the early nineteenth century to the fight for the Civil Rights Bill in 1964. It is in one direction and that direction is towards the equality of citizens before the state and the public order.

THE SPEED OF CHANGE

The society of the United States was a relative latecomer to Western history. Emerging precisely at the point in time where scale was rapidly increasing, it was itself one aspect of increasing scale in western European society. From the beginning it was a dependent part of international markets and empires. Its closest approximations to a peasantry, the chattel slaves of the South and subsistence farmers of the frontiers, were really a far cry from the remnants of feudal agrarian society. Its class system, weakened by distance from Europe and the opportunities of the frontier, never resembled the harsh outlines of government based on feudalism and conquest and, with early independence from the British system, the feudal concept of estates evaporated. The society of the United States thus maximized those aspects of increasing scale which destroyed the age-old agrarian society and exalted the rational producer.

"Americanization" has been a derogatory term for the changes which have occurred at a rapidly accelerating rate in the western European countries. The process of increasing internal inclusiveness is not, however, a characteristic unique to the United States. It occurred here earliest, and progressed most rapidly, because fewer aged structures constrained the process. The lack of hereditary ruling and taxing elites elevated the role of the entrepreneur in the cities, while the availability of land on the frontiers allowed millions the opportunity to become free and rational producers. The political norms invoked by the Declaration of Independence and the Constitution led easily and logically to the political and intellectual enfranchisement of the total population. This, in turn, led to the economic enfranchisement won, at least in principle, in the 1930's and 1940's.

But such is the irony of history, that the society of rational producers was hardly realized before its radical transformation into something new and strange became evident. World War II energized and activated the American economy to an enormous extent. In the process the technologies of production, given a chance by the unlimited demand and the shortage of manpower, raced ahead towards the maximum application of nonhuman energy to work. In the postwar years the results became obvious: American society was not only the wealthiest in the world, it was also far wealthier than it had ever been before. That wealth, distributed through collective bargaining between corporations, unions, the free market, and the government, raised the resource level of millions of American households. Leisure increased, as the forty-hour week and the three-week vacation became the norm. The average income was more than double that of the early years of the twentieth century. Higher levels of formal education, made easier by a late start at work and increasing educational facilities, marked each succeeding generation. The goods of the market, the pleasures of leisure, and the rich and novel symbolic worlds of the mass media became part of the "American way of life."

The society of rational producers accepted all this as its due. The enormous spurt of prosperity was a just reward for self-control, parsimony, and labor. The American people expressed its values through the major investments of the postwar years: the deification of the family was evident in the rapid spread of home ownership. Appetite for movement and privacy was satisfied by the flood of automobiles which carved new concrete channels through fields and city neighborhoods. Commitment to the children was evident in the increasing "child market" for commodities, the "adolescent culture" of the mass media, anxieties and plans for higher education, and, always, the preference for the single-family house in the neighborhoods of the likeminded.[11]

The suburban move did not create these values. The suburbs have been felicitously and accurately called "new homes for old values." What occurred was the result of release from those constraints of poverty and space which had prevented the average American from living as he had wanted to do all along. Now with new consumer freedoms the old working-class culture could express itself in many new ways. That culture was evident in the conservatism of the "new middle classes"—their focus upon the child population, their pious religious participation, their concern with earning, buying, and planning to buy.

David Riesman has called them the "nouveau riche" of leisure.[12] He has pointed out their great new opportunities for learning, for development, for the creation of a new social

11. Scott Greer, *Urban Renewal and American Cities: The Dilemma of Democratic Intervention* (Indianapolis: Bobbs-Merrill, 1965).
12. David Riesman, with Reuel Denny and Nathan Glazer, *The Lonely Crowd* (New Haven: Yale University Press, 1950).

character appropriate to the economies of plenty. But it is important to note certain concomitants of the new society which actually prevented learning, in old ways, important norms required for life in the society of increasing scale and internal inclusiveness. The knowledge, skills, and norms of good "consumership" are hardly adequate for a round of life; taste is no substitute for morality. And what was happening to morality?

Morality is that aspect of the common culture which emphasizes duties rather than rights. But the new affluence provided little in the way of guidelines to responsible public action. Indeed, through its cushioning effects, it tended to pull the teeth of older protest movements. Labor unions, their jurisdictions firm and their members' paychecks increasing, found little cause or profit in militancy. The socialist movements, committed to a reevaluation of work and social class, found the workers content with their "fair share" and uninterested in radical change. Feminism virtually disappeared, as the female became the captain of consumption and director of child-rearing in a child-oriented society. Aside from the continual pressure of colored ethnics for fuller inclusion, little action in the public domain reflected the duties, as against the rights, of citizenship.

In reality, the inherited social character of the rational producer had never had more than slight relevance to the demands of the public interest. Oriented to the maximization of profit at the entrepreneurial level, to parsimony and security at the level of the rank and file, the public purpose was assumed to be automatically fulfilled through individual aggrandizement—even the protest movements were powered by a concern with equal opportunity to aggrandize. No wonder the vast increase in energy, leisure, and symbolic communication has not resulted in the education of adults to a concern with public affairs and the high culture.

The Gross National Product is shared out among millions

of households, where it is consumed in private. Much is undoubtedly being learned in the process—styles of dress and furniture change; child-rearing and sex practices are exposed to questioning and conscious thought; many of the peripheral crafts and skills of the society are diffused in the do-it-yourself manner. But the hard core of responsibility for the public affairs of society and one's action in them is not an area where adult education has flourished. "Public affairs" programs on the mass media remain public charges because there is little effective market for the dramatization of dilemmas and promises in the larger society.

This weakness in the political culture is maximized by the processes which are transforming the organizational shape of the society. The continuing changes in the space-time ratio (the cost in time of traversing space) result in a continuing process of national integration. The corporations safeguard market and resources through continuing mergers. As this occurs, the effective center of control shifts from the city, where the major industry is now a branch plant, to the national headquarters, where real decisions occur. Parallel changes take place in labor unions. (A labor leader described, ironically, a dozen bargaining sessions around the country waiting the word from New York—where the management of the telephone company and the president of the union were settling the issues.) Increasingly, even at top levels of local control, the industrial-commercial empires are manned by salaried workers.

The local political community is also changing, *pari passu*. While the nation becomes overwhelmingly urban in its residence, the city loses its governmental form. The increasing command of space incident to the diffusion of the automobile has allowed the development of endless tract housing on the peripheries. These settlements, separately incorporated, live within the ecology of the metropolis but are not subject to any public powers at the local level. Typically, small residential enclaves and suburban municipalities are stewards for highly local interests; they are little concerned with the great issues of the metropolis as a whole and, like dogs in the manger, prevent any broader power from acting. Thus the governmental fragmentation of the metropolitan area prevents the generation and solution of significant issues at the place where they occur—the local political community.[13]

Public action is learned through participation in the near-at-hand. It is learned through membership in a group, where one's private vocabulary is measured against the common culture, and where one's individual enthusiasm or grievance can be turned into social fact through communication and collective action. But study after study has shown that Americans are poor participators in the social groups accessible to them. They are most apt to participate in the voluntary organizations of suburbia—those groups devoted to the problems of household, family, and neighborhood. And of those who do participate, some must learn at least the ABC's of public action. But they are a minority and their public affairs tend to the trivial and the parochial.

For the rest, true significance is no longer local. The shifts in space-time ratio have radically changed the meaning of space and it is more useful now to speak, not of statute miles, but of what John Friedman calls "interactional space." The very concept of space is reduced to its effects as a barrier to and a channel for social interaction. In this sense, many of the most significant leaders of American thought and action are not primarily citizens of any local community. With national and international roles, the nation is their community, O'Hare Airport their crossroads, and the airstrips from Boston to Norfolk their Main Street. Even at the bottom of the occupational pyramid, where men engage largely in routine jobs seldom taking them beyond a plant or neighborhood, some dimensions of the world are supralocal. Each evening when they turn on the Big Screen their attention

13. Scott Greer, *Governing the Metropolis* (New York: John Wiley and Sons, 1962).

moves through interactional space to the national society. It is the locus of true significance, but it is far away and it is not experienced as personal action in a concrete social group.

While the organization of work and distribution of consumption goods have been radically changed, a more basic dynamic has continued to revolutionize the *process* of production. We have seen the origins of intensive urbanization in the progressive mechanization of the extractive industries, which released workers from the rural areas. We have noted that agriculture is the most automated of our industries. But the process has not stopped there. The "secondary" industries of fabrication are increasingly staffed, not with men, but with machines operated and controlled by other machines and powered by nonhuman energy resources. Production soars while the blue-collar labor force declines. As this occurs, more labor has moved into the white-collar jobs of sales and clerical tasks (the processing and diffusion of orders), into service jobs and the professions. Men increasingly work, as Riesman points out, not with "hard" materials but with "soft" symbols and social structures.[14]

Many of these jobs, however, are now in danger. The development of electronic data processing has provided a new kind of machine, one which can process orders at lightning speed with a far lower rate of error than the fallible human being could ever achieve. Digital computers with "canned" programs perform analyses in one minute which took, only a few years ago, several hundred man-hours on hand calculators (and let us recall that the computer is only about a decade old). Meanwhile, the service industries are increasingly applying new machines and sales activities are being revolutionized by prepackaging. Even the teacher is experimenting with teaching machines—devices which minimize error and improve learning through the abolition of the "human relationship" between pupil and mentor. The revolution which be-

14. Riesman *et al.*, *The Lonely Crowd.*

gan with agriculture bids fair to permeate the traditional worlds of human work.

The world of the rational producer is working itself out of a job. The society based upon the economy and logic of scarcity becomes a monster cornucopia of production; the world focused upon cities, hinterlands, and regions, becomes involved and almost dissolved in the giant national system; the economy exalting the value of hard work and self-control produces a set of tools which threaten to make work as we have known it obsolete. The results are a set of massive problems, a fierce tension between the common culture, the social character, and the politico-economic situation of Americans.

THE PROBLEMS OF PLENTY

Each year production in the United States increases by two or three percent and personal income moves steadily upward with it. The vast array of consumer goods spreads further: to color television, pastel sports cars, power-driven reels for deep sea fishing. The number of millionaires passes 100,000. Yet the unemployment rate in 1968 was around 5 percent; it was 14 percent for the youngest entrants to the labor force, 30 percent for those of the latter who did not finish high school, and 50 percent for those in the latter category who are colored. "Silent firing" becomes the rule. The author recently visited one of the major steel plants, economic resource for a populous valley, where no one had been hired for a couple of years and no one was going to be hired for several more. A large proportion of the stock of conventional jobs is disappearing.

These are the results of substituting machines for routine human work, for *drudgery*. Norbert Wiener believed that anything which could be done better by machines should be, for machines allow "the human use of human beings." The difficulty is that human beings can be used in American society only in a job, and jobs are not multiplying as fast as would-be workers. Then, since the job is one's claim to economic citizenship, the society dichotomizes into the relatively skilled, honored, and prosperous holders of increasingly technical jobs, on one hand, and the unemployed on the other. Subsisting on inadequate doles, the latter are "social basket cases," casualties of increasing scale.

The unemployed are a minor proportion of the citizenry at present, but there is no assurance this will remain true. By Adam Smith's definition, less than half the labor force is now employed in "productive" work, and some economists believe that in two decades it will be more like 15 per cent. The accumulated labor force, meanwhile, is accelerating, as the child crop from the war and postwar years makes ready to marry and procreate. The society faces more than a temporary problem: as one in which the right to economic citizenship is affirmed it must generate millions of roles to confer that citizenship. The political rights of the unemployed (as well as the vulnerability of complex orders to sabotage) will force that duty upon whomever holds political authority.

In a global perspective, it does not seem a grim or tragic predicament. When one considers the problems of nations whose wealth per capita is less than one-twentieth of ours— the energy-poor and inefficient producers who dominate world society—it seems no problem at all. And, indeed, certain solutions to the problem seem clear and feasible. These solutions would require either a change in the assignment of work, a change in the nature of the role which guaranteed one economic citizenship, or a change in the nature of work. Given our certainty of production, any of the three would have the major effect of distributing economic citizenship to the increasing population of the republic.

The sheer number of human hours required by our productive plant is decreasing faster than our standard work week. (And probably faster than we can see from statistics, for featherbedding is a concomitant of silent firing.) It is not difficult to see that shortening of work weeks and the outlawing of "overtime" could easily effect a redistribution of jobs. The cost of production would increase somewhat in the short run, but the long-run human costs of multiplying the unemployed would be greatly minimized. Further, the resulting increase in leisure could be counted as a social good.

To go further, the very requirement that economic citizenship depends upon the job could be amended. The guaranteed household income is a distinct possibility and, as the authors of *The Triple Revolution* point out, the total cost of guaranteeing $3,000 a year for every American household would run less than two percent of the Gross National Product.[15] Such a minimal level would not attract many people who had the opportunity of earning the average income for the nation—over twice as much. But it would have the advantages of shoring up broken households where middle-aged women are busy raising a significant proportion of our next generation, of removing some of the stigma of failure from the older men whose skills are obsolete, of providing some kind of base on which the unemployed youth of the poor might lay the foundations for a rise to useful employment. In short, those bred to a society which once demanded menial, casual, and heavy physical labor would not have to bear alone the burdens of transition to a world where such labor was of decreasing value. Even though they might remain net charges upon the society, the effects upon the middle-aged miners in the worked-out coal fields of Illinois or West Virginia could be counted as a suitable social investment.

The foregoing are means of adjusting to the decline in our conventional stock of jobs relative to our burgeoning population. More important, however, is the long-run possibility of using labor, released now from manual drudgery, in a wide variety of spheres where the chief resource demanded is simply human action itself. From a strictly economic point of view, what is needed is work which is highly labor intensive, which produces negotiable goods, and produces goods

15. Robert Perucci and Marc Pilisuk, compilers, *The Triple Revolution: Social Problem in Depth* (Boston: Little, Brown, 1968).

which do not compete with themselves in future market situations. From a social point of view, what this writer prefers is work which enhances the quality of human life, for producers and consumers alike. The kind of work that is immediately apparent is that focusing upon the human services: education, health, the arts and sciences.

Indeed, we can already see a shift of investment towards these areas of production. The recreational industries, from tourism to fly-tying, are booming; the most important generator of new jobs in the economy today is education; even health is an increasingly big business. But the shift is not fast enough to accommodate the new generations of job-hungry youth and it is unlikely to accelerate fast enough to provide work for the millions of new households that will form in the next decade. This is in large part because the fields of health, education, welfare, and the arts, at best supplied by a very imperfect market, have been wards of the government. As such, they have been as stunted as most charity cases.

The obvious solution is a massive increase in governmental investment in these areas of production. Where the market is incapable and the task is crucial, the public sector must act, as even the late Senator Taft acknowledged. Education is a public task by general acknowledgment, and so, increasingly, is research. The massive increase of resources in these areas could produce a rapidly professionalizing labor force with increasingly powerful tools for solving human problems.

Research, justified by a concern for all of mankind as well as the national interest, could face other crucial problems than that of exploring space. These include, at least (1) the discovery of new sources of nonhuman energy, to take the place of our depleting reserves of fossil fuel and to make this power available to people now the victims of the erratic distribution of coal and oil; (2) the delineation of the social and physical causes of overfertility and the implementation of population control in the variety of human societies; (3) the discovery of the basic principles of learning and the development of a variety of educational techniques, suited to the varieties of persons and cultures and the different capabilities required; and (4) perhaps the most important of all, the delineation of the nature and constraints of social organization in our rapidly expanding and increasingly complex society, with a concern not only for inexorable constraints on collective action, but also for the conditions of increasing freedom to choose. In short, our abundance of material goods and services could subsidize an increase in knowledge and techniques which would help the entire global society to achieve "the American standard of living," a goal impossible at present.

The above policies have all been suggested by reasonable men, yet they have a wildly utopian ring. Emphasizing the interdependence of the total society and, in the process, the necessary interaction of government and the economy, they violate the common culture of the American as a rational producer. They sound immoral to him and therefore, impossible to the observer. To pay people more for not producing, to pay an adequate livelihood whether people work or not, is anathema. Further, to increase the amount of the wealth distributed by the federal government and then to invest that wealth in the "nonproductive" work of health, education, welfare, research, and the arts is to violate both the norms concerning who should have power and those concerning what should be done with it.

The social character of Americans is based upon the discipline of poverty and the religion of work. Their moral armature depends upon the mortification of the flesh through toil, a debt paid to the self-controls which constitute conscience. Leisure itself is a problem for such a character, and the prevalence of moonlighting on the one hand and do-it-yourself tasks on the other testifies to the use of make-work as a means to security. The harsh character suited to the subsistence job or the subsistence farm, inappropriate though it is to the soft life of routine employee and aggressive consumer, continues full force in the absence of a replacement. For the threat that one's character is obsolescent is also a threat that one's self is obsolete: hence the anxiety over work, the threat in leisure.

Leisure for others, particularly for those who cannot find a job at productive labor, is the same threat doubled. Used to privatizing his economic life, the rational producer has only a personalistic vocabulary for achievement or success; the failure of others is proof of their incompetence and hence their lack of character. Even as his own life is organized around the armature of threat, scarcity, and work, so he cannot believe men will work hard without these whips—and he cannot accept the morality of men who do not work for a living. His harsh judgments of others are the mirror images of his own concept of self.

His privatization of public issues is simply a continuation of his heritage, the common culture of the merchant, farmer, and laborer. It is evident in his alienation from public responsibility and in his suspicion of the political process and public affairs. Since he is involved only peripherally, through the ritual of the vote and his spectatorship of the big screen, government is unreal and far away. Where he lives dwell only consumers of goods and compliers with order. Only in the small scale world of the local polity does he have access to a concrete political process; its trivial issues generally fail to arouse him to public action, save for sporadic efforts to impose a veto where his minor interests are considered in danger.

Democracy is an aristocratic concept, and the ideal political norms of the United States imply a common culture stressing noblesse oblige, the duties as well as the rights. The duties begin with the obligation to understand, take positions, and contend. They continue through the obligations to serve the public interest and to pay the price in the form of goods, services and powers surrendered to the public purpose. Democracy is, then, the socializing of political responsibility.

Judging from our data on American politics, the common culture has diffused these duties only as vague desiderata. The average citizen has not integrated them in the essential armature of his social character. His knowledge of the high culture, including his own political history, is typically vague and inaccurate. His knowledge of public affairs, even the burning issues of his politics, is hardly any better. (In one recent referendum for metropolitan government the slogan of the opposition was: "If you don't understand it, don't vote for it!") His education is typically already obsolete by the time he takes his place in the ranks of householders and citizens; it is not kept up by lifelong learning. Under the circumstances, it is easy for him to lose all perspective on the vast issues of the continental nation. He has no idea of the relative share of the Gross National Product going into governmental expenditures, or the relative importance of armaments in those expenses, much less the share spent by local, state, and federal governments. Illiterate of statistics, he is unable to read the alphabet, much less the language necessary to understand the world of national policy.

He translates these issues, then, into his own vocabulary of everyday action. The federal government is defined as a small business man, forever on the edge of bankruptcy. With the imperative of thrift and parsimony held sacred, he hardly understands, much less appreciates, the importance of research and development, risk capital, and the long view that attempts to predict and control the future. It would help if he could improve his economic notions to take account of, at least, the imperatives of big business enterprises, but he does not understand big business. His economic folk thought omits the most important aspects of the contemporary society: rapid technological change, the complexity of organization, and the interaction of political and economic goals.

He confronts opposition, from the world without and from ideological opponents within, in the crude dichotomy of chauvinism. All that threatens is inherently evil. His ethnocentrism is so pronounced that he continually underestimates the power of other nation states and overestimates the importance of his domestic enemies. His political illiteracy is perhaps most dangerous in the areas where he should be competent—the values behind the Bill of Rights and the history of governmental oppression which gave rise to that bill.[16] His inability to accept the problematic nature of the real world blinds him to much of the reason for controversy and, therefore, to the basis for protecting the person with a minority opinion. Life to him is simple in principle: thus the anxiety generated through his blurred awareness of the Communists as radical critics of his way of thought. His response is a religious reaffirmation of what he takes to be his "way of life"; the deification of small business (though 200 corporations produce 80 per cent of the economic values in the society), the decrial of the federal government's spending (though most of it goes for the wars of past and future which he supports in principle), opposition to "growing federal power" (though most of his security is a by-product of the welfare programs and economic stewardship of the national system).

But he is not really given to political contention. In his everyday social relationships, he avoids conversation about politics if there is any genuine difference of opinion, for it is "controversial." (He imagines a politics without controversy.) His chief source of political information is in the mass-media figures who agree with him, and his outlet for political opinions is the circle of kin and friends upon whom he can count to share his assumptions and pieties.[17] But political questions do not really limit his friendship circle, for he tempers the winds of conversation to the company, excising if necessary all subjects of general import. (In an unpublished study of a

16. Raymond W. Mack, "Do We Really Believe in the Bill of Rights?" in *Social Problems*, 3:264–67.
17. Scott Greer, *Metropolitics: A Study of Political Culture* (New York: John Wiley and Sons, 1963).

middle-class Oregon population, Robin Williams and his associates found no relation between friendship and similarity of values.) While such behavior probably reflects, rather than creates, the lack of significance found in public issues, each opportunity lost perpetuates the existing situation.

Half-in and half-out of the large-scale society, the "typical" social character sketched in above is a changeling. One can see traces of the peasant villager, the vague fear of the unknown and the lack of confidence that the world is in any way subject to one's choice and efforts. One can see, in many cases, a "daemonic universe" in which the President of the United States is a "conscious agent of the Communist conspiracy," while fluoridation of the water supplies is a plot by Communists to weaken the bone structure of American bodies. One can see also the hard carapace of the rational producer's social character: the suspicion of political leaders and the public enterprise, hatred of positive government of all sorts and especially taxes, contempt for controversy and the political process. The common culture has not produced a social character adequate for a broadly based democratic polity; it has produced a society of employees, spectators, and consumers who think they are free enterprisers.

Yet so constituted is the American polity that its ability to act rests finally upon the consent of the average citizen. The local political community is based upon their agreement and must return to them for changes in taxes, in powers, and in its formal structure. The rules for the local community are, in turn, frozen into the constitution of the states, while the latter are given conditions for the integration of governmental action in the society. At each level the political leadership must have the assent of the citizens. Only thus can government action be legitimated through the common political culture, and the law which is that culture frozen into statutes and charters.

One might well ask how, under the circumstances, the country is governed at all? And indeed, the history of the

United States includes some vast hiatuses in which little governmental direction was evident—whether we speak of the lawlessness of the western territories before statehood, the "lynch law" of the South and the Indian "wars," or the uncontrolled development of our giant corporations and our vast and ragged cities.[18] In the past, the society, simpler in its organization and protected from its enemies, could live with a modicum of governmental responsibility. Today this becomes less possible by the minute: the anxieties of the cold war with its threat of thermonuclear holocaust, and the anxieties of economic change with its threat of disastrous depressions inevitably increase the responsibility of the federal government and the national political leadership.

National leaders dominate the big screen and the issues they confront are the most salient in modern life. But they are far away from the social presence of the citizens and they achieve support only through the delegation of trust to party or person in the forced choice of a two-party election. But indeed, this distance from the voters is probably the only reason they can act at all. When we look at the states and their polities, we are struck with their incapability to act with respect to their legitimate problems. This inability of state governments to organize consensus probably rests, in turn, upon their very exposure to the rank and file of their constituencies. We hear much about the overrepresented rural vote as the cause of state incapacities, yet the only careful studies of the problem indicate that urban delegations to the capitols get what they want—they simply cannot even agree among themselves on what it is. The doctrine of states' rights has foundered in our complex society upon the inabil-

---

18. For examples see Robert Wood, *1400 Governments* (Cambridge: Harvard University Press, 1961). For the weakness of the national government in crucial times see Matthew Josephson, *The Robber Barons: The Great American Capitalists* (New York: Harcourt, Brace and World, 1934). On genocide, one of the many poignant accounts is that of Theodora Kroeber, *Ishi in Two Worlds: A Biography of the Last Wild Indian in North America* (Berkeley: University of California Press, 1961).

ity of the states to act as semi-sovereign governments. They have been, instead, veto groups—brakes upon the policies generated at the national level.

Equally rigid has been the hold of popular democracy upon our city governments. Limited in their abilities to tax, their abilities to expand their jurisdictions and powers, and their abilities to reformulate their structure, they have been passive victims of the powerful transformations associated with expanding scale. Their limits are, in turn, due to their exposure to the population through the referendum, that plebescite which assumes competence and concern on the part of everyone aged eighteen or more. Unable to act under these limits, unable to reorganize themselves (so they could act) under the state constitutional limits, cities have increasingly turned to devices which evade the vote of the electorate. Special district governments with their own taxing power can integrate jurisdictions and increase governmental control—at the expense of being virtually invisible to the citizens. State and federal grants-in-aid for new purposes break the deadlock of local indifference and stalemate, but at the expense of being administered by professional bureaucracies hardly exposed to the citizenry. Positive government evaporates from the local democracy in the process, leaving the mayors of our cities in the role of "caretakers." As such they try to update the services legitimatized in the past and to increase the flow of nonlocal funds into their bailiwicks. Prisoners of the common political culture, they attempt to "wire around" the dead cells of the local democracy.[19]

THE UBIQUITY OF CHANGE

To recapitulate, social character has been identified as typical ways of acting in important social situations. Based upon a culture created to handle the everyday situations that must be confronted, social character perpetuates that culture as

19. Greer, *Metropolitics.*

individuals attempt to adapt the new to the framework of the familiar, applying wonted behavior to the emerging world. Thus the social character appropriate to the rational producer, the laborer, the small businessman, and the peasant, has been applied to the rapidly urbanizing society of the twentieth century. In the process, its inadequacies are evident; it fits neither the situations of the individual actor nor the demands of the large-scale system. It is perpetuated in the rhetoric of politics, the folk theory of economics, and the cliches of popular morality. Yet one suspects that it can give lip service in these areas only because of their lack of salience to the ordinary citizen (as burial rites are among our most conservative customs largely because of their unimportance to the ongoing society). Let us examine, then, the changes in those situations where Americans *must* be competent and concerned with outcomes.

The typical American worker is becoming a white-collar employee and his work is changing to the control of symbols and people. Further, he is apt to work within a large-scale formal organization, one which integrates the behavior of hundreds of men with that of hundreds of machines on one power grid and one time schedule. This means that the work he does is demanding, for error can cumulate geometrically. What is more, the action demanded is *rational choice* in respect to the larger system. It rests upon a precise knowledge of abstract theory applied to the concrete facts at issue; it encourages rationality in the formulating and resolving of the question at issue.

The increasing scale of the organization within which the individual acts has other consequences. At the bottom of the skill hierarchy the workers are conscious of the sheer complexity and integration of behavior in the corporation. At the top, the managers are aware of this complexity as it persists, thrives or fails within a complex organizational environment, national in scale. The very scope of their roles is conducive to wider horizons; the North Carolina textile industry is integrally related through the world market to those of Japan and Hong Kong, while many major American corporations do a large minority, or even a majority, of their business overseas. With jet aircraft, the executive life can literally be lived in an international network of organizations. This is a far cry from the squires of the Pennsylvania mill towns still described by nostalgic novelists.

Meanwhile, back at the plant, the squires have given way to the experts at social engineering. David Riesman (as so often) first underlined the significance of the "human relations in industry" approach to the problems of authority in economic organization.[20] The solution of brute mechanical problems of production has been accompanied by an increasing awareness of the problems of social coordination, integration, and morale. Perhaps a decline of the social character called the "rational producer" among routine workers has accompanied the post war prosperity and the increase in security. At any rate, "labor commitment" is a problem not only in the underdeveloped countries.[21] The role of the organizational engineer is increasingly one which requires an understanding of the varieties of humanity which, together, constitute "the firm." Labor leader, personnel man, arbitrator,—all are in the same profession, and provide major reference groups for management.

The changing nature of everyday life is evident also in the world of leisure. Here it is important to remember that, for the first time in history, the whole range of men has the right of *choice,* and in many different areas. Increased formal education and access to the mass media means a broadening of cultural equipment, for many different vocabularies run through the collage of noise and images on television and, when they are new, allow alternate definitions of known events. The increase in household incomes means an im-

20. Riesman *et al., The Lonely Crowd,* pp. 302–37 and 330–38.
21. Wilbur Moore and Arnold Feldman, editors, *Labor Commitment and Economic Development* (Princeton: Princeton University Press, 1962).

proved power to act; it is evident in the growth of what some have called the "ardent amateur." This wealth is invested in fields as diverse as sports, movie-making, and the arts and crafts. Perhaps most important of all, the increase in leisure has increased our life-space, allowing action in a variety of realms.

In a recent national poll it was reported that six percent of the adults interviewed had taken an active part in a theatrical production within the past year. This finding is to be read along with a recent statement that there are now over 10,000 little theaters in the United States. Galleries for the arts multiply in the metropolitan areas and spring up in the smaller cities, while the sale of books—both soft and hard cover—has increased faster than the population.

All in all, it seems possible that the release of man from the iron role of the laborer is beginning to produce an efflorescence of man as a maker and man as a social actor. It is, to be sure, a phenomenon broadcast throughout the population. It is most evident in the hobbies and crafts, pursued and consumed in the privacy of the household. It is least evident in social action, the significant role in public space. Yet the consistent finding that a large minority of the citizens in the suburban municipalities is involved in their local community at a number of levels may indicate an increasing preference for social and political action as leisure pursuits. Equally important is the finding that public life in the suburbs is accessible to and engaged in by women as frequently as by men.

Another realm of everyday life that is not amenable to the old norms of the rational producer is that of child-rearing. The authoritarian norms of the past assumed a clear congruence between the world of the fathers and that of the sons; only the most obtuse can believe that this holds true today. Instead, children are given the most general norms and discover for themselves how they are applied in the large-scale, formal group such as the junior high, the high school, or the university. Nor do the norms of self-control, parsimony, and work fit very well in the relations between parents and child; there is so little real work for the child in the ongoing round of the household, that it penalizes the parent more to find it than it does the child to perform it. Indeed, the work of the household is not the proper task of the child. With the widespread realization that formal education is the key to the future, the pressure on children is calculated to ensure commitment to the goals of the educational system. With this achieved, the child is rewarded with his "fair share" of the consumables, a share calculated by comparison with his peers. For the parents, this is an expected cost of rearing children.

The major cost in rearing children, however, is the burden of uncertainty. With the breakup of the scarcity economy and its ways, parents are involved in the enterprise of inventing a rationale for child-rearing. The thorniest problems in learning theory, authority relationships, and depth psychology are innocently posed and somehow settled by these amateur social scientists who struggle with the unknown. Grappling for certainty, they swing between the discarded norms of their own childhood and the efforts of social scientists to generalize about the complex and delicate process which transform the neonate into the American citizen of tomorrow. Their effort to be rational and their consequent uncertainty are, again, not likely to reinforce the norms of the authoritarian social character.

The everyday life situations which the contemporary American must handle show certain recurring attributes. One is the pervasiveness of the *problematic:* on the job, in the children's bedroom, or facing the big screen. The intellectual answer is demanded and it cannot be intuited or remembered; the social answer which resolves the impasse is required yet it does not come "naturally." Both kinds of uncertainty can lead to what Riesman calls "the other-directed character," the person without any intrinsic standards for the good or the true. It can also lead, however, to belief in the possibility of rational consensus, a solution to the problems of the intellectually uncertain. And it can lead to a belief that one must take the standpoint of the other in order to understand him and solve the problems of the socially uncertain.

Perhaps a new American social character is emerging from these recurrent problems of everyday life. It would be one organized around the armature of intellectual control and socially created agreement. It would emphasize the necessity to think, in abstract terms, of a larger and more problematic world than was ever assumed by the rational producer. Particularly in respect to facing, on television and elsewhere, the variety of social worlds, pluralism and scale would require that an immense value be placed upon taking into account the role of the other person. Projecting these demands upon the events revealed by the big screen, the public world in which one is totally involved (through the bomb, conscription, taxes, the danger of depression or inflation), such a social character would require a general education and source of information far beyond what has ever been available in the past to either common men or privileged elites.

Such an education is possible in the United States today and is approximated for some of the oncoming generation. Should the above speculations be correct, that generation would be the first to realize and formulate a new American character type. It would be congruent, not with Americanism but with the human world of large-scale society. Freed from the older constraints of poverty, parochialism, and authoritarianism, our first postwar generation is still an enigma to its parents. It has not known the depression of the 1930's, a catastrophe which unnecessarily reinforced and prolonged the dominance of a scarcity culture, nor has it known the appalling experience of watching a Hitler dominate the proudest societies on earth. At the same time it has been educated in schools immensely superior to those of older generations (schools which Dr. Conant says have much that is right about them and, generally, only minor arrangements which are wrong). Finally, it is a generation which has grown up with the world in its living room, with the White House, Little Rock, Khrushchev and De Gaulle before it on the big screen. Its perspectives should be broader, its pieties more relevant to reality, and its questions more significant.

In the meantime the American society is not filled with either the "ideal type" of rational producer nor with the new character type sketched in above. What seems the likely case is a complex mix of social characters, with old styles, new styles, and hybrids galore. (Anyone's social character may vary greatly between the realms of work, politics, leisure, kinship, and the high culture.) One would expect the new style to predominate where the task was most inexorable and the new norms most requisite, while the older style would be common where it could be maintained without difficulty.

The fundamentalists of religion, politics, and work should be found in the remnants of the smaller-scale society and in the roles of small scope within the larger world. The small towns of the rural areas, the open country neighborhoods, the South, should be heavily loaded with the older types; they should be common among small businessmen, farmers, ranchers, miners, and common laborers. They should also be found among Negroes and other ethnic groups cut off, by segregation, from full participation in the wider society.

The new social character should be most common in the metropolitan areas, in the most rapidly expanding and large-scale economies of the Middle Atlantic and the West Coast. They should be common among such workers as those employed in mass communications, entertainment, education, government, and distribution. They should be most common in those jobs requiring broad decisions and exceptional technical expertise, though one would expect them to appear in force among the ranks of the service workers—maintenance men, restaurateurs, landscape gardeners, and the like. For it is in jobs where the intellectually and socially problematic are most crucial that one would expect a major alteration in the ethic of hard work, parsimony, and self-control.

But both are extreme types, and it is not likely that either will be found to dominate the social positions indicated. Between the old style and the new, lies the tolerant middle, the rational producer whose carapace of habit and character is softening in the sun of prosperity and leisure, the new-style American who still commits himself erratically to the grim conscience and religion of work. The middle range is made up of the changelings: arbitrating between the extremes, it is the cushion which prevents the war of norms from utterly hamstringing the society. It was sorely pressed in mediating between the southern sheriffs and the Student Nonviolent Coordinating Committee. It is that part of a generation torn between mutually irreconcilable commitments. Its bad conscience and its overconstrained leisure, its fetishism of commodities and privatization of action are alike, symptoms of a social character no longer adequate to its world. The tensions will probably not be resolved in this generation, however; for that resolution we must look to the next crop.

Meanwhile, the mix is changing. The present generation controlling this country is one which remembers the great depression, a bench mark of poverty. Like children who never had enough to eat and thus become, as adults, compulsive eaters, this generation has been obsessed with the consumption goods of the private market. But as new generations come on, we shall find a differing hierarchy of values and a new set of norms. The passing of the depression generation will be accompanied by the declining importance of those who spent their earliest years in small towns and open country. (The true meaning of urbanization is obscured by their presence for, so rapidly have our cities grown, that a large proportion of our "metropolitanites" is really made up of country boys in the suburbs.) Increasing quantities and qualities of formal education should radically alter the cultural equipment of these new, city-bred, post-depression citizens.

Perhaps, from all these trends, one could hazard the prediction that the people of the United States are busy inventing the social character appropriate to the large-scale society. As they do so, they will be laying the foundations for the first truly democratic civilization in the history of mankind. No effort is more important than this, for we are committed, willy-nilly, to a democratic solution to our problems. This means that our public policy cannot long remain far above the common culture and the social character of the usual citizen.

17

Policy
and the Urban Future

It is my assumption that images of the future determine present actions. They may or may not determine the nature of the future—that depends upon a much more complex set of circumstances. But willy-nilly, much of our behavior is postulated upon images of a possible and/or desirable future. Furthermore, it seems useful to assume that certain assumptions about the immutable, the changeless and inescapable, limit and to a degree determine images of a possible and/or desirable future. Thus images of the future invasion and decline of a neighborhood influence the behavior of investor, dealer, and seller of real estate: the prophecy is fulfilled. But contrariwise, images of growth lead some to invest in worthless acres of Western desert: the prophecy was not fulfilled but the action was determined.

A very common image of cities in the United States is that of disorder, regression, decadence—in short, disorganization. There is neither space nor purpose for expanding this observation, nor for allocating responsibility for its currency. Suffice it to say that muckraking political scientists, welfare-oriented sociologists, and doomsday-identifying demagogues have tended to end with a similar image: "Things fall apart, the center cannot hold. Mere anarchy is loosed upon the world."

Of course, changes in organization will look like disorganization if one compares them only with a past state of affairs. Thus the processes of rapid urban settlement in the nineteenth and early twentieth centuries were widely regarded as a species of disorganization. The city was seen as intrinsically evil and evil in its results: some went so far as to organize the planned movement of urban youth back to the villages (while tens of thousands were sent back, however, other hundreds of thousands came forward).

Later the process of suburbanization was regarded as equally immoral. The growth of the horizontal neighborhoods on the peripheries (called slurbs), the proliferation of suburban municipalities (called a governmental crazy quilt), the declining dominance of the old downtown (called decay at the center) reflect a tacit comparison of current change with the real or imagined city of another age.

In similar fashion, changes in the ethnic mixture of the society were regarded as calamitous. Whether we read Thoreau's description of the Irish countryman who built his hut near Walden Pond or Henry Adams' reflections on the mongrelization of the United States, the comparison implied is the same. That ethnic mixture was richest in the cities, and there we find concern with Americanizing the immigrant, the decline of political standards with machine politics, the dominance of racial and religious differences in the urban polity. Moving, however, to a new state of the system, the release of ethnic votes from machine dominance and the release of social energy among the ethnic poor, black and white alike, provoke further alarm; some become nostalgic for the older situation where these energies were impounded by the bloc politics of the machines.

In short, our images of the urban future have been calamitous and catastrophic in their tonalities, for they have taken the past as norm and change as evil. Now changes *are* disorganizing, but only when they are partial and run contrary to fixed structures that predominate. But when a given change is congruent with other changes in the structure, it is possible that a *new* pattern will predominate. Universal literacy was seen as a potential disaster by those who felt it would be impossible to keep the lower orders in their place; as it turned out, literacy allowed for a transformation of the economy that radically improved the place of these orders. Of course, it is always a gamble as to just how change in one aspect will affect and be affected by other changes; my aim is to draw attention to it as a hazard, a gamble, and not an intrinsic evil. (We may note in passing that stability may also be disorganizing. When it is partial and contrary to a changing structure that predominates, it becomes as much a threat as partial change in a static structure. Racism in America is such a stability, destructive in its conflict with expanding economic and political scale.)

Thus I will reformulate the earlier proposition. While present policy is based upon images of futures and these are, in turn, limited by our notions of the immutable, these notions of the immutable are essentially ways of hedging our bets as to just what will prevail. Since what prevails is, to some degree, dependent upon what we do at present (as our efficacy depends upon the accuracy of our assessment), it is clear that we need the most rigorous standards for our images of the future city if our policy is to be more than sympathetic magic and public ritual.

IMAGES OF URBAN FORM

Our most prevalent image of the city is still one based upon the railroad centers of the *fin du siècle*. It is a clearly bounded, dense, centralized container for people, goods, and activities. Its boundaries—economic, political, and other—are congruent in space; the headquarters of each order is located near others at the center of the city. Center city is organizational hub and symbolic hearth of the metropolis as a whole; here power and wealth, style and grace, are on exhibit; here the urbanite communes with the meaningful symbols of his life.

The image rests upon a belief that centrality is an immutable necessity for an urban order. A single dominant area is thought to be required if a city is to persist (functionalism), if it is to maximize its wealth and numbers (boosterism), or if it is to optimize its contributions to social life (utopianism).

The policy directives of such an image are clear enough. One must try to effect a recentralization of those activities and structures that have got away from the center; one must maintain those that remain; to do these things one will most likely have to rebuild the core. One must also reincorporate activities outside the boundaries into the city, discouraging scatteration and sprawl.

The first set of policies, concerned with maintaining centrality, are clearly the inspiration for most of what is known as Urban Renewal. Believing central position has immutable value, urban renewal efforts consist in making that value accessible for new investment. The second set of policies, aimed at reincorporation of the suburban areas, is clearly the base for the "metropolitan government" movements. Believing that clearly defined boundaries including all the relevant urban population are necessary for meaningful city government, such movements aim at a redefinition of the city's political form.

But there is a second and competing image of the city. This image is of a vast, horizontal network of settlement held together by rapid means of transportation. In this image there is no single center; instead, there are many subcenters of activity and urbanites orient their activities to one or two of these, ignoring the others and ignoring the city as a whole. In this image of the city boundaries are vague; urban area, fringe, and hinterland merge; and growth at the peripheries is continuous. Such a view is sometimes called "conurbation";

I prefer to see it as an urban *texture* replacing the older urban *form*.

Underlying the image is the notion that the immutable process is that of decentralization. Decentralization is seen as an absolute requisite. For the city to persist as a functioning unit, decentralization is necessary, for a single center simply could not handle the transactions when population and activities pass a certain point. For the maximization of population one must maximize space; to maximize production one must also maximize space; thus the decentralized city is necessary to maximize profits. Finally, to optimize such amenities as private houselots, horizontal structures for industry and commerce, playgrounds and parking lots, decentralization is again necessary.

Should one accept decentralization as ineluctable and the horizontal urban texture as the accurate image of the city, certain policy directives follow. Ignoring the older core, once a center by historical and technological accident, one encourages decentralization by means of a developing, efficient transportation grid. One tries to guide the spreading texture of activity, to plan the subcenters so that they will provide the range of necessities and desirables, and to allow for adequate communication within and between the various subcenters. Policy is less interested in the incorporation of all the urban settlement within a single governmental unit—indeed, the boundaries of settlement may be so hazy that units are quite arbitrary. Instead, one looks for viable governmental subunits and ways of relating them to each other and to the larger whole, insofar as that is necessary.

CONCERNING IMMUTABLES

Of course, neither centrality nor decentralization is immutable and ineluctable. The first is not required, the second is not inescapable. A great deal of the dialogue between proponents of the two images simply rests upon generalizations from past views of one's favorite cities. But some of it rests upon major structural variables in the American political economy. They are givens, from the point of view of those concerned with any given city, but they are not inescapable for the nation as a whole.

Let us state these constraints in another form: *if* the national government allows local option in land use, and *if* it allows private option in location, *then* there can be no local urban policy. The free movement of the factors of production means that the economy, most basic in structuring the city, is beyond local control; that in-and-out migration, most basic in creating the city's human structure, is beyond local control; and finally, of course, that capital for new development and maintenance is also beyond local control. However, there cannot be a *national* policy for urban form either; local option in land use prevents it, and private option in mobility reinforces that prevention.

Given such limits, the most useful image of urban America is one based on the national playing field. The given urban settlement is a specialized part within a grid of locations ultimately determined by national markets in land, labor, and capital, and large-scale organizations (including governmental agencies) are the major players. For this "national city" there is no national policy; it is a collective output, the result of a great many aggregated and interacting decisions.

We may note a case parallel to that of urban form in the way civil rights have been handled. *If* we have local option in the definition of rights and their protection, and *if* we have private options in migration, hiring, lending and selling, *then* we have no possibility of local policy (because of private option) nor of a national policy (because of local options). But if we continue the analogy we note an important change: when political forces at the national level call civil rights a major problem for the national government, "immutables" are shifted around and changed. The result has been a decline in both local and private option, based upon increase in the national government's power.

When the shape and texture of our cities becomes a problem of major national interest, one would expect a similar development. The given dichotomies of control, between local and national, private and public, would be shifted in the direction of increasing national and public powers. For many purposes the corporation boundaries of the given city would become irrelevant, and even the metropolitan region would be subordinate to a larger image—that of the continental city-state. In an age of instantaneous communication and very rapid movement of men and materials, the national metropolitan network is as easy to move across as is any one of the great metropolitan complexes now emerging.

A National Urban Policy

What would a national urban policy be like? First, remember that any policy has several dimensions; one we have discussed earlier—should we try to aim at a minimal order, at the simple persistence of a given state of things? (Most structural-functionalist theory really deals with no more than survival.) Or, should we aim at maximizing certain values— as the production and consumption of automobiles or the size of the Gross National Product? (Both require shoddy construction and rapid obsolescence to succeed.) A third alternative, more difficult intellectually and politically, would be to optimize a wide range of values for the cities, of which private profits and civic mercantilism would be only two. Let us look at some aspects of urban structures that a national policy should consider and form or reform.

Location and Transportation. A national policy would certainly handle the question of the desirable size of population centers at given locations, in terms of a wide range of values. We get a notion of some of them through looking at the assorting process now going on. Population sometimes clusters around such natural resources as the factors of material production, but increasingly it is attracted by such resources as climate, landscape, foliage, and topography. Then too, accessibility of resources—whether it is the desert and beach, or clusters of universities, or the Broadway theater—has attraction. This leads us to ask: how would one so distribute the sites of action as to maximize choice and minimize the friction of space? Another perspective: How large should various cities be? How much concentration is required to provide a given range of opportunities? And, what ranges are desirable in terms of the present preferences of the population, as well as the preferences they *might* have if they were available?

The questions of efficiency of economic production and distribution remain. These, however, are not absolutes; our laissez-faire ideology has allowed them to become so. We must think in terms of opportunity costs, realizing that maximizing production of automobiles may vitiate esthetic and moral values. As a crude example, it is possible to minimize the death and disfigurement of human beings by automobile traffic through the use of engineering, layout, enforcement, and education programs. We can actually estimate the cost, in dollars spent (or average speed per mile traveled), of a human life. It can be programmed; but, when we do it, it becomes clear that we pay either way. How shall we decide how to optimize? What counts in the layout of urban America?

Thus far the marketplace, modified by temporary threats and bribes from state and local government, has been decisive. If we find we cannot afford this method of land allocation, then our only alternatives are overall control, either through administrative decree or piecemeal through the polity. Choices among values are finally amenable to neither science nor technology.

Science and technology do constitute dynamics in the process of policy formation: they increase our degrees of freedom. On the one hand, it is possible today, for the first time, to handle the enormous details of land-use data rapidly: with computers we can finally understand where we are without losing five years in gathering and processing data. On the other hand, we are increasingly free to engineer topography, climate, and amenities. Changes in transportation and communication shift the cost of separation in space, and the substitutability of materials makes the "resource base" city a candidate for extinction. Thus any policy for the location of urban sites and their integration must be sensitive to the changing limits of policy choice as well as the changing value hierarchies among the population.

Homogeneity and Heterogeneity. A national urban policy would also deal with the problem of specialization versus given mixes of activity, economic and otherwise, for both the city as a whole and subareas within the city. Some specialization is already evident today, in university towns, resort towns, and various resource-based settlements. It could go much further; those who speak of the "Science City," or the "Educational Park" are proposing systematic and extreme forms of spatial concentration (and therefore segregation), of functions and of the populations that perform them.

One can argue for such concentration in terms of economies of scale. If it is necessary to have a special environment for a given activity, then the overhead declines per unit as we increase the action. At the same time, we would benefit from the multiplier effect. Thus if two physicists working together (or near one another) are more than twice as effective as when working alone, then concentration is the directive. Such activities as research, development, education and health, will undoubtedly absorb an increasing proportion of human time and energies; it is possible to build cities around such armatures, as we once built a Pittsburgh around iron and coal or, more to the point, a Las Vegas around sunshine and roulette wheels.

Within the city one can also argue for concentration and, therefore, segregation. To take an extreme case, one can argue for the utility of the ghetto for East European Jews; it provided a familiar shared environment, a protective community, and a specialized market for distinctively Jewish goods and services, including temple and school. Some argue for the utility of the present black ghettos; though there is an element of rationalization here, since most urban Negroes will probably live in black slums all their lives, there is also some validity. The argument for the Jewish ghetto holds in large part; in addition, it can be argued that there is more chance for a Negro child to grow up with self-respect and confidence when surrounded by his peers than when integrated with more affluent children of different pigmentation. And, at the same time, there is more possibility of political leverage, thus political education, in the bloc politics of the slum.

Both types of concentration, and the middle category, the planned suburbs (miscalled new towns) produce similar costs. They structure intergroup differences by using physical distance as barrier; they result in reinforcing the boundaries between the components of the society. They act to perpetuate existing differences and to generate new ones. The schism resulting may easily become parapolitical, political, or violently antipolitical. The latter result is, of course, most frightening to American sensibilities; it represents riot, rebellion, and revolution. However, we should not dismiss such alternatives out of hand; it may be argued that there is no way out of our impasse short of revolution.

Another objection offered to concentration and segregation is the sheer fact of separating the components of the world. Interdependence exists but is not perceived; and it gives the citizen a dangerously misleading map of his world. He knows, if he is white, that the black ghetto is strange, dangerous, and explosive; he does not know how important the black labor force and market are in the economy of the United States. In turn, the black man in the ghetto knows the white suburbs are exclusionist if not racist, snobbish, and wealthy and callous. They are exploiters. He does not know how critical to the working economy of the country are the droves of technicians, entrepreneurs, managers, and professionals who crowd the freeways in the rush hours.

And one may multiply such examples. Age and sex segregation are also well structured. How fares the middle-class male child who has never seen his father work? The women who have only the vaguest notion of where their money comes from? Businessmen, in their self-pitying moods, claim that nobody understands them; the toughest politician will occasionally say the same thing. Both are nearly correct and the same holds for many other specialties in our society. Increasing segregation, through Science City, might promote understanding within what is, after all, a narrow segment of the population, at the cost of increasing the superstitious popular view of the scientist as humanoid.

To summarize: if we concentrate, we segregate. The results may maximize the values of a specialized environment, may have a multiplier effect (for physicists or black politicians), or may be seedbeds for new cultural variations and inventions. They will certainly reinforce intergroup differences, actual and perceived, which has political dangers as well as dangers for the city as a teaching machine.

How shall we optimize? We experiment today with transportation as the binder, busing children out of their "neighborhood school" to others where the racial mix is different. We struggle for integration in an increasingly specialized and intellectually segregated world through experiments with "general education." But powerful knowledge, as Whitehead remarks, is specialized knowledge. How to avoid the ruts of social stereotype and intellectual narrowness—and the frightful dangers each represents for the human community? Would it help to mix activities on the same or adjacent sites, to bring work closer to the home? Would John Dewey's ideas, once tried for a while in the Gary schools, yet work? Could we, as the Soviets do, combine real work with study for youngsters, and systematically vary their work experiences? These questions are implicit in the major policy dilemma:

how shall we relate a heterogeneous population so as to maximize, and thus optimize, both social creativity and social integration?

And again, we must accept the likelihood of major change. There will be, through public education and the mass media, a continuing acculturation to the broad normative and belief system of lumpen-middle-class America. This system will also be in motion with new inputs from a society increasingly college-educated. Technology, which already makes many locational decisions of the past obsolete, will continue its dance of Shiva, destroying as it creates. As the labor force continues to move from industry to the services and professions, the reasons for towns change. And, as the quinary industries—health, education, welfare, research and development, the arts and crafts—become increasingly important, we may forego the massive urban complex for a reticulated system of land use, with areas of high concentration in one activity shading off into areas where the activity is cognate but different. Thus, one could imagine an urban fabric without sharply demarcated spatial boundaries. As for social and cultural integration, we have hardly begun to put our minds to it; our policies have been hand-me-downs from an earlier era, strongly tinctured of Social Darwinism and minimal charity.

Local and National Government. A national urban policy is contingent on a reordering of local government and would make such a reordering possible. The problem is still that of the relationships possible and desirable between the smaller community and the large, between part and whole. With our federal system we have maximized the freedom of the states and, through them, the municipalities to control their own destinies at the cost of stalemate, confusion, and inaction. We have tried to increase citizen participation and the adequacy of representation through using small communities as polities; we frequently achieve citizen indifference and do-nothing representation. One of the reasons is the trivial issues of local government, due to what Robert Wood calls the "segregation of needs from resources," and due also to the limited scope of the jurisdiction.

To be specific, this range of values is involved: (1) a working consensus, thus legitimacy, for local government; (2) democratic processes at the local level; (3) efficacy in resolving conflict and in directing collective enterprises; and (4) a scope of action adequate to the empirically problematic situation. The first is required of all government; the second is the American solution to the problem, "Whose ox shall be gored?"; the third is the difference between government and custom; the fourth is implied by the third. Thus we must find in local government answers to such questions as: who should control the use of land? How shall we tax and whom and how much? Failing consensus on issues, whose norms shall be honored in such matters as civil rights, urban renewal, educational policy?

In optimizing values at the level of local government we shall have to recognize the increasing interpenetration of the nation and the city. Many of the major decisions, for any given city, are made far away; if the city is to have any say in its destiny, it must depend upon a *national* interest brokerage, a national policy, to guarantee it. Equity in taxing and spending must be national, for the notion of minimal standards (in housing, education, health) implies redistribution of income from rich regions to poor. Planning, as we have already noted, must in its broad outlines be national for the whole playing field is involved.

Yet the local community may still be viewed as a laboratory for the discovery and improvement of democracy. At the local level of government, as in more private enterprises, there is a potential of creativity and sensitivity that are worth nurturance. Thus within an increasingly national policy it would be possible to allow for the maximum freedom to vary congruent with national goals. The smaller communities are interrelated within the framework of the larger; this is an obvious fact, yet our eighteenth-century jealousy of central government has blinded us to it. But this is true only for government. Everyone knows his profession, his corporation, his union, to be deeply dependent upon a larger network within which his state or city are only parts—as each profession, corporation, or union is only one part of his city. The problem is, in short, to reform government in view of the organizational topography of the total society.

And this must be done within a context of change; thus we should not repeat the mistake of those who, believing history was over, wrote constitutions "once and for all." We can expect the space-time ratio to continue to shrink, accessibility among the parts of the country to increase. We can expect organizational and physical space to change in their relationships as a consequence. We once saw centralization as the dominant fact in our social organization; with today's technology one sees, in many enterprises, a centralization of control and a decentralization of activities. Publishing is centered in New York City, but printing is a much more decentralized activity. Television broadcasting is centered in Hollywood, but the consumption is as scattered as households are. In short, our use of physical space changes our social organization. Government must accept and, if possible, use this fact.

Decentralization of the routine functions of local government is beginning to appear in a number of cities. More important, there is considerable interest in decentralizing certain classes of decision-making; who after all should be concerned with the location and design of a neighborhood park, street lights, or traffic signals? There are certain broad limits, since the neighborhood is part of a larger matrix of activity, but within these limits probably the people who live there.

CODA: CAN WE GET THERE FROM HERE?

The basic problem is still the expansion of national public power, at the expense of local and private control. And a national policy is, as noted, contingent on changing local-national relationships. How can it come about? This chapter deals with the study of futures, not with controlling them, yet it is important to note that accurate study is in some degree dependent on control—who leaves political change out of his forecast does so at his peril.

I see several trends moving us toward basic decisions on the proper state of the nation. First, the crescive changes, the massive trends that are not the result of policy but whose effects and side effects condition and trigger policy. Rising educational levels, instantaneous communication through electronic media, increasing prosperity, all point toward increased leisure for political learning and action among the masses. If it is true that responsibility is a luxury that only the powerful can afford, we are socializing the potential for power at a great rate. It may result in a demand for a national government.

This trend will be reinforced by the continuing harvest of our present policies. By default we have concentrated "outsiders"—poor, black, and volatile—at the vulnerable centers of our metropolitan complexes; besides them we have concentrated others, "semi-outsiders," poor, white and volatile. We have given over the function of policing to still others, barely insiders, who have bitter memories of racial competition and conflict. We have built self-perpetuating enclaves of people who are indifferent to, if not enemies of, the dominant moral order of middle-class white society, and they can be moved against the physical structure of that society.

The result is pressure for national urban policy. That policy may take into account the range of values I have been adumbrating in this paper; it may move through the expensive and difficult and unpredictable paths of innovation and amelioration. We have many signs of such a movement. It may, of course, result in the brutal logic of suppression, with the troops who today patrol a large part of the non-

American earth recalled to patrol the centers of our great cities. Much depends upon the efficacy of our education, formal and informal; what have Americans learned from their public school, mass media, and the community—their teaching machines?

We may have learned enough to demand or at least accept a national urban policy. It would allow us to break the stasis that has left us without the will or tools to shape the communities where most of us are at home; it would be frightening to many, for it would mean a final rejection of many myths of the agrarian past.

One such is the belief that urban government is general government, rather than specialized and limited; another is the conviction that the inhabitants of a given area have some basic right to govern themselves; another is the continuing belief that the city is "hallowed ground," with a putative immortality. These are aesthetic yearnings at best, fraudulent claims at worst; in any event, they have resulted in tunnel vision. Focusing upon the given concrete sprawl of buildings and activity, we have been unable to see the vast, interrelated network that is urban America. Until we do so, our urban renewal and governmental reforms are, in Norton Long's words, "civic fig leaves," sops to outraged conscience.

REFERENCES

Norton E. Long, *The Polity,* edited and with an introduction by Charles Press (Chicago: Rand McNally & Company, 1962).

Alfred North Whitehead, *Science and the Modern World* (New York: The Free Press, 1967).

Robert C. Wood, *1400 Governments* (Cambridge: Harvard University Press, 1961).

Name Index

Subject Index

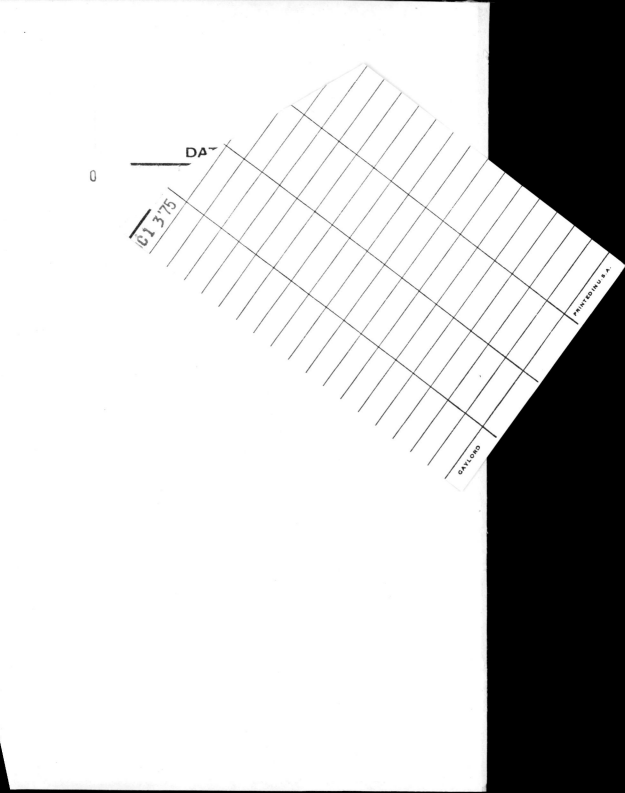

DA

OC 1 3 '75

GAYLORD   PRINTED IN U.S.A.